HELL AND DAMNATION

———✦✕✕✦———

A SINNER'S GUIDE
TO ETERNAL TORMENT

MARQ DE VILLIERS

University of Regina Press

Printed and bound in Canada at Friesens. The text of this book is printed on 100% post-consumer recycled paper with earth-friendly vegetable-based inks.

Cover and text design: Duncan Campbell, University of Regina Press
Cover art: Devil mask glyph by Icons Producer for the Noun Project.
Copy editor: Ryan Perks
Indexer: Sergey Lobchev, Brookfield Indexing Services

Excerpts from the Canaanite Baal saga copyright J. C. L. Gibson, 1956, *Canaanite Myths and Legends*, T&T Clark International, an imprint of Bloomsbury Publishing Plc. reprinted by permission. Verse and chorus from Paul Simon's *The Afterlife*, copyright © 2011 Paul Simon. Used by permission of the Publisher: Paul Simon Music. Passages from *The Epic of Gilgamesh* by permission of the Assyrian International News Agency (AINA). Passages from Philip Almond's *The Devil: A New Biography*, by permission of the publisher, Cornell University Press.

Library and Archives Canada Cataloguing in Publication

De Villiers, Marq, author
    Hell and damnation : a sinner's guide to eternal torment / Marq de Villiers.

Includes bibliographical references and index.
Issued in print and electronic formats.
ISBN 978-0-88977-584-8 (softcover).—ISBN 978-0-88977-585-5 (PDF).—
ISBN 978-0-88977-586-2 (HTML)

1. Hell. I. Title.

BL545.D4 2019   202'.3   C2018-906027-1   C2018-906028-X

10 9 8 7 6 5 4 3 2

University of Regina Press, University of Regina
Regina, Saskatchewan, Canada, S4S 0A2
TEL: (306) 585-4758 FAX: (306) 585-4699
WEB: www.uofrpress.ca

We acknowledge the support of the Canada Council for the Arts for our publishing program. We acknowledge the financial support of the Government of Canada. / Nous reconnaissons l'appui financier du gouvernement du Canada. This publication was made possible with support from Creative Saskatchewan's Book Publishing Production Grant Program.

THIS BOOK IS DEDICATED TO SKEPTICS EVERYWHERE. Like Thomas Tailour of Newbury, England, punished in 1491 for denying the power of prayer and doubting the survival of the soul after death. When a man or woman dies in the body they also die in their soul, he declared, for as the light of a candle is put out by casting it away or in other ways quenched by blowing or shaking it, so is the soul quenched by death. Tailour died a heretic, gladly unrepentant.

Eternity is a very long time,
especially towards the end.
—WOODY ALLEN

I am on my way to look
for the great perhaps.
—RABELAIS, ON HIS DEATHBED

INTRODUCTION

READERS WHO MAKE IT THAT FAR WILL NOTE THAT many of my sources, especially those from the Christian tradition, are rather less than canonical. Thus, I've incorporated passages from many early Christian and proto-Christian accounts, such as *The Apocalypse of Peter*, *The Apocalypse of the Virgin*, and *The Gospel of Nicodemus*, that were rejected by the compilers of the Christian Bible. These early gospels, some of them gnostic texts newly (re)discovered, were considered by the early church fathers to be lamentably off-message, and therefore to be either suppressed or ignored (pronouncing them anathema was a favourite tactic). In my defence, consider the alternatives. It is hard for anyone in these skeptical days to consider, say, Genesis as a historical account; and bemusement is the only proper response to the editors/compilers who thought to place Revelation into the canon with a straight face. I can reasonably argue, therefore, that both Nicodemus and Bartholomew, who have given us wonderful eavesdropped accounts of the petty squabbling between

Hades and Satan as Jesus descended for the harrowing of hell, are as theologically useful as any of the accepted gospels, contradictory as they are. Sure, it is the right of any reader to reject as reportage the accounts of hell in Arda Viraf and Gilgamesh and Ishtar, as well as in Virgil and Dante and Milton and Tundale and the various apocalypses; but then I am attempting to assemble an overview of humanity's bounteous (not to say riotous) imaginings about the afterlife, not to argue a coherent theological case. That these non-canonical texts conflict with the canon and with each other is okay. In fact, that is sort of the point.

What theological case is made comes only at the end, in the epilogue, where I ask the reader to consider the multiple florid, even lurid, versions of hell in the world's religious texts, and to wonder why anyone would give credence to any of them as a depiction of how the world and the supposed afterworld really are.

ACKNOWLEDGEMENTS

FOR MY PREVIOUS BOOKS, I TRIED TO TRAVEL AS much and as often as possible to the places that appeared in the text, and to interview as many people as I could *in situ.* Clearly, this time there were certain . . . logistical difficulties in so doing. Lack of solid check-in data . . . uncertainty about return tickets . . . certain meteorological anomalies . . . a paucity of trustworthy guides. So I relied on people who have "been there," and people who have written about people who have been there, and people who have commented on people who have written about people who have been there. Many of these sources are mentioned in the text.

Three people (organizations?) need to be acknowledged off the top: the anonymous writer for *The Economist* who assembled the altogether engaging piece "Hell: A Rough Guide," which was the trigger for this book; Eileen Gardiner, the editor of the hugely impressive scholarly website called Hell-On-Line, where she has assembled a unique (and exhaustive) catalogue of texts on hell from multiple cultures around the world; and the editors of Project Gutenberg, who have placed into the public domain literally thousands of works, some obscure and others renowned, to the immense benefit of human knowledge.

Gardiner, especially, needs to be singled out. I have tried to give credit where it is due in the text, and have quoted briefly from her work, I hope without missing any attributions. But she is more valuable than that. Many of the otherwise obscure works (tracts, polemics, apocalypses, gospels, visions) that I was able to find and to use, I only knew about because Gardiner had been there before. Those, too, will be acknowledged in the text.

My bibliography indicates some of the other sources I have found useful. It's hard to single out some and not others, but Philip Almond, Elaine Pagels, Miriam Van Scott, and Marvin Meyer stand out, as do the mystics like Saint Teresa of Ávila, the Irish monk Adamnán, and the medieval gadfly Tundale, who saw the devil *in person*. Not to mention the great poets of our tradition—Virgil, Dante, and Milton. Of the modern commentariat, Ross Douthat is significant—I disagree with him on almost everything, and he would not like what I have to say, but I admire his fidelity and unwavering moral compass, so lamentably in short supply in these parlous days.

A few other names to be showered with gratitude (they will know why): Shaun Bradley, Sheila Hirtle, Philip Slayton, and Bruce Walsh.

WHAT KIND
OF PLACE
IS THIS
?

CHAPTER 1

WHO INVENTED HELL,
AND FOR GOD'S SAKE WHY?

What is this thing called hell?

HELL IS A PLACE OF PUNISHMENT. BUT NOT ALWAYS.

Hell is a place where sin can be purged and the sinner purified. But not always.

Hell is eternal, at least for those faiths that follow the arrow of time.

Hell is merely a staging post in the endless cycle, at least for those faiths for which the Wheel turns.

Hell is populated by demons and ruled by a devil. Sometimes.

Hell has many rulers.

Or only one.

Sometimes no one is there but the dead.

Hell is the endless void, where dust returns always to dust, ashes to ashes.

Hell began only when Sin did. Lucifer's fault. Or Adam's. And Eve's.

Hell expresses god's righteous, ever-burning wrath. Or maybe his eternal sorrow. Or perhaps just his impatience.

(Or *her* wrath, and *her* sorrow, and *her* rancour.)

Satan's navel marks the very centre of the earth, the innermost Pit.

Hell is meant for heretics and unbelievers.

Hellfire is in the armoury of multiple gods. But the Christian furnaces are the hottest of all.

Many hells freeze over.

Yes, there are cauldrons of boiling oil.

Hell is a single giant chamber full of stench and noise and pain, torment its sole purpose, wailing and gnashing of teeth its signature sound.

There are many hells. Each sin has its own hell. There is no end to the catalogue of sins.

Hell is watching a child die.

Hell is just a state of mind, a radical separation from god.

ALL OF THESE things were true, at one time or another, in one place or another, and some of them still are.

But . . . why? Where did all this—all the elaborate cosmologies and geographies of hell and all the quarrelling, devilish personalities and the demonic cast of thousands and the horrid instruments of torture and the never-quenched fire—come from?

In our Eurocentric way, we sometimes believe *our* hell is *the* hell, but the Judeo-Christian world was far from alone in developing theories of hell—virtually every human society (with some interesting exceptions, including to a degree the Judeo part of the Judeo-Christian world; see next chapter) has imagined a version of sometimes ever-lasting horror. Hell is generally outside time and beyond physics, twin characteristics it shares with heaven—at least in our world, heaven and hell are intertwined and codependent, the fate of one bound up with that of the other, the ultimate Upstairs, Downstairs story. Thus some opening questions:

What is the nature of the first hells, and their origins?

When were the first hells conceived? How old is hell?

What does the invention of hell tell us about the systems of belief that conceived of divine authority and infernal punishment in the first place?

And the devil? He was not always the master of hell, and not even present in multiple hells of history—just as many hells don't have associated heavens (the many Buddhist traditions, for example).

In those hells where the devil does preside, how did he go from an angel, to a messenger, to god's mischievous servant, to one of the Fallen, to jailed, to jailer, to the grotesqueries of torture imagined by medieval Christendom? How did he go from a tool of the oppressed to a weapon of the oppressor?[1] In Christianity, he grew in malevolence the further away we got from Christ himself, a measure of the hardening of religious arteries over time.

THERE ARE SEVERAL speculative theories about hell's origins. Some of them conflict, some overlap, some reinforce others. They may all in some respects be "true."

For the moment, we can set aside revelations from Gilgamesh, Arda Viraf, Ishtar, Virgil, Saints Peter and Paul,

Dante, and the rest of the tour guides to hell we will meet in
due course, since their hells are often poetic in inspiration,
though they are usually intended as reportage of a sort.
(Dante's descent into the inferno, for example, was part
of a grand allegory for how to approach the divine, but it
was, in a curious way, also excellent travel writing—and it
did have its tattle-tale aspects, as we shall see.) And in any
case, they were all reporting on what *already was*, in their
view—few of them, except possibly Milton, had much to
say about how hell came about: what they encountered
had been around, as far as they knew, forever.

In the darkness, perhaps, were dreamers

ONE THEORY IS that sapient creatures dream, and their
dreams seem real, and gods and demons give those dreams
structure and coherence.

A useful place to start thinking about the origins of
human dreaming is Tanzania, home of the so-called
Laetoli footprints. There they are, in a dusty gorge, in
an unprepossessing ravine made up of grey rocks and
gravel, in a landscape marred by boulders left over from
an unimaginable cataclysm long in the past, in a region
ravaged by drought and hard times, where hardly anything
lives but thorn trees and adders and scorpions. But there,
left on a once-muddy stream bank and subsequently fossil-
ized, are the imprinted bare feet of our earliest ancestors.
Two of them passed by that day so long ago, leaving one
large set of prints and a smaller one, presumably an adult
and a child. They stride purposefully across the mud,
surrounded by the prints of creatures larger and much

more dangerous than they. The Tanzanian conservators, scrupulous caretakers of these enigmatic images from the distant past, have carefully covered them over to preserve them from the ravages of nature, but it is possible to superimpose onto the site a mental picture of the two little upright hominids as they made their careful way up the path (perhaps hand in hand, for the small prints are alongside the larger ones).

It is easy, looking at those impressions, to conjure up a picture of how it might have been. Here, after all, walked our ancestors, 3.6 million years ago, dreaming no doubt their wary dreams of warmth and wealth and well-being, bequeathing these dreams and their genes to the endless generations to follow. It is a humbling thought that all the world's saints and all the world's sinners, down over the endless millennia, can be seen in these tiny impressions—every warlord who was ever born, every mystic, every murderer, every poet, and every politician descended, somehow, from the people (or their kin) who left behind these small traces. The two of them passed this way only once, but once was enough to make them immortal. Perhaps they were a family, going home, making their way carefully through the many hazards that beset them. It would be nice to think they had full bellies, and that they made a fire there in the African night.[2]

We can imagine that they would have been "dreaming their dreams"—but did they? Imaginings are not evidence, not even speculative evidence. How can we know they even had dreams? Or should we impute dreams only to *Homo sapiens*, the big-brained idiot now so diligently wrecking the planet?

There is some evidence to suggest that dreams do pre-date *Homo sapiens* and even the genus *Homo*. In the same year I saw the Laetoli footprints, I took a small boat onto Uganda's Lake Edward to Izinga Island, a kilometre or so offshore, where Ugandan conservation authorities had set up a sanctuary for orphaned chimps, most of them confiscated from poachers. I wasn't allowed ashore—the chimps were afraid of humans, with good reason—but I moored a few metres out and watched them feed. There were about a dozen animals. Chimps are social beings, and these ones were taken from their parents too young to be able to fend for themselves. Only one had learned to make a nest, and she mostly made a botch of it. The rest had discovered a cave on the other side of the island, and were excavating it deeper to make a shelter: like human children, they were afraid of the dark. Sometimes they'd cry themselves to sleep in the darkness, breaking the game warden's heart.

Do they, the chimps, our nearest relatives, dream? It seems they do. Did the little people who left the Laetoli footprints dream? Of course they did. Did Lucy, whose three-million-year-old bones are now "resting," in the parlance of funeral directors, in a glass case in an ill-lit hall in Addis Ababa's national museum, dream? Of course she did. All these creatures, our earliest fathers and mothers and aunts and uncles and cousins, dreamed their dreams . . . but of what?

We can take it they dreamed of pleasure, for it seems all sentient creatures do that. No doubt they dreamed of comfort, and out of comfort comes companionship and out of companionship comes love. Or maybe love comes from something more primal, with no need of dreams. We can take it they also dreamed of fear, and of pain, and possibly of the monsters that produce them: all sentient creatures seem to do that too, to explain the anguish they feel.

Did they dream of loss? Did they grieve? Did they cry in the night, when one of them was taken? Why wouldn't they? The chimpanzees do.

Did they wonder how it happened?

Did they ask, then, the crucial question, *Why?*

Someone must have.

Because it is from the *why* that religion comes, religion and the whole tottering apparatus of gods, demons, and, crucially, the afterlife. Including the notion of hell and its modern corollary, damnation.

There must be a reason, after all, why things go wrong

IF YOU DISMISS the frankly naïve origin stories of the world's peoples, including those of the major faiths, how otherwise could gods and devils have been derived? The admittedly sketchy evidence from surviving Stone Age cultures, taken with the even more sketchy evidence found in early art and funerary artifacts, suggests that just like cosmological origin stories, supernatural beliefs derive from an early empirical attempt to explain the world and how it works.

The philosopher A.C. Grayling, in the explication of humanism he called *The God Argument*, got it about right, if you can ignore the slightly condescending tone. To early cultures, he said, "natural phenomena are most intuitively explained by seeing them as the work of purposive agents who variously cause the wind to blow and the rain to fall, whose footsteps on the clouds are thunderous, and who are responsible for the cycling of the stars and the growth of vegetation in the springtime." No doubt, he suggested, imputing agency to natural events was used by analogy on people's own experience of agency and purpose, projected onto nature. "This was after all the only resource that early humans had to explain how things can be made to happen. They could feel themselves to be causes of events, as when they threw a stone or pushed an object along the ground: how could things happen in nature unless caused, and how caused except by an agent? It is a simple argument by analogy from their own case, and as such is an empirical argument."

Such a belief system is what anthropologists call "animism," and they, too, usually mean it in a mildly condescending way. Animist gods were local gods in a very literal sense. There was not *a* stream god—there was a god of this stream, over here . . .

In this view, religion is an ancient way of making sense of the world, and persists in our times for no other reason than parents passing it to children down the ages. For his part, Grayling suggests that the explanation and systemization so derived amounted to an early version of science, one that did exactly what science does now: offer explanation through observation, based on what was known, or at least inferred. In this view, prayer, sacrifice, and taboo amounted in their turn to the earliest technology, the instruments of change. Religion gives meaning to the meaningless, our species' first cut at explaining how the cosmos works. Absent physics and chemistry, it was not a bad try.

Shakespeare understood, in *A Midsummer Night's Dream*, how humans like to make patterns, give names to the mysterious:

> The poet's eye, in a fine frenzy rolling,
>   Doth glance from heaven to
>   earth, from earth to heaven;
>   And as imagination bodies forth
>   The forms of things unknown,
>   the poet's pen
>   Turns them to shapes, and
>   gives to airy nothing
>   A local habitation and a name.[3]

The cosmologist John D. Barrow, in his book *New Theories of Everything*, makes a similar point: early people (early worriers) needed "to embroider a tapestry of meaning within which the authors could represent themselves, and with respect to which they could evaluate the status of the unknown and the mysterious." By doing so they could justify their society by suggesting that it was similar in form and structure to the way the world itself operates. The belief in cause and effect, Barrow explained, "pays due respect to the natural forces which hold life and death in their hands. If one's view of nature involves a personification of natural forces, then this search for reason reduces to the attribution of blame."

In this view, gods and demons were invented because they offered at least some control over nature. Their role was to serve as intermediaries between the hard world of things and the mysteries of causation.

After animism came polytheism, whose adherents believed the world controlled by a clutch of strong gods with wider-than-local powers (the Fertility God, the God of Storms, the God of Death, the God of the Gut and the Liver, and so on) who collectively controlled the entirety of nature. Sometimes, as with the Greeks, the pantheon was a family affair; in other cases it was a series of alliances between more or less equal but unrelated gods. As the Israeli historian Yuval Harari put it in his book *Sapiens*, "much of ancient mythology is in fact a legal contract in which humans promise everlasting devotion to the gods in exchange for mastery over plants and animals."

Not always mastery, though. There had to be *some* reason why things went wrong—a skilled hunter struck down by an unthreatening creature, earthquakes, floods, pestilence, "sore boils," . . . demons!

The subsequent invention of monotheism didn't contradict this point of view, but rather amplified it. Demons, always the obverse of gods, became the devil, the obverse of god. But it is not obvious why this should be so. Why should (how can) an all-powerful god have rivals? And why is his rival necessarily evil? In some traditions, the answer was a simple dualism, in that evil and good existed simultaneously, co-creators and co-creatures of the universe. But sometimes hell was the creation of God, a place to park his enemies, the devil merely his tool—the monotheistic religions were not always clear on this point. (The theism not always as "mono" as advertised).

Monotheism is actually not that old, and is not really to be found very much before the Jewish, and then the Christian, era (a brief Egyptian flirtation with it, under Akhenaton, notwithstanding). But it changed everything. In the polytheistic system, battles were won and lost depending on which god was stronger on any given day; outcomes were never predictable. Some gods won, some lost, some prevailed, some failed—the God of Storms, for instance, overcoming the God of Agriculture, or vice versa. After the Hebrews invented a single, omnipotent god, this could no longer work. A single god, after all, can't be seen to fail. Thus humans had to be at fault, not omnipotent God, a notion enthusiastically adopted by the Jews and then the Christian cult. *We may have been battered and beaten in battle and exiled and subjected to plagues and famine and catastrophe*, this theory goes, *but it was really our fault for not believing and behaving properly. We're lucky he didn't wipe us out and start over. God is great.*

In any case, Plato's widely accepted notion that souls were immortal and migrated to new corporeal vessels at the body's death, turned out to be a poor fit for this emerging monotheistic world view. Aristotle's notion worked better; he argued that a soul is what makes a body whole—that soul and body were separate but interdependent. This was precondition for a more direct relationship with the creator, for survival into the afterlife, and for reward—and punishment.

And because there was now only one true God, it was incumbent on all adherents to discredit the gods of others, just as it was incumbent on God and his human agents to chastise those who believed with insufficient conviction, and then to find some place to imprison and punish them. As the philosopher Adam Kotsko put it in his book *The Prince of This World,* "It was no longer that we have our gods and you have yours, but rather that we have *the* god and you have a delusion at best and a dangerous lie at worst."

Therefore hell, the new home of heresy.

Hell explains why wrongness is always with us

HELL MUST EXIST because plague, famine, and war never go away. Prayer never helps. God seems useless, his "miracles" impotent. The devil, lurking in hell, must therefore be at fault.

What if an angry god is watching?

PERHAPS BELIEF IN post-life punishment is inherent, a useful evolutionary adaptation, helping humans overcome selfishness.[4]

If god is in the gaps between knowledge, where's the devil?

IT'S COMMONPLACE AMONG the religiously skeptical to assert that god resides in the gaps between knowledge—which is not so different, after all, from the ancient Epicurean notion that gods were composed of a different, thinner type of matter than other entities, living between the worlds, affecting only dreams and the imagination, not the material world. That is, as more of the world is explained—and ends up being not so divine after all—faith increasingly resides in the gaps in what we know. Its home may have shrunk, but there is still room for things that have to be taken on faith—and for faith itself. As Christopher Hitchens once put it in *The Portable Atheist*, "religion comes from the period of human prehistory when nobody—not even the mighty Democritus who concluded that all matter was made of atoms—had the slightest idea what was going on."

We are better off now, in some ways. In others, not. The late David Sullivan, a "professional cult infiltrator," told an audience at a public forum on cults in 2010 what it would have already found obvious: "When people want to believe what they want to believe, they are very hard to dissuade. . . . There's a deep desire for faith, there's a deep desire to feel there's someone up there who really cares about what's going on. . . . A desire to have a coherent worldview, [to believe] that there's a rhyme and reason for everything we do, and all the terrible things that happen to people—people die, children get leukemia—there's some reason for it." Before humans learned how to make tools, or how to farm, or how to write, Sullivan suggested, they were telling stories with a deeper purpose—the hunter who killed his prey wasn't just strong: the spirit of the hunt was smiling. The rivers were stocked with fish because the river king was benevolent. Conversely, whenever something went wrong—a devil was to blame. In society after society, religious belief, in one form or another, has arisen spontaneously. Anything that cannot immediately be explained must be explained all the same, and the explanation often lies in something bigger than oneself, for good or evil.[5]

In addition, religion and politics have long become codependent (the Ten Commandments are essentially morality made political). "At first . . . purposeful agents were at work in nature itself—water nymphs, dryads in trees, thunder gods, and so on," as Grayling put it, and then Zeus, Poseidon, Hades, and the rest took over the government of nature, and they resided in heaven, not in the trees or the water. As knowledge of the natural world increased, and as our mastery of it progressed, these godlings were obliged to relocate themselves, at first to mountaintops, then to the sky. The more our ancestors came to know of the universe's workings, the further out the gods had to move. I well remember a columnist for the *Toronto Telegram* concluding in all seriousness (in the 1960s!) that the only reason the space-faring Yuri Gagarin didn't see the angels "up there" was because he was a godless Communist. Now, the divine apparatus has moved beyond space and time altogether.

This relocation had consequences. As the gods moved away, moving beyond the horizons of scientific knowledge, their usefulness to political rulers—kings and chieftains and their henchmen, priests and shamans—increased. Gods who could no longer be importuned on an everyday basis needed skilled interpreters, and these interpreters saw to it that their systems of belief did not merely survive but flourished. Soon, they became a privileged caste. Priests and rulers were a unified elite, especially as human society developed (settled agriculture allowed elites to be fed and housed without working themselves, and made possible oppressing armies). Like any privileged elite, they privileged themselves first. It became their business to assert an unchallengeable truth, revealed in all its fullness, any opposition to which could only be condemned. Thus beliefs became codes of conduct, and then conduct came to be judged by the tenets of belief. Hence the new notion of heresy. The judging of morality implied, in turn, a verdict that needed enforcement. Consequently, one place was set aside for the good (including rulers and priests) and quite another place for the not-so-good.

Heaven and hell were the necessary constructs.

In time, Satan became the chief heretic. And the chief jailer.

Therefore hell is a form of social control

THE SECOND-CENTURY BCE Greek historian and snob Polybius had a skeptical, not to say cynical, view of how hell came about. In the first volume of his *Histories*, he suggested that the whole thing was a crock cobbled together to control the mob, albeit necessary because of that. Gods had nothing to do with it:

> If it were possible to form a state wholly of philosophers, such a custom would perhaps be unnecessary. But since the multitude is ever fickle, full of lawless desires, irrational anger and violent passion, the only resource is to keep them in check by mysterious terrors and scenic effects of this sort. Wherefore, to my mind, the ancients were not acting without purpose or at random, when they brought in among the vulgar those

opinions about the gods, and the belief in
the punishments in Hades: much rather
do I think that men nowadays are acting
rashly and foolishly in rejecting them.[6]

Polybius wasn't the only one to think hell a contrivance of the authorities. Seneca famously described the notion of hell as a "fable"; Cicero, for his part, was sniffy too, calling the stories of hell "silly absurdities and fables"; so did Lucullus. Plato as well, though he had a different spin. Still reeling from the death of Socrates, he theorized about a place (or places) where citizens would have either reward or punishment, depending on their character; his hell was meant to keep rulers honest (i.e., from descending into tyranny). In his idiosyncratic view, hell was a form of democratic control.

The leader of the Thirty Tyrants in Athens, Critias (Plato's uncle), put it even more bluntly, if more poetically:

> Then came, it seems, that wise and
>   cunning man,
> The first inventor of the fear of gods. . . .
> He framed a tale, a most
>   alluring doctrine,
> Concealing truth by veils of lying lore.
> He told of the abode of awful gods,
> Up in revolving vaults, whence
>   thunder roars,
> And lightning's fearful flashes
>   blind the eye. . . .
> He thus encircled men by bonds of fear;

Surrounded them by gods
in fair abodes,
He charmed them by his spells,
and daunted them—
And lawlessness turned into
law and order.[7]

The early (or not-quite-so-early) Christians adopted this "pagan," social-control view of the afterlife, albeit absent Polybius's cynicism and Plato's spin. It didn't start right away. Even the apostle Paul, whose life's work was to persuade the Gentiles that they could be saved through Jesus, never believed that those not so saved would burn in hell. There was no hell then, so they could not be consigned there: they would just not have everlasting life—they would be dead. It wasn't until the second century that the church fathers, needing better sanctions against deviations from doctrine, began to conflate extant scriptural references to fire and judgment with earlier, pre-Christian notions of hell, and decided that those not saved would therefore burn in this newly discovered place: *if you don't follow our rules, this is what fate awaits you—you'll see!* This altogether grimmer notion can be seen most clearly in *The Apocalypse of Peter*, written sometime early in the second century (we will meet this "Peter" in more detail later). His apocalypse was constructed as a chatty dialogue between Peter and Jesus, and shows an unwholesome obsession with tortures of all kinds. Thus is Gentle Jesus, the Jewish rabbi, transformed into a vengeful Christ, who would "stand before humanity in judgment, hurling men, women, children, and infants not swearing allegiance to him into the torment of eternal fire."

None of this transmogrification gave the church fathers pause. Instead, the new view seemed to them an improvement, a useful doctrine à la Polybius. Loaves and fishes and healing the sick and *sharing* were all very well, in their place; but now the Big Men of the church had more pressing things on their minds than salvation and blessing the poor. Like preventing deviation and ensuring adherence to dogma.[8] A world populated by angels wouldn't need much governing or many rules—but *ours* does.

In the ninth century, Charlemagne's son and successor, Louis the Pious, neatly outlined the "it is all our fault" case for holy (and churchly) chastisement: "Is there anyone who does not feel that God has been offended and roused to anger by our most wicked deeds? . . . Our sins have done this, for which we are rightly chastised by him and through which we greatly offended him, so that we may correct our faults."[9]

What can fix this? Why, faithfulness to correct dogma!

Divine punishment is, therefore, a prime reason for hell.

As the former Episcopal bishop and apostate John Shelby Spong acknowledged in 2006, "religion is always in the control business, and that's something people don't really understand. It's in a guilt-producing control business. And if you have heaven as a place where you're rewarded for your goodness, and hell as a place where you're punished for your evil, then you sort of have control of the population. And so they create this fiery place which has quite literally scared the hell out of a lot of people, throughout Christian history. And it's part of a control tactic." The Christian church, said Spong, "fired up its furnaces hotter than anybody else." As the philosopher Aku Visala once put it, "you can have a god without causal [and control] powers, but from a religious point of view he would be kind of useless."

All a little unfair, no doubt. Religion has given comfort to millions of the deprived and bereaved, and still does. Nevertheless, soul control worked for the early church fathers, and it seems it still does.

Or maybe hell was needed because life was so damned unfair

IN ANOTHER THEORY, both hell and heaven were invented because of the world's evident unfairness. If the purpose of god, or the gods, was to put order into the universe, the devil was there to restore a balance fatally disturbed by life on earth. From this perspective, the devil was a virtuous earthling's revenge on the wicked, "a tool of the oppressed." A moral universe, which we supposedly inhabit, necessarily requires judgment and retribution. While it should be evident that the wicked *should* not prosper, it was nonetheless obvious to all that on earth the wicked *did* prosper far too often, whereas the virtuous, like Job, were too often struck with disasters and covered with those damned "sore boils." Ouch! Robbers and thieves and murderers got away with their malfeasance as often as not—that was plain for all to see. The rich were often evil, rulers oppressive, the feckless successful—that was plain too. Thus, after a while it really didn't seem fair for sinners to lounge away eternity in bucolic peace along with the virtuous.

As hundreds of writers have pointed out, dating back to Origen in the second century, god is meant to be love, and his creatures are meant to live in a just world. So how could gluttons, adulterers, killers, and whoremongers prosper? As Tobias Swinden indignantly put it in 1727,

> Indeed if there be a God, and his Providence be allowed, it must be supposed he will do right: And since things happen promiscuously in this World, so that there is one Event to the Righteous, and to the Wicked; nay, since it oftentimes cometh to pass, that the Troubles of the Righteous are many; that they have none, or little of the Enjoyments of this World; that they are cut down and withered, while the Wicked flourish like a green Bay-Tree, are in no fear of Death, come into no Trouble neither are plagued like other Men: I say, since these things are thus, how can exact Justice be done if there be not a future State? How can the seeming incongruities of this Life be reconciled and made even, but by the equal Distributions of the next, wherein good Men shall be mightily rewarded and evil Men as mightily punished? [10]

Many early Jewish (and Old Testament) texts make the same balancing assumption. For example, Malachi 4:1–3 puts it this way: "For, behold, the day cometh, that shall burn as an oven; and all the proud, yea, and all that do wickedly, shall be stubble: and the day that cometh shall burn them up, saith the Lord of hosts, that it shall leave them neither root nor branch. But unto you that fear my name shall the Sun of righteousness arise with healing in his wings; and ye shall go forth, and grow up as calves of the stall. And ye shall tread down the wicked; for they shall be ashes under the soles of your feet in the day that I shall do this, saith the Lord of hosts."

The devil, then, is an explanation for evil. On the one hand, there must be a devil because so many evil things happen that cannot possibly be attributed to god—therefore there must be a god-obverse, to cause evil. On the other hand, the devil is there as a way for god to punish the wicked. The contradictions in these stances were not always obvious. But in sum, it was surely obvious that in the afterlife god would, at last, reward the virtuous and damn malefactors—that there would be one place of punishment, and another of reward, and in this sense whether the devil was god's agent or god's enemy was not really relevant. Either would do. Supernatural sanctions would be the great leveller. Malefactors would be shown to a reserved suite in a prison of despair and desolation—*that* would serve them! Hell would be the locus of god's unappeasable revenge. As *The Economist* pointed out in "Hell: A Rough Guide," just as man has always made god in his own image, so he projected his own notions of fairness onto the world to come, and ended up with a horror show.

Or, hell is a self-improvement spa

SOME HELLS, SUCH as many of the Hindu and Buddhist versions, have no devils or even demons; their hells were self-policing. Sure, there is management of a sort, but the managers are there to help, not hinder—to help souls improve their thinking and thus their deeds. There is torture aplenty, but it is for the souls' own good, not punishment for punishment's sake. There has to be some way, after all, for the dead to work out the evil deeds they did in this life before they can move on to the next one—and what better method to concentrate the mind than bodily flaying and boiling and burning and cutting and mincing and crushing? All souls, no matter how virtuous, must go to hell in Buddhist and Hindu doctrine, there to be sorted into classes—virtue, relative virtue, not-so-good, pretty bad, thoroughly evil, and more. True, the really virtuous get to skip the bad parts and gain early checkout, but they do have to show up anyway—it is not enough for souls to judge themselves virtuous; hellish record-keepers do that for them. The punishment in these hells is never eternal: the souls merely have to wait until the karma of previous incarnations has been worked through and the soul purified. This could take a very long time, but was not forever.

Fitness regimens, you might say, tailor-made for all.

Or, hell is just an amplification of death

IN YET ANOTHER view, hell began simply as an amplification of death, which otherwise remained mysterious. At first, it was merely an underworld (*hel* in Old German meant something like "to cover"), a land of shadows, a cavern for the dead where decomposition was the norm, a gathering place for ghosts and goblins, the locus of dreams, the one place where the gods were not. This was the majority view in Old Mesopotamia, for example. It was also the early Jewish view. Later hell became a place for parking the enemies of heaven, and after that it became the proper place for the Unredeemed, an abode of evil and despair, where sinners pay the price for their wickedness. Sometimes they paid that price forever.

Put all these parts together, and hell begins to grow in the human imagination.

There is one more theory: hell is real

IN WHICH CASE, we just have to decide which one.

CHAPTER 2

HELL-FREE ZONES

EVEN SO, WHY ARE SOME CULTURES HELL-FREE AND others hell-bent? As argued above, heaven and hell are codependent, and so are religion and politics. How, then, are malefactors dealt with in those societies without the controls of hell, and what is the "afterlife" like in those cosmologies, if indeed there is one?

We're rather prone to thinking of an animist world filled with multiple gods and goblins as primitive, but that's a pejorative even more condescending than Grayling's tone in *The God Argument*. In fact, the animist view is in a real sense less primitive than our own closely held beliefs about the incarnate dualism between eternally divine good and eternally infernal evil. We also tend to think of the life so portrayed as, per the Hobbesian phrase, nasty, brutish, and short. Most writing about the pre-agrarian era assumes that a world governed by capricious spirits and demons must have been a world of terror, with our early ancestors huddling around a fire, fearful of the night—or even the day. But was it? It may have been short, but it might not have been either brutish or nasty. Indeed, there is considerable evidence, from studies of the few hunter-gatherer societies still extant, that it might have been a great deal more pleasant than that. And even its presumed brevity is now under scientific review.

No hell in Old Africa

AS HUMAN POLITICS developed, the supernatural became stratified and ever more complicated. But even so, there were sophisticated cultures that found no reason for hell and little point in punishment. Generally, but with some interesting exceptions, those are the same cultures that equally resisted the notion of heaven and salvation, a heresy that greatly distressed early Christian missionaries to, say, Africa, who saw only what they were pleased to call "ancestor worship," and took it as further evidence of the ignorance of the benighted heathen. Of course, from our own perspective, eternal hellfire seems hardly more progressive, but there it is. It is plausible that monotheisms must necessarily be authoritarian—and arbitrary—in nature.

IN MOST TRADITIONAL African societies, and in other widely scattered cultures—such as those of the Aboriginal peoples of Australia—there was really no need for hell. Sure, the world had a creator, who had to live somewhere, often in what seems rather like a summer resort for himself, his family, and various magical minions, but this had little to do with ordinary people. For them, there was no clear dividing line between life and death: these were not mutually exclusive. Death didn't end, and barely altered, the continuous person. Life's journey was a dynamic process involving the acquisition or loss of "power," or life force, and death merely caused a small change in the continuum of existence. So the dead continued to live in the community, and to take part in communal decision-making. The only difference was you couldn't see them, and had to communicate in sometimes annoyingly indirect ways. In this view, there was no need to fear a hell (or, indeed, to anticipate paradise). Punishment was for those who were alive, not dead. The afterworld was mostly just a replica of the normal world, and was really "here."

As a consequence, the after-death was not unpleasant, or not any more than the here and now. The greatest risk for the dead was to be forgotten: the dead can live forever, but only at the pleasure of the living—those who were no longer alive in the communal memory (in "top of mind awareness," in advertising-speak) could fade away, and eventually diminish to nothing. In Old Africa, that was the worst of hells.

This is not to say that death was not dreaded—it was. And there are exceptions to this idea of continuity, to the notion that all are welcome in the afterworld. Wizards, murderers, thieves, malefactors—they may be doomed to punishment in the afterlife as wandering ghosts, and they may be beaten and expelled by the ancestors according to the seriousness of their misdeeds. But death also became the beginning of another journey—the dead person's deeper relationship with creation. The goal of life was to become a proper and respected ancestor, one who could help link the here and now and the hereafter.

Logically enough, this human-centric view of the afterworld applied equally to gods. Among the Igbo, for example, a god who seemed ineffectual (who failed to enable his followers to harness his supernatural powers for their own benefit) would have his earthly totems—shrines, figurines—destroyed, and his memory forgotten: deicide was common against gods who failed to put out. By contrast, bad behaviour on the part of the deity is not supposed to dim a Christian's belief. To Christians, God can be a moral imbecile—think of all those mighty smitings of tribes that angered him—and yet not come in for criticism. He took the Jews out of Egypt, a good thing, surely, but at what horrendous cost to the Egyptians? The Bible doesn't seem to care, and nor do theologians. (Though it is true that the Bible does hint at the Almighty's moral failings: Abraham, after all, denounces God's plans to slaughter everyone in Sodom and Gomorrah, the righteous and the unrighteous alike, by asking the less than rhetorical question: "Shall not the Judge of all the earth do right?" Didn't work, but at least he tried.)

In Old Africa, hell, in the end, just seemed pointless, which is also a very modern point of view.

No longer. Africa was colonized by Christians and Muslims, and traditional beliefs faded. Thus heaven came to Africa. And hell.

Kur and the rise of the One Percent in Old Mesopotamia

A SUCCESSION OF cultures dating back as far as the Egyptian Old Kingdom flourished in the Tigris–Euphrates

Valley—the Sumerians, followed by the Akkadians, supplanted by the Babylonians, and finally the Assyrians and Canaanites, who were still around in the seventh century BCE. In most of these cultures, eternal bliss was largely reserved for the gods, with one human exception—the Noah-like flood survivor called Utanapishtim. Everyone else, even kings, were consigned to Kur, a dreary place where the only activity was eating and drinking, which doesn't sound so bad except that the only edible substance was dust.

This was not a place of either purgation or damnation— it was simply the eternal lot of all mortals.

In an early instance of the One Percent, though, the rich could take with them as much food and as many luxury goods as they wished, along with servants to please them. The royal tombs at Ur, in southern Mesopotamia (now Iraq), are a good example: the burial chamber of the queen contained a rich hoard of fancy stuff, plus the bodies of personal attendants, who had been obliged to perish with the royal person. Gold and lapis lazuli were commonplace, often in the shape of eight-pointed rosettes. In addition, on the ramp down into the pit was a train of fifty more dead attendants (they all drank poison so they could be with Herself forever), plus chariots and carts and their drivers, with oxen and horses bearing even more goods to the grave.[1]

In other periods the afterworld was more hellish—a land of no return, a fortress barred with seven gates, governed by a succession of Hades precursors. How do we know? From early sagas that described persons (demigods or mortals or shades, it is not always clear) descending to the underworld and returning with edifying tales. The best known of these is the Sumerian tale that recounts the heroic exploits of Gilgamesh and his friend and companion and possible lover Enkidu, which ends with the latter's death—the earliest instance of a literary downer. Other to-hell-and-back sagas from the region include the *Descent of Inanna* (*Ishtar* in the Akkadian version) *to the Underworld*, which includes piquant details of her struggles with her sister Ereshkigal, Queen of the Dead, and the saga of Baal, a colourful Canaanite tale about Baal's struggle with Mot, or Death. (Baal won, sort of.)

A dull hell for the Jews

THE EARLY HEBREWS, though an otherwise inventive people credited with (or blamed for) creating monotheism, were never very good at hell. Jewish hell was dull stuff, in fact. Most forms of Judaism didn't share the sunny Christian notion of the immortality of the soul, whether for punishment or exaltation, and in the earliest times the dead simply went to Sheol, all of them, without exception. Sheol was not a place of punishment, unless you define darkness and eternal silence as torment; like the Kur of the Mesopotamians, it was just *there*, though with none of Kur's menu of dust, for the Jewish dead didn't need food. As Ecclesiastes put it, "there is no work nor devising nor knowledge nor wisdom in Sheol."

In this regard, early Jewish thought overlapped with the surrounding cultures. The Canaanites, the Philistines, and the Ugarites (from the city of Ugarit—a subculture of the Canaanites) believed that the afterworld was a gloomy place, dank and mouldy, but that's all it was. True, Baal was a Canaanite god, and he did descend to the underworld to confront Mot, the God of Death, but none of the dead ever re-emerged from the down-under, either for punishment or reward.

The Jewish view of the afterlife changed as Israelite fortunes changed, as we shall see in more detail later. The book of Daniel, a late addition to the canon, is a case in point. A few centuries before the Christian era, Sheol was finally divided into a neighbourhood for the righteous and another for the wicked, and at the time of Jesus some Jews, though far from all, had come to believe that the dead would one day be resurrected, either to live in the bosom of Abraham, or to face a more active torment. Gehenna (originally Geh-Hinnom) then became the preferred place for punishment. Gehenna was derived from the valley around Jerusalem, which was used in pagan times for human sacrifices to the god Moloch and later as a dump for bodies and animal carcasses, and a ripe place it must have been. (Even so, some rabbinical sources say the dead wouldn't stay in either Sheol or Gehenna for any more than a year, at most, so that's not so bad.) The Greek Septuagint and the resulting Old Testament lamentably translated both Sheol and Gehenna as "Hades," and then confused Hades with hell, thereby puzzling a hundred generations of readers.

In ancient Egypt, death but no hellish torture

THE ANCIENT EGYPTIANS (the *ancient* ancient Egyptians, the ones of the early Old Kingdom) had no concept of hell either. This changed as the centuries wore on. Egypt of the Pharaohs lasted a very long time, and obviously beliefs changed considerably over the millennia, and differing views of a "hell" began to creep in. For the full three thousand years that Egypt flourished there was considerable curiosity about the transition from *here* to *there*, from life to afterlife. Behind the whole apparatus of massive tombs and the preservation of the body was the belief that the body had to remain intact, and receive regular nourishment, after death. In later centuries all the dead, except for rulers and priests who were above that sort of thing, had to undergo judgment. Bad souls were not tortured, just destroyed, and that was the end of them. For much of Egyptian history, that was that. Not only was there no eternal torment, there was no torment at all—and thus no hell.

In later dynasties, this changed. Lack of punishment came to be seen as increasingly unfair. That would soon be fixed.

The afterlife for the Japanese was as boring as it was for the Jews

SHINTO (WHICH MEANS "Way of the Gods" in Japanese) is in every definition unusual. It is a religion that really isn't a religion. It has gods, but they aren't that important, except occasionally. It has no devil, and no enforcement mechanism for sinners. It has no scripture, no holy writ. In reality, it is more a way of connecting the past to the present, an homage to tradition, than a supernatural theory—it is mystic, therefore, rather than religious.

Nevertheless, somewhere around four out of five Japanese "adhere" in some way to Shinto ways of thinking.

For our purposes, what is important is that Shinto has no hell.

True, there is an afterlife, but it is no more worked out than the Jewish Sheol. Yomi is where the dead go after life. It is neither a heaven (to which one may aspire) nor a hell (which one has to fear). It has some connection to the present world, but in reality is a gloomy and shadowy place where the dead spend perpetuity: a dull sort of afterlife indeed. The only hellish part is that the dead would know there could be no escape: as the eighth-century chronicle *Kojiki* puts it, "Once one has eaten at the hearth of Yomi, it is impossible to return to the land of the living"—thereby echoing Persephone, Orpheus, Nergal, and Ishtar: the dead are dead, stay dead, don't come home. Sinners, whoever they were, didn't need punishing. They were already dead. Enough, already.

The Druids were flexible about death, but the soul was immortal

JULIUS CAESAR, WHO was impressed with the bravery (and the ferocity) of the Celtic warriors he encountered on the field of battle, attributed these qualities to the fact that they feared no afterlife, neither heaven nor hell. "The Druids in particular wish to impress this on them that souls do not perish, but pass from one to another after death, and by this chiefly they think to incite men to valor, the fear of death being overlooked," wrote Caesar. He added that at funerals all things that had been "dear to the dead man," even living creatures, were thrown on the funeral pyre, and at times slaves and beloved retainers were also consumed, which seems a little unfair. Diodorus Siculus, a Roman historian of Caesar's time, added this piquant detail: "At the burial of the dead, some threw letters addressed to dead relatives on the funeral pyre, believing that the dead would read them in the next world." Other Roman writers compared the Celtic doctrines to those of the Greek followers of Pythagoras. One such example comes from Valerius Maximus, who wrote his popular histories at the time of Jesus. "They [the Celts] would fain make us believe that the souls of men are immortal. I would be tempted to call these breeches-wearing folk fools, if their doctrine were not the same as that of the mantle-clad Pythagoras."[2]

A few other places, too, were no-hell zones

A FEW OTHER cultures remain hell-free. The Baha'i, wisely, take a pass on the whole notion, merely saying that both heaven and hell should be understood "symbolically." Christian sects like the Jehovah's Witnesses don't believe in hell, except as the common grave of mankind. In the Americas, the Aztecs had an afterlife, and the dead soul had to go to considerable trouble to reach its goal, but they had no hell. As John Buckley put it in his ever-curious *Prophecy Unveiled*, "the perils ahead included mountains, deserts, confrontations with serpents and lizards, and a place where the wind would drive with obsidian knives. Once the person had overcome the perils of the Underworld Way, the soul would arrive before

Miclantecutli, where it would stay for four years. The final stage required the help of the man's dog, sacrificed at his death, to travel across the Ninefold Stream, and then, hound and master, to enter the eternal house of the dead, Chicomemictlan." No choosing, no judging, no fear of rejection—just a long slog.[3]

The early inhabitants of New Zealand (the Maoris) and Australia (the various Aboriginal tribes) had similar beliefs. For the Maoris, you needed to cross a river to get to the afterlife, at which point you would be greeted by long-lost family and friends in a kind of joyous reunion. Sure, you had to get past the usual array of monstrous creatures, precipitous cliffs, and nasty winds, but pretty well everyone made it, nice or not, and hell as a place of punishment never came into play. A few of the Aboriginal peoples of Australia believed in a post-death place "somewhere across the sea," but most reckoned that the dead hung around, pretty much where they had lived, and got on with post-life in common with the spirits of other ancestors and the life embedded in the land itself. In Australia as in Africa: no hell.

CHAPTER 3

WHERE THE HELL IS IT?

Probably down there somewhere
. . . but where's the gate?

IF YOU'RE GOING TO HELL, WHERE IS IT? HOW DO
you *get there?* And *get in?* And what is the journey like?

For those societies that did and do believe in an
actual hell, where was (and is) it to be found? Well, the
London *Daily Mail*, if you can remain undiverted by
the self-exclamatory "explosive interview" with Victoria
Beckham on the same page, believes it knows where Hades
was: in the cavern named Alepotrypa, in Diros Bay, Mani,
in southern Greece, which was recently "re-discovered
by a man walking his dog" (a nice rhetorical detail). The
Mail's evidence is sketchy: the paper says archeologists
"claim" that the cavern "may" have generated (or "sparked"
in *Mail*-speak) the "age-old myth" of Hades. The fact that
this cavern was well known for decades, even centuries,
before it came to the *Mail's* attention (Patrick Leigh Fer-
mor wrote about its history in his quite splendid travelogue

called *Mani*) doesn't detract a whit from the newspaper's excitement. The size of the cavern, a full 1,000 metres, with its own lake, is advanced as further evidence, as is the ruin inside it of a Neolithic village, long abandoned. Well, the kingdom of Hades had to be somewhere. Rather lacks the teeming demons and sulphurous fumes and "villainous smoaks" that eyewitnesses like Virgil and the Venerable Bede recall, but why not?

Naturally, there are other claimants, even in the modern era. The Italian news agency Agenzia Nazionale Stampa Associata (ANSA), for example, reported in 2013 that another team of archeologists had uncovered the entrance to Pluto's Gate to Hell (a.k.a. the Plutonion) in a small cave near a temple to Apollo, just outside the Phrygian city of Hierapolis, in southwestern Turkey (now known as Pamukkale). This gateway had also been known for millennia, though its location had been mislaid; it appeared in the writings of Cicero and the geographer Strabo, who died in 24 CE, both of whom reported having visited it.

It's a puzzle how they could have lost track of the place for all those centuries. It is, after all, a cave in the earth's crust from which foul-smelling toxic gases emerge (birds unfortunate enough to fly through these emanations die, and the entrance is strewn with their corpses). Strabo himself recorded the same thing. In his time, pilgrims were wont to sacrifice bulls to Pluto by the simple expedient of leading them to the entrance and watching them keel over. "This space is full of vapor so misty and dense that one can scarcely see the ground. Any animal that passes inside meets instant death. I threw in sparrows and they immediately breathed their last breath and fell." In one of his more colourful quotes, Strabo wrote that the eunuchs of the goddess Cybele were able to enter the cave, through the fumes, unaffected. "They held their breath as long as possible and gained immunity either from their menomation [their castration], divine providence, or certain physical powers that are antidotes against the vapor."[1]

For the pedantic, these fumes are called mephitic gases—named, as Austin Considine recounted in a hilarious piece for *Vice*, "after the Samnite love goddess, Mephitis; common skunks are called *Mephitis mephitis*."[2] (In a footnote to history, the Samnites are remembered for being a tribal people of southern Italy who fought three wars with Rome, losing every one. They are also fondly remembered by romantics because their goddesses greatly outnumbered and out-manoeuvred their gods, who seemed a particularly thick lot.)

Francesco D'Andria, the archeologist who announced the Hierapolis discovery, said his team found the remains of a temple at the site, and a pool used by pilgrims, with a series of steps. "We could see the cave's lethal properties during the excavation," he told ANSA. "Several birds died as they tried to get close to the warm opening, instantly killed by the carbon dioxide fumes."[3]

Another possible hellish location is in Turkmenistan, but the geologists who discovered it in the 1970s set it on fire, and it has been burning ever since. This claimant, predictably known in the local tourist literature as the Door to Hell, is outside the little village of Derweze (or Darvaza), in the Karakum Desert, about 260 kilometres north of Ashgabat, the Turkmen capital. This, too, was the topic of a breathless piece in the *Daily Mail*, which clearly has a fondness for netherworldian addresses. The hole, a massive 70 metres in diameter, was opened up by Soviet geologists drilling for oil, resulting in a methane blowout. The ground beneath the drilling rig collapsed into the hell below, and the geologists decided to burn off the gas to prevent atmospheric contamination. They optimistically hoped the burn-off would take only days, but forty-five-and-counting years later it is still going strong. In April 2010, the country's strongman, Gurbanguly Berdimuhamedow, ordered that the hole be closed. So far, no one has found the means to make it so.[4]

The old sagas knew what hell was, but were vague on where

THE EGYPTIANS, FOR example, sometimes seemed to believe that the underworld—even they occasionally used the term, though "afterworld" was more common—actually surrounded the upper world. But not always. Wherever it was, it was some distance away. Egyptians of the Middle Kingdom and later had to travel a good distance to get there. Not surprisingly, considering Egypt's dependence on the Nile, the journey entailed a boat trip along a river, barred by seven (or eight) gates, which let only the righteous through. This river flowed in Tuat, the land of the dead. The ultimate destination was the kingdom of Osiris, where select souls could enjoy eternal life. The others? They ended up in a shadowy underground realm, "somewhere," a river divided in turn into burning regions, with caves, lakes of hellfire, and cauldrons of burning rock.

Though these notions were to become cross-culturally familiar, even clichéd, the texts are silent on where this shadowy realm is located.

As reported, Baal, the potent god of the Ugaritic (Canaanite) culture of the second millennium BCE, set off to visit hell to wrestle with death; he found it in a hole along with the "earth gods" ("earth" meaning hell in this context), though he doesn't say where this hole is located. The Baal sagas do say that the entrance to the underworld is at "the base of the mountains at the end of the desert"—presumably it was known which desert was meant, so the fragments are silent on the subject. Baal's city sounds a challenge to promote in tourist brochures: the city was called Swamp, Baal's own palace was Sludge, and the surrounding lands were Phlegm.[5] Baal's sister, as we will see, is an even more potent deity than Baal himself, and a lot angrier.

The Kur of the Mesopotamians and much of the ancient Middle East was, as indicated in the previous chapter, a dark underworld realm, sometimes home to the gods of, or related to, the earth, the so-called chthonic gods, but mostly it was merely a repository for the dead, a dark and gloomy place without features or relief. Everybody went there, but where it was located remained largely unreported.

Almost all the old sagas mention a "descent" on the journey to hell. Just so, the *Underworld Vision of an Assyrian Crown Prince* put hell deep underground. The *Book of Arda Viraf* doesn't say where hell is, but then Viraf was caught up in quasi-pornographic descriptions of the torments awaiting the damned, and geography wasn't high on his list of skills. Ishtar, famously, visited "the land of no return," the underworld itself. As the saga says,

> To the land of darkness,
> Ishtar, the Daughter of Sin,
>   directed her thought. . . .
> To the house of shadows, the
>   dwelling of Irkalla,
> To the house without exit for
>   him who enters therein,
> To the road whence there is no turning,
> To the house without light for
>   him who enters therein,
> The place where dust is their
>   nourishment, clay their food.
> They have no light, in
>   darkness they dwell.
> Clothed like birds, with
>   wings as garments.[6]

Grim enough, but it could be almost anywhere, judging from that description. Underground is all we know.

Greco-Roman Hades was surely down there, somewhere . . .

THE GREEKS, AS we will see when we deal with hell's architecture, had a meticulously detailed vision of how hell (or Tartarus, part of Hades) was organized and something of its politics; but they were vague as to its address, except that it was surely a shadowy place beneath the earth. (But see Hierapolis and Alepotrypa, above.) Other early Greek writers located it variously in a field in Sicily, a cave at Taenarum on the southern tip of the Peloponnese (that's how both Orpheus and Hercules got there), and where the river Acheron still plunges into its gorges. Maybe it was in all of these places, and had more than one gateway.

The Romans of the Caesars disagreed with all the precursor locations—they more or less adopted the Greeks' quarrelsome family of gods in its entirety, but since Rome was the centre of the known universe, both Olympus and Hades must perforce be found within the empire. Some writers suggest the gates to hell could be found along the Rhine, or the Danube. Vulcan, blacksmith to the gods, located his forge under Vesuvius, or Etna, or Vulcano in the Tyrrhenian Sea north of Sicily; the exact location depends on your authority, but at least they were all nicely within Roman jurisdiction. There he made mighty weapons for the endless wars waged by his brothers and sisters—this surely was the most argumentative clutch of gods in world history. The hot lava fragments and clouds of dust erupting from Vulcano (or Etna, or Vesuvius) came from the forge itself as the armourer Vulcan beat out thunderbolts for Jupiter and weapons for Mars. (Venus, famously, cheated on Vulcan with Mars, which made him surly and more warlike than ever.) If Vulcan was there, Hades couldn't be far away, surely. Slowly, by consensus, the entrance to the underworld came to be located at Avernus, a crater near Cumae, outside of Naples. In any case, that's where Aeneas entered, as Virgil reported; the locals built temples to Apollo and Jupiter there, and excavated a tunnel leading to the grotto of one of the nastier sibyls.

Trivial as the *Daily Mail*'s fascination with gates to Hades may seem, at least their cavern was reliably underground. With a few exceptions, pretty much anyone who has been to hell, or has professed to knowledge of the topic, understands that much. The Greek geographer Pausanias, who made it his life's work to find this sort of thing out, located hell "as far beneath Hades as Hades is beneath the Earth." It seemed obvious to him, as to almost all the ancients, that the dead and living, especially the bad dead and the good living, had to be kept far apart.

Jesus never said where hell was, nor did the Prophet

TO THE EARLY Jews, Hades or Sheol was far below the ground, dark, silent, and without memory, a grievous lack. Sheol, like Homer's Hades, is a dark, dreary, shadowy pit where most are "gathered to their people." As suggested earlier, Sheol came eventually to contain separate divisions for the righteous and the wicked, a notion picked up and embellished by the Christians, who earlier had pictured an underground cavern shared by all, good and bad, for eternity—not unlike, in point of fact, the *Daily Mail*'s thousand-metre cavern inhabited by the various divisions of Hades. Jewish lore is vague on hell, because the Hebrew Bible basically ignores the place: it is nowhere mentioned in the first five books of the Old Testament; God created the earth and moulded man from clay, but seemed to neglect a netherworld. At death, the person becomes "a dead breath," the body returns to dust, and the spirit returns to God. So much we have already recounted. But how you actually get to the dust place is never described.

The earliest books of the Bible described an underground cavern where all people, good and bad, spent eternity after death. Later books were more informed, if rather opaque. For example, Ezekiel 31:16 has God declare of Lucifer, "I made the nations to shake at the sound of his fall, when I cast him down to Hell with them that descend into the pit: and all the trees of Eden, the choice and best of Lebanon, all that drink water, shall be comforted in the nether parts of the earth." Colourful, but not something you can plug into your GPS. Still, Lebanon is a hint. If Eden was there, why not hell?

Jesus never said where hell was. He was good on the wailings and gnashings of teeth there, but where all this happened he didn't deign to say, not even after visiting the place to rescue Adam.

Neither the Qur'an nor the Prophet in his many *hadith* located hell. Modern imams are vague: "No one knows its exact location but God," is a common hedge. Still, Muhammad did reveal that the ungodly would go there: "And surely, hell is the promised place for them all. It has seven gates, for each of these gates is a class of sinners assigned."[7] Each gate got its share of the damned, each according to his deeds. When unbelievers are brought to hell, its gates will open, they will enter it, and stay in it forever. It is true that in certain readings of certain *hadith*, hell is located in the heavens, where Allah could keep an eye on it, but mostly it is assumed that it is in lower earth, the underworld or netherworld, which is where pretty well everyone else places it.

In the medieval Christian imagination, many travellers reported seeing hell's smoke coming up through holes in the ground, so it must be downstairs. Dante, the Western world's most famous infernal chronicler, agreed: Satan was at the bottom of hell, with his navel marking the very centre of the earth. Hell wasn't very large, though: Dante managed to tour the whole afterworld in less than a week, and this even includes his later trip to heaven.

Milton, in *Paradise Lost*, was even vaguer than this. Since his great poem was set in the time of Adam and Eve, when the earth was still unsullied by sin, hell was mostly unpeopled; his descriptions of the place as well as his depictions of its management will be recounted in a later chapter. Still, Milton did say it took Satan nine days to fall from heaven to hell, so if heaven is above, as assumed, hell must be down there somewhere.

Perhaps hell is beneath Ireland?

YET ANOTHER CANDIDATE, admittedly rather a hell-come-lately, surrounds the cult of Saint Patrick, who located the entrance gate on Station Island in Lough Derg, a popular pilgrimage site in County Donegal.

Whether Patrick, a fifth-century saint popularly credited with bringing Christianity to Ireland, ever visited Station Island remains doubtful. The legends say that Patrick was having trouble persuading the local heathen of the righteousness of his visions, so God showed him the entrance to purgatory, the newly invented antechamber to hell, so the recalcitrant could see for themselves the horrors that awaited them *sans* conversion. Its real popularity stems from a later legend, that of the Knight Owayne (or Owein). The *Tractatus de purgatorio sancti Patricii*, written somewhere around 1179, describes how Owein entered the gloomy entrance to purgatory, where he met a group of men, one of whom told him to mention Jesus wherever he ran into difficulties. He was also told not to turn back, however attractive the offers to do so, until he had finished his tour. By later medieval standards, the travails he found were modest enough—a wheel of red-hot nails, a hall of boiling cauldrons, whirlwinds, stinking rivers, and a pit with demons: so far so conventional. What was new was that these punishments were for all the dead awaiting judgment, not just for sinners, a bleak enough vision—this was a time when the notion of purgatory was entering mainstream Catholic thought. Still, the name of Jesus turned out to be the proper passcode, just as he had been informed, and when he had safely reached the antechamber to heaven he was sent back the way he came, now piously impervious to demons.

Because of its purgatorial association, a number of medieval writers produced tracts on Station Island; a 1492 world map shows it as one of the principal landmarks of Ireland. It remained a popular sanctuary until it was abruptly shut down by Pope Alexander VI in 1497, for reasons that remain obscure. It was reopened after the pope's death, and though it never quite regained its cachet, a splendid basilica was built on the spot, subsequently refurbished. It now serves as a retreat, not a portal to hell. As the retreat's website (www.loughderg.org)

puts it, "Lough Derg is . . . set in calm lake waters, offers no distraction, no artificialities or interruptions. Instead you are warmly welcomed and cared for: there are no strangers here. The island, made holy by the prayers of millions of pilgrims over the centuries, continues to provide a safe haven for rest, reflection and renewal to all who wish to 'come away to a quiet place and rest a while (Mark 6:31).' "[8] In this atmosphere, the tortures Owein witnessed seem a long time ago.

Modern science puts hell in the sun—so proved in 1727

THERE ARE EXCEPTIONS in the literature to this notion of hell being below. Even the Christian texts weren't unanimous: most place hell where the ancients put it— the centre of the earth, entered through caves, bogs, volcanoes and so forth—but some place hell in the upper atmosphere. For instance, in 1696 William Whiston put it in a comet "ascending from the Hot Regions near the Sun, and going into the Cold Regions beyond Saturn, with its long smoking Tail arising up from it."[9]

Tobias Swinden's massive and argumentative 1727 tome, *An Enquiry into the Nature and Place of Hell*, put hell in the sun, the hottest place imaginable, and also the farthest in his scheme of things from the Empyrean, or heaven. At the time, these placements in the air represented a "modern" gloss on ancient knowledge, scientific savvy having improved some since Virgil, or Dante for that matter. This is certainly what Swinden himself asserted— that the natural philosophers of his time looked with scorn on the ignorant imaginings of their predecessors, dismissing them (Dante very much included) as "such light, airy and fantastick Stuff will better befit a dreaming visionary Writer, than one that pretendeth to be awake and to design nothing but Reality and Truth." That was a bit rich, no? Accusing Dante of fake news?

Swinden spent his opening chapters arguing for the very existence of hell. There must be one, he argued, "for if these things were not in themselves true and real, how could the Ideas of them be so powerfully imprinted on the Minds of all Mankind, so that no Nation of the World was ever so barbarous as not to own them? Nay, it is utterly impossible to eradicate the Notions of them out of any one Person without the Faculties of whose Mind are not disordered by Phrensy, or disabled by Stupidity."

Okay, but where is it, this hell? It was believed by the ancients ("the heathen") that it was in a certain large and dark place under the earth.

> Some of the Latins, from the Grecians, placed it in subterraneous Regions, immediately under the Lake Avernus in Campania a Country of Italy in the Realm of Naples; it was through a dark Cave near this Lake, the Poet Virgil saith, that Aeneas visited the infernal Kingdoms. Others placed it under Tenarus a Promontory of Laconia in Peloponnesus; only because it was a horrid dark Place, full of thick Woods, into which if any enter they were very rarely known to return, being usually lost, either through the vast Extent and inextricable

Windings of the Woods themselves, or
by the Fury of Wild Beasts that devoured
them. And by this way, the Poet Ovid saith,
Orpheus descended into hell. Others fan-
cied the River or Fountain of Styx to be the
Spring-head of hell because the Waters of
it were so venomous, that they surely kill'd
any thing that drank of them.

No, Swinden argued. This was all poetic fancy, or
stupidity, or both. On the contrary, hell must be in a
place as hot and as far away as possible. This must surely
be the sun, and he devoted several chapters to his proof.
The headings say it all: "That the Fire of Hell is not Met-
aphorical but Real"; "On the Improbability of Hell Fires
being in or About the Center of the Earth"; "A Conjecture that the Body of the Sun is the Local Hell, with an
apology for the Novelty of it"; "Reasons for the Aforesaid
Conjecture"; "Objections from Atheism and Philosophy Answered"; "Objections from the Holy Scriptures
Answered; and Objections from the Benefits of the Sun
to us in this World, Answered."[10]

Strong evidence for hell near the city of Fengdu, in south-central China

ONE OF THE most famous Asian explorers of the netherworld was Governor Kwoh, who somewhere around
1573 personally inspected hell, which he found outside
Fengdu, in Sichuan province; it was 200 feet below the
surface, he reported, and he reached it by being lowered

on a rope. (We will meet Governor Kwoh again in a later chapter where he gives a first-person account of his exploits.) Other Chinese Buddhists suggested that the afterworld was just west of China, on the other side of Mount T'ai, safely out of the empire's grasp, but much closer to China than the Indian Buddhists claim. A Taoist tract, the *Treatise on the Infernal Regions*, fixed the site, or rather the entrance to it, somewhere in the province of Sichuan, as Governor Kwoh had said, close to Fengdu. Outside hell there are mountains, a wide sea, and massifs of iron. The actual entrance, in this version, is also in the side of a mountain close to town of Fung-U-hsien (a.k.a. Fengdu). Twenty years later a naval officer, Wang Ming, stumbled ashore near Fengdu and came across the ghost of his dead wife, newly married to the equally ghostly P'an-kuan. The blissful couple was living in the suburbs of hell, and Wang was given a guided tour.[11]

Or maybe hell is under the Gulf of Mexico

XIBALBA, AS THE Mayan afterworld was called (the bad part as well as the good), lay "far to the west," and it was therefore popular among the influential to be buried as far west as Mayan territory went. Xibalba had several "entrances"—either on the "islands of Campeche" off the west coast of the Yucatan Peninsula, which no longer seem to exist, or through a cave near Coban, in Guatemala. "Xibalba was entered through a cave or area of still water in Tlalticpac, which was the surface of the earth and the first of the nine underworld levels. The Milky Way was also considered an entrance to Xibalba and the road along which souls walked to meet their fate. The Maya, believing the underworld had nine different levels, represented this idea in the gigantic stone pyramids they built as tombs for their kings which often have nine tiers."[12]

Wherever it is, you probably have to pass through gates

HELL, SOMEWHAT LIKE heaven, is generally a gated community. Dante's gate is famously inscribed, "Abandon all hope, ye who enter here." Less famously, this is only the last of a nine-line inscription, which includes the claim that the realm within was created by the "Highest Wisdom and the Primal Love," which seems doubtful, and a trifle sacrilegious.[13]

In Milton's *Paradise Lost*, the Western tradition's second most famous description of hell, there are nine gates—three made of brass, three of iron, and three of adamantine rock—and they are guarded by Sin, Death, and the ever-barking hounds of hell.

This notion of gates is a device that goes back a long way, almost to the beginning of recorded history. Many of the ancient Egyptian texts, the so-called Coffin Texts, that deal with the afterlife describe gates—and their guardians, demons all. The dead souls were queried by each demon in turn and needed to know the secrets that would let them pass—hence the existence, in many ancient coffins, of spells to serve as passwords. None of the texts say where the gates are, only that they exist. Only one ancient text suggests a route map, and that is *The Book of Two Ways*, found on coffins near Hermopolis (modern Al-Ashmūnayn) dating from the Middle Kingdom.

You couldn't tell from the context where the two ways actually went, but the text does describe the seven gates and the nature of the demons that controlled access. Judging from their names, these demons would not win any sociability contests. They are the One Who Cuts Them Down; the One Who Eats the Excrement of His Rear; the Noisy One with Opposed Face; the One with Upside Down Face and Numerous of Forms; the One Who Lives on Worms; the One Who Raises His Voice in Flame; and, somewhat cryptically, the One Who Stretches Out the Prow-Rope. Most of the spells insist that the deceased person tell the appropriate demon that he is "the ... sharp [end] of the striking force (of god), which has no opposition"; this is apparently a *laissez-passer* for all occasions.[14]

Virgil took up this gate motif in *The Aeneid*:

> In front stands a huge gate, and pillars of solid adamant, that no might of man, nay, not even the sons of heaven, could uproot in war; there stands an iron tower, soaring high, and Tisiphone [one of the Furies], sitting girt with bloody pall, keeps sleepless watch over the portal night and day. . . . Then at last, grating on harsh, jarring hinge, the infernal gates open. Do you see what sentry sits in the doorway? What shape guards the threshold? The monstrous Hydra, still fiercer, with her fifty black gaping throats, dwells within. Then Tartarus itself yawns sheer down, stretching into the

gloom twice as far as is the upward view of
the sky toward heavenly Olympus.[15]

The Mesopotamians encountered gates too. When
Ishtar visited the underworld on her ill-fated visit to her
sister, she had to pass through seven gates, each more
humiliating than the last.

Islam, which isn't as obsessed with hell (or Jahannam,
a.k.a. Geganna) as the Christians, nevertheless had its
views—and its gates.

Hell is a fiery pit, hot and dry like the desert itself,
enclosed by seven gates, far below the surface of the
earth. "The Qur'an mentions 7 regions of Jahannam [each
with its gate]: Jahannam proper, Latha (flaming inferno),
Hutamah (destroying blaze), Sa'hir (blaze), Saqr (scorching fire), Gahim (fierce fire) and Haiyeh (great abyss). As
the skin of the damned burns away, Allah regenerates
it so sinners can suffer anew. But Allah is also merciful,
and can redeem souls from this punishment."[16]

Merciful, sure. And it wasn't forever. That was good.

Not just gates—bridges too

BRIDGES WERE ANOTHER common entryway to hell.
Often enough, souls crossing the bridge would be just
fine (and go to heaven) if they were pious, but would likely
fall off if they weren't, and be consigned to whatever grim
fate awaited them. Critical to the Zoroastrian notions
of hell was the Chinvât Bridge (Bridge of Accountants),
which served just this purpose.[17]

The bridge motif was taken up by Pope Gregory I (a.k.a. Gregory the Great), who was pontiff from 590 until 604; in his case it crossed the "infernal river," and was just as perilous as its Zoroastrian predecessor. Islam adopted a bridge too, though in that case the Bridge of al-Sirat led to heaven, not hell. It was also picked up by the medieval tract called *The Vision of Tundale*, whose eyewitness description of Satan we will encounter later; Tundale had to take a cow across his bridge, a nice rustic touch. Tundale was himself influenced by writings attributed to the Irish mystic called Adamnán, bishop of Iona, who died in 704, and who was fond of bridges too. We'll come back to Adamnán's description of hell in more detail later; a quick reference to his bridge, from Boswell's translation, will suffice for the moment: "His guardian angel brought him to visit the nethermost hell, with all its pains, and its crosses, and its torments. Now, the first region whereunto he came was a land burnt black, waste and scorched, but with no punishment at all therein. A glen, filled with fire, was on the further side of it; huge the flame of it, extending beyond the margin on either hand. Black its base, red the middle, and the upper part thereof. Eight serpents were in it, with eyes like coals of fire."

Then he spotted the bridge:

> An enormous bridge spans the glen, reaching from one bank to the other; high the middle of it, but lower its two extremities. Three companies seek to pass over it, but not all succeed. One company find

the bridge to be of ample width, from beginning to end, until they win across the fiery glen, safe and sound, fearless and undismayed. The second company, when entering upon it, find it narrow at first, but broad afterwards, until they, in like manner, fare across that same glen, after great peril. But for the last company the bridge is broad at first, but strait and narrow thereafter, until they fall from the midst of it into that same perilous glen, into the throats of those eight red-hot serpents, that have their dwelling-place in the glen.[18]

Obviously enough, the three groups were the pious, late converts, and sinners.

Finally! Hell's geographic coordinates

ONE OF THE "ninety-two questions" answered by the Zoroastrian seer Dastur Manuschihr in his *Religious Judgments* was this: in which direction and in which land is hell, and how is it?

Hell is divided into three districts, he wrote. One is called "that of the ever-stationary [purgatory] of the wicked . . . and the place is terrible, dark, stinking, and grievous with evil. And one is called the worst existence, and it is there the first tormentors and demons have their abode. . . . And one is called Drujaskan, and is at the bottom of the gloomy existence, where the head of the demons rush; there is the populous abode of all darkness and all evil."

In Manuschihr's telling, the word "hell" is just the collective name for all three regions together. Hell as a whole "is northerly, descending, and underneath this earth, even unto the utmost declivity of the sky; and its gate is in the earth, a place of the northern quarter, and is called the Arezur ridge, a mountain which, among its fellow mountains of the name of Arezur that are amid the rugged mountains, is said in revelation to have a great fame with the demons, and the rushing together and assembly of the demons in the world are on the summit of that mountain, or as it is called 'the head of Arezur.'"

How do you get there, and how are you greeted? "A soul of the wicked, the fourth night after passing away, its account being rendered, rolls head-foremost and totters from the Chinvât Bridge; and Vizarash, the demon, conveys him cruelly bound therefrom, and leads him unto hell."[19]

And a pleasant journey to you too.

II

WHO'S
IN
CHARGE
?

CHAPTER 4

HELL'S EXECUTIVE SUITE

The folks in the corner office . . .

BEFORE WE LOOK AT HOW HELL ACTUALLY WORKS, quick sketches of top management, the Big Men such as Hades, Tartarus, Beelzebub, Satan, and the rest, and the occasional Big Woman, along with a sense of the grave matters that preoccupy (and sometimes roil) them and their underlings.

At least in the West, Hades and Satan are widely regarded as the CEOs of hell. Sometimes they serve together, but not always—Hades usually predates Satan. And joint bossdom is seldom harmonious, as we shall see.

After the Egyptian gods (Horus and Ra and the rest) and Ereshkigal, the Assyrian Queen of the Dead, and before Satan came fully into his own through the Christian and then the Islamic traditions, the chief celebrity hell-keeper was the Greek/Roman Hades, along with a copious middle management of demons and so forth—among them his ferryman Charon, whose task was to take all the newly dead across the River Styx, where they were met by Cerberus, the many-headed hellhound. (The pious pilgrim Arda Viraf, as recorded in the Zoroastrian chronicles, met a hideous damsel instead of Cerberus, and it's hard to know which is a tougher challenge—Viraf was a little vague about what the hideous damsel actually did, except take the poor sinner in tow. Perhaps nothing. Perhaps her hideousness was enough, a mirror of the sinner's hideous soul.)

The eminences who judged the souls after arrival at the portals to hell/heaven were various. For the Greeks and Romans it was sometimes Hades himself, who in the older traditions was not a tormentor but a jailer, though more usually you could find presiding three Zeus-appointed judges, Minos, Radamanthus, and Aeacus.

In the Christian tradition, all souls are ultimately judged by God, but usually in a lesser guise, or by one of his agents; in the pop version, this would be Saint Peter at his Pearly Gates (it would be a boring job for the Almighty himself). But in mainstream Christianity, God already knew what you'd been up to, and had no need to hold court after death. In Islam, too, Allah already knew all, and the partitioning and directing of sinners was therefore pretty routine, virtually automatic—a well-worn algorithm. And once you'd been directed below? These days Lucifer (a.k.a. Satan), once an angel of light before his revolt against God, is down in the middle of the earth, imprisoned in ice, though his malice still floats free and entices sinners to sin. No longer beautiful, he is a winged fiend with cloven feet, horns, and a tail. (Like Dante, perhaps, you can peer over the edge of the eighth circle to see the Fiend below.)

Old Egypt used Horus or some other underworld god to do the judging, the sentence against those who failed carried out by the usefully named Devourer of Souls. The Mesopotamians didn't need gatekeepers or overseers, since in their view there was no upside to the afterlife—there was no heaven and everyone went to the same dreary place, just as the Japanese and the Jews did: entrance was automatic and sinners didn't need screening. The Hindus, too, had no chief demon, though Yama, the God of Death, is sometimes described as dwelling there. Yama may be the lord of the dead, but he is also (mostly) helpful, guiding individuals to the path to salvation best suited to them, quite unlike the imperious Jehovah (Yahweh) of the Old Testament, whose mind is always made up and who has, if you want to be critical, an overly rosy view of the virtues of hellfire. Buddhist hells generally have managers rather than judges, with a detailed bureaucratic structure to keep sinners on track, everything very orderly.

There is a second management rank too, an assortment of minor devils with pitchforks and haloes of brimstone, imps and demons, the Furies "guarding the dungeon's adamantine doors, and combing the black snakes hanging in their hair,"[1] cruelly beaked crows ready to rip out your intestines, along with the shades of the dead, personality-free, generally stupid, occasionally screeching like bats—the place is hellishly crowded. Dante saw centaurs and harpies (foul and loathsome birds with women's faces), the Minotaur, and three-headed Cerberus. Michelangelo includes Charon the boatman and Minos, one of the judges of the Greek underworld. Even

Milton, whose hell was set in the time of Adam and Eve and therefore still unpeopled, locates Medusa and the Hydras there. When he coined the phrase "all hell broke loose," he was really referring to demons attempting a jailbreak (hell contained demons and mighty angelic sinners aplenty, in his view). The Titans are still present, in some versions.

These demons get quite an airing in the Bible. The apostle Matthew mentions demons no fewer than eleven times, often when Jesus drives them out of possessed humans, at least once transferring them to pigs, which seems a little unfair and would get PETA on his case. Mark has ten mentions of demons, and Luke a handful. There were other mentions in Acts and of course Revelation. Indeed, it sometimes seems from the New Testament that Jesus's homeland was thick with demons; many of his miracles were aimed at winkling them out. Jewish demons, popular in early writings, were generally not of or from hell—they were mostly regarded as the souls of the wretched who "refused the place prepared for them." Hindu imps were usually just contract workers whose task it was to shepherd the souls along their path to improvement; they didn't have much autonomy.

And don't forget the few celebrity guests to be found in hell—not as part of the executive branch, merely as long-term tenants. Sisyphus, for example, was in Tartarus for killing guests at his castle and for seducing his niece (his real sin was to consider himself godlike, which really annoyed Zeus): his boring task was to forever roll a rock up a hill, a tedious punishment, to be sure, but pretty mild by hellish standards. Another was King Tantalus, banished to Hades after he cut up his son Pelops and served him as the main dish when dining with the gods. (He also stole ambrosia from the gods and blabbed about its secrets.) In hell, he is forced to stand in a pool beneath a fruit tree with low branches, without being able to drink the water or eat the fruit. Then there is the giant Tityos, who tried to rape the goddess Leto, urged on by Zeus's current wife Hera, for Leto had given birth to the twins Apollo and Artemis, fathered by Zeus, which angered Hera no end. In the stories, Hera seems constantly angry, mostly because Zeus apparently insisted on seducing all and sundry whenever he had the chance. Tityos, the "nine-acre giant," is punished rather like Prometheus—tortured by vultures feeding on his liver.[2] Virgil's *Aeneid* gives a graphic description of the awfulness of his punishment, as we will see when we follow Aeneas to hell.

Of course, then there are the short-term tourists to hell, introduced in subsequent chapters, along with a few tour guides. Here just a quick summary: heroes, for example, are often celebrated in Hades lore—Hercules for one, since he was the only mortal ever to defeat Cerberus, that damned dog, and return to the world. Orpheus, for his part, was the only one who ever melted Hades's iron-clad heart. In other traditions, Hinduism for example, kings could descend into hell for "harrowing" (essentially a rescue operation), a notion later borrowed by the Christians—Mary descended into hell in *The Apocalypse of Mary*, and so, more famously, did Jesus. Many Christian texts maintain that Jesus, sometime between his crucifixion and resurrection (or in one version, while he was still nailed to the cross), descended into hell to free the souls of those who had died before his death (we have some eyewitness accounts below). This adventure mirrors both the Zoroastrian belief and an early Jewish text, *The Testament of the Twelve Patriarchs*, which described a saviour travelling to the underworld to free his allies from Satan's grasp. In their turn Aeneas (eyewitness: Virgil) and Dante himself made it there and back, though without attempting a rescue.

Has Hades been given a bum rap?

IT CAN GET confusing, because it depends when you tap into the histories. Hades usually came before Satan, but in the early Christian stories they coincided—in the gospels of Nicodemus and Bartholomew, for example. Later, Hades faded into history in his lesser role as an innkeeper, and Satan grew in malice, reigning for more than a millennium before fading in turn under the scrutiny of the rationalists of the Enlightenment.

Hades was a place as well as a god, which adds to the confusion.

Beelzebub was a figure of mystery: sometimes he was Hades, sometimes a synonym for Lucifer. He doesn't make an appearance in the Old Testament except as an oracle consulted by Ahaziah. He first shows up in the Ugaritic Baal sagas, as Baal-Zebub, which translates, sort of, as Lord of the Flies, though it could mean Lord of the High House, or the locus of Baal's palace, up there in the clouds; then he finds a place in many of the Semitic religions before taking his place as Hades in the Greek pantheon. The medievalists confused him with Satan himself.

Hades hasn't had good press. Both Homer and Hesiod described him as "pitiless," "loathsome," and "monstrous." But to some degree this is a bum rap. He could also be regarded as the put-upon little brother.

Hades had a long tenure as the chief of the underworld. He was the son of the Titans Cronos and his wife Rhea; his brothers were "Zeus the loud-thunderer," as Homer called him, later chief of the Olympians, and Poseidon, the God of the Sea. His sisters were Hera, wife and sister to Zeus, Demeter, also at various times wife and sister to Zeus, who was the Goddess of Fertility, and Hestia, Goddess of the Hearth and Family. By no means was this an exemplary family. Hades was devoured by his father Cronos shortly after his birth, along with several of his siblings. Zeus, showing the early initiative that later made him chief, forced his father to vomit up the family, then the children banded together to drive the Titans from heaven and lock them up in the pit prepared for them in Tartarus.

Thus Greek hell began with a ferocious and deadly revolt in a pre-existing heaven. The rebels, Zeus and his siblings, won their war (unlike the Christian hell, which also began with a revolt against heaven. But the rebels lost that war, and Lucifer and his fellow angels, defeated, were dumped into hell, at first no more than a hole in the ground, with sharp rocks heaped overhead . . . but it grew from there).

In both cases, imprisoning revolutionaries was the first purpose of hell.

Newly victorious, the three brothers, Zeus, Hades, and Poseidon, drew lots to see who would reign where. Hades drew the short straw and was given the dark and dismal underworld, there to be jailer to his father. In fairness, he also acquired some positive characteristics—he was the god of the hidden wealth of the earth, including precious metals, and the seeds that nourished humans. The Romans had a softer view of him than the Greeks, naming him Dis, or Pluto, the Lord of Riches; he is often shown in Roman art, dark-bearded and regal, pouring specie from a cornucopia. He was the only god not to live on Olympus.

He was also the only known lord of the underworld to have a consort, unless you count Queen Ereshkigal's grumpy companion Nergal, a story recounted in a later chapter. The "trim-ankled" Persephone was the daughter of Zeus and the harvest goddess Demeter, and was conceived, as the myths tell us, as they "mated, like two snakes"; she was an unwilling consort, according to most versions of the stories. Persephone was abducted by Hades as he passed by in his chariot, in literature's earliest obsessive-lover tale. According to Homer's adjective-friendly *Hymn to Demeter*, Zeus was complicit in the whole thing:

> I begin to sing of rich-haired Demeter, awful goddess—of her and her trim-ankled daughter whom Aidoneus [Hades] rapt away, given to him by all-seeing Zeus the loud-thunderer.
>
> Separated from Demeter, lady of the golden sword and glorious fruits, she was

playing with the deep-bosomed daughters of Oceanus and gathering flowers over a soft meadow, roses and crocuses and beautiful violets, irises also and hyacinths and the narcissus, which Earth made to grow at the will of Zeus and to please the Host of Many, to be a snare for the bloom-like girl—a marvelous, radiant flower.

And the girl [Persephone] was amazed and reached out with both hands to take the lovely toy; but the wide-pathed earth yawned there in the plain of Nysa, and the lord, Host of Many, with his immortal horses sprang out upon her—the Son of Cronos, He who has many names.

He caught her up reluctant on his golden car and bare her away lamenting. Then she cried out shrilly with her voice, calling upon her father, the Son of Cronos [Zeus], who is most high and excellent. But no one, either of the deathless gods or of mortal men, heard her voice, nor yet the olive-trees bearing rich fruit: only tender-hearted Hecate, bright-coiffed, the daughter of Persaeus, heard the girl from her cave, and the lord Helios, Hyperion's bright son, as she cried to her father, the Son of Cronos.

But he was sitting aloof, apart from the gods, in his temple where many pray, and receiving sweet offerings from mortal men.

> So he, that son of Cronos, of many names,
> who is Ruler of Many and Host of Many,
> was bearing her away by leave of Zeus on
> his immortal chariot—his own brother's
> child and all unwilling.[3]

Demeter was furious at Zeus's treachery, and demanded her Persephone back, threatening a prolonged famine until Zeus made it happen. In the chaos that ensued, Zeus was forced to relent, but not before stipulating that Persephone's extraction from hell could only be done if she hadn't tasted any of the food in the underworld. Alas, Hades had tricked her into eating seven pomegranate seeds, and that was that—it meant she could return for only half of the year, presumably summer. Nothing in the myth cycles indicates whether Persephone had any preference in the matter—maybe she was abducted, or maybe she just grew to like Hades, down there in the dim. Ovid, in his *Metamorphoses*, hinting at an ambiguity, has Persephone herself reporting to her mother:

> I saw
> Myself with my own eyes,
>   your Proserpine.
> Her looks were sad, and fear
>   still in her eyes;
> And yet a queen, and yet
>   of that dark land
> Empress, and yet with
>   power and majesty

The consort of the sovereign
lord of Hell.[4]

Our new conventional wisdom is that she was a kid-
nap victim and an abused spouse. So there Hades sits,
glum and joyless, with a reluctant consort, in perpetual
darkness. Who wouldn't be pitiless?

Satan has had unfairly bad press too

NOW SATAN'S IS a more complicated story than Hades's.
It is possible to argue, in point of fact, that Satan (Lucifer,
Mephistopheles, sometimes Beelzebub, Ha-Satan, the
Adversary, Iblis, Shaitan, occasionally Belial, also known
in various biblical texts as the Old Serpent, the Great
Red Dragon, the Accuser of the Brethren, the Prince of
Darkness, the Great Corrupter, and more, and to children
whose parents should know better as the "boogeyman"
or Old Nick) has also suffered thoroughly bad press
through the ages, worse than Hades's, culminating in the
grotesque libels of the medieval period. (Even so, the *Trés
riche heures du duc de Berry*, quite late in the Christian
period—1413—was still able to describe Satan lounging
around a brilliant blue hell in blue robes, reclining on
"a blazing grill, inhaling and exhaling the souls of the
damned. A trio of demons work[ing] the bellows to keep
the fires going."[5] Pretty enough. No hairy, horned Fiend
there, though there were tortures aplenty.)

The scholar Elaine Pagels points out that in the early
lore of the Hebrews, Satan was not a being but an atti-
tude, *satan* being the Hebrew word for adversary. Later,

the Satan was one of God's angels, a being of superior capacity and intelligence—that's where the Christians discovered him. But as Pagels put it, "in the Hebrew Bible, as in mainstream Judaism to this day, Satan never appears as Western Christendom has come to know him, as the leader of an evil empire, an army of hostile spirits who make war on God and humankind alike; on the contrary, he appears in the books of Numbers and of Job as one of God's obedient servants—a messenger or angel . . . on the staff of the royal court."[6] (Or, as Mark Twain would have it, Satan was a chum of Gabriel and Michael in heaven, and visited earth to find out what the hell God had wrought by fashioning man, his findings recorded in a series of appalled letters home.)[7]

Sometimes, too, Satan can act as a provocateur—still doing God's will, but with a new sense of malicious mischief, if not yet malice. Take the story of Job, in the biblical book of the same name, cited by Pagels. God has been boasting to Satan and other "children of God" how faithful and obedient his people were, and Satan cajoles God into trying to prove it. God plays along with the gag, and authorizes Satan to inflict all kinds of miseries on Job, renowned (until then) as "the greatest of all men of the east." Among those miseries were the famous head-to-toe "sore boils."

There were two kinds of trials for Job: the first was to lose his property and his position, the second was more physical. The Book of Job sets the scene: "There was a day when the sons of God came to present themselves before the Lord, and Satan came also among them to present himself before the Lord. And the Lord said unto

Satan, From whence comest thou? And Satan answered the Lord, and said, From going to and fro in the earth, and from walking up and down in it."

Not much of an answer that, was it? A bit evasive. But God let him get away with it:

> And the Lord said unto Satan, Hast thou considered my servant Job, that there is none like him in the earth, a perfect and an upright man, one that feareth God, and escheweth evil? And still he holdeth fast his integrity, although thou movedst me against him, to destroy him without cause.
>
> And Satan answered the Lord, and said, Skin for skin, yea, all that a man hath will he give for his life. But put forth thine hand now, and touch his bone and his flesh, and he will curse thee to thy face. And the Lord said unto Satan, Behold, he is in thine hand; but save his life.
>
> So went Satan forth from the presence of the Lord, and smote Job with sore boils from the sole of his foot unto his crown. And he took him a potsherd to scrape himself withal; and he sat down among the ashes.
>
> In all this did not Job sin with his lips.

Sure, Job's faith is up to it, but you have to wonder at the character of a god who would take up a cruel dare like that, even if it was only meant as a test. No wonder Satan was a cynic.

Soon, in Hebrew writing, Satan got up to more and more mischief, and was blamed more and more for whatever bad things happened. Pagels gives two more examples. At least one writer (in 1 Chronicles 21) blamed Satan for persuading King David to conduct a census. Why was this so bad? Because David intended it to be used as a database for (the horror of) taxation, and faced an army revolt as a consequence. God, apparently, hated counting his folk, and hated taxation even more (though burnt offerings to him were okay). This is possibly why some of the early gnostic gospels considered David a creature of demons, as was his son, Solomon, "who built Jerusalem with the aid of demons."[8] Even after David apparently saw the error of his taxing ways and debased himself, Jehovah remained mightily annoyed, and, in what surely set a record for overreaction, offered David three bad choices: three years famine in Israel, or three months to lose constantly at battle, or pestilence in the land. David, not wanting to be either hungry or a loser, chose pestilence, and the Lord sent an avenging angel to destroy 70,000 Israelites with plague. Indeed, the Lord's pique was so great that he barely restrained himself from destroying Jerusalem. ("And God sent an angel unto Jerusalem to destroy it: and as he was destroying, the Lord beheld, and he repented him of the evil, and said to the angel that destroyed, It is enough, stay now thine hand.")

The other instance was when the exiled Jews returned from Babylon, causing some resentment among those who had stayed behind. As the Remainers (to borrow a Brexit term) complained, the prophet Zechariah, among others, blamed a *satan* (Hebrew for "adversary") for putting them up to it. Thus began the process of turning Satan from a helper to a mischief-maker to an adversary of God.

In the early days, there were a few upbeat appraisals of Satan

THERE WERE SOME early resisters to the steady infernalization of Satan (though they were promptly denounced as heretics, themselves agents of the chief heretic himself). In some accounts Satan was not the devil of later ill repute but a wise person.

In one of the gnostic gospels found at Nag Hammadi, *The Testimony of Truth*, the anonymous author turned the whole Adam and Eve story on its head. In this version, God was the villain for falsely threatening the First Couple with death if they ate from the forbidden tree; the snake on the other hand, "who was wiser than all the animals that were in paradise," told them their eyes would be opened, and they would gain in knowledge and stature. And guess who was right about that forbidden fruit—God or the snake?

In any case, after Adam and Eve donned their fig-leaf aprons, God came along, looking for them, and the couple hid themselves, a giveaway for the Almighty, who knew at once that they had done what he had told them not to, and that they now knew too much. Who instructed you to do this? asked God. Eve, said Adam, passing the blame along. The snake, said Eve, passing it further. "And God cursed the snake, and called him devil. And he said,

Look, Adam has become like one of us, knowing evil and good. Then he said, Let us cast him out of Paradise, lest he take from the tree of life, and eat, and live forever."

At this point, *The Testimony of Truth* lets God have it:

> What sort is this God? First he begrudged Adam from eating of the tree of knowledge, and, secondly, he said Adam, where are you? God does not have foreknowledge? Would he not know from the beginning?
>
> And afterwards, he said, Let us cast him out of this place, lest he eat of the tree of life and live forever. He has certainly shown himself to be a malicious grudger! And what kind of God is this? For great is the blindness of those who read, and they did not know him. And he said, "I am the jealous God; I will bring the sins of the fathers upon the children until three (and) four generations."
>
> And he said, "I will make their heart thick, and I will cause their mind to become blind, that they might not know nor comprehend the things that are said." But these things he has said to those who believe in him and serve him!

The second-century gnostic text called *The Origin of the World* was even more cynical (and decidedly proto-feminist). In this version, when Adam awoke after his creation, he was urged by Eve (who was already there) to stand on his own feet, instead of crawling around like that. "He at once opened his eyes and he saw her [Eve] and said, you will be called the Mother of the Living, because you have given me life."

Then "the authorities" (creators of the world, a.k.a. God) saw Eve talking to Adam, "and they said to each other, who is this enlightened woman? She looks like what appeared to us in the light. Come, let us seize her and ejaculate our semen into her, so that she may be unclean and unable to ascend to her light, and her children will serve us. But let us not tell Adam, because he is not one of us. Instead let us put him to sleep and suggest to him that Eve came from his rib, so that the woman may serve and he may rule over her."

This cynical ploy by God did not, however, fool Eve for an instant. "Since Eve was a heavenly power, she laughed at what they had in mind. She blinded their eyes and secretly left something that resembled her with Adam."

In both these gospels, God was bamboozled, Adam a dupe, Eve smarter than they—so there. In both versions, too, the serpent (Satan) was wiser and more generous than God. To punish Satan for his presumption, God caused him to creep on his belly thereafter, a fairly typical act of petty revenge.

Another early text, *The Nature of the Rulers*, told a very similar tale. There were slight differences: God is called "the Archons," who are described as having "bodies that are both male and female, with the faces of beasts"; and Eve (also created first) disguised herself as a tree when the Archons wanted to ejaculate on her in order to discredit her. Again, Eve prevailed, and again Adam was a mere dupe. Later, Eve "became" the serpent. God made the world, but Eve/Satan remade it.

This revisionism was strong stuff, but it didn't go as far as the later Cathars in their more comprehensive heresy, who believed that Satan actually created the world and everything in it after being unjustly expelled from heaven. Philip Almond, in his *The Devil: A New Biography*, has a succinct description of the Cathars' main belief: "It was [Satan] who made Adam and Eve (not so called) and aroused their lust, so she could have sex with a serpent, created from Satan's spit. After that, God decided to send his son so that the people could recognize the devil and his wickedness. To this end, he first sent an angel, called Mary, the mother of Jesus. When Christ descended, he entered and came through her ear. In response, Satan sent his angel, John the Baptist." No wonder Pope Innocent III was determined to suppress the Cathars—and did—in his catastrophic Albigensian Crusade.

As the Christian story developed, the conventional satanic history was codified. Lucifer, as he was then, the Bringer of Light, was the most beautiful and radiant of God's angels, if the most willful and proud. It was Origen (born 185, died 253), an early Christian gadfly and pundit, who identified the devil with Lucifer, a fallen being of light: Lucifer, Origen wrote, "has fallen from heaven. For if, as some suppose, he was a being of darkness why is he said to have formerly been Lucifer or light-bearer? In this way, then, even Satan was once light, before he went astray and fell from this place."[9] Unsurprisingly Origen, who subsequently suggested that Lucifer could himself be redeemed, had some of his writings "anath-

emized" by the early church fathers, despite his ingra-
tiating self-castration. After all, Lucifer's pride was the
original sin, predating Adam's, in that he freely chose
to turn away from God—a notion that has troubled
theologians ever since: after all, how can angels, created
perfect, rebel against their perfect creator? On the other
hand, why bother with a devil if even the devil can be
saved? But Origen had a point. From this perspective,
Lucifer more or less resembled an ambitious lad wanting
to take over the family business from dad—pushy, maybe,
but understandable. God, then, merely looks peevish.
Banishing Lucifer (and his many rebellious companions)
from heaven and heaving him into a pit seems arbitrary
and excessive—and really bad politics, since what he
created was an implacable enemy.

The transformation into the Fiend

ALL THIS HAD gone by the Middle Ages, when Satan
more and more took on his sinister shape as chief villain
and chief prisoner, locked away by God yet with the abil-
ity to indulge in unlimited malice. The twelfth-century
Vision of Tundale was an early formulation of this notion;
it remained popular for three hundred years, to be finally
supplanted by Dante.

Unlike Dante's masterwork, the Tundale poem has
been disparaged as "structurally chaotic, dramatically
pointless, and doctrinally slender. To the Middle English
poetic version in particular one might add linguistically
repetitive and rhythmically pedestrian."[10] Still, it was
vivid enough. An angel takes Tundale through hell to

a great pit where he would see a hideous sight: Satan bound in chains, with a hundred heads on his body and as many mouths, a mouth above the chin with a hundred tongues, as black as could be, great and strong, a hundred cubits long and twenty broad, capable of swallowing a thousand souls in one gulp. He had a thousand hands, with nails of iron, a long snout with huge lips, and a great tail with sharp hooks, the better to grasp the souls who tried to flee—and so on and so on. Tundale, in the much-disparaged Middle English poetic version, is a difficult read, but worth puzzling out:

> He was bothe grett and strong
> And of an hundryt cubytes long.
> Twenty cubytes was he brad,
> And ten of thyknes was he mad.
> And when he gaput, or when he gonus,
> A thowsand sowlys he
>   swoluwys attonus.

> Byfor and behynd hym was kende
> On his body a thowsand hande.
> And on ylke a honde was ther seyn
> Twenty fyngrys with nayles keyn,
> And ylke a fyngur semud than
> The leynthe of an hundryt sponne
> And ten sponne abowt of thyknes;
> Ylke a fyngur was no les.

> Hys tayle was greyt and of gret lenthe,
> And in hit had he full gret strynthe.

With scharpe hokys that in
 is tayle stykythe
The sowlys therwith sore he prekydthe.[11]

And so to the grotesqueries of the witch trials

SO IT HAS come to this: here is a scaly horned beast, with serrated tongue and iron claws; in this way Lucifer Light Carrier disappeared into some grotesque caricature of a demon conjured up by the ever-descending visions of a long succession of seers. As the Middle Ages progressed, even this caricature became caricatured, and Satan became a creature with a bifurcated penis as long as an alder bush and made of iron, with scales and semen as cold as ice, who mated with an ever-increasing number of witches, anus and vagina at once (bifurcation has its advantages, apparently).

Reading those accounts now, they seem comically ridiculous, except that literally thousands of women (up to 100,000 over two hundred and fifty years by some accounts), mostly alone or homeless or spurned by their families, were burned alive at the stake or hanged for consorting with the devil—centuries of agony in the service of a demented scholarship. The saintly church founder Augustine, who died in the year 430, cannot be exempted from this dismal litany: his writings gave comfort to many a witch-hunter of later years. It's true that he considered witchcraft to consist mostly of idolatry and illusion (and that there were no actual witches), but he also said, in his prolix *City of God* (book 21, chapter 6), that sorcerers existed who were in league with devils. "For to this inextinguishable lamp we add a host of marvels wrought by men, or by magic—that is, by men under the influence of devils, or by the devils directly—for such marvels we cannot deny without impugning the truth of the sacred Scriptures we believe." That was enough for the medievalists.

In 1597 King James VI of Scotland (who in 1603 became James I of England) complained about the "fearefull abounding at this time [and] in this Countrey, of these detestable slaves of the Divel, the Witches or enchaunters."

One of the more notorious witch-killers of the seventeenth century was the Englishman Matthew Hopkins, a self-promoter who billed himself (without any authority) as Witch Finder Generall (*sic*) of England; he was personally responsible for bringing torture and death to around three hundred "witches" during the hysteria of the English Civil War (and his malign influence was felt in the colonies, since Governor John Winthrop of Massachusetts admitted that Hopkins's techniques for unearthing witches, such as "pricking" women with knives to find dead spots on the skin touched by the Devil, were used to good effect in the Salem trials of the 1690s). Among other leaks from the netherworld, Hopkins claimed to have often eavesdropped on the devil's seduction of errant women. A typical quote: "What will you have me doe for you, my deare and nearest children, covenanted and compacted with me in my hellish league, and sealed with your blood, my delicate firebrand-darlings?"[12]

Right in the European mainstream was the French theologian Claude Tholosan, who presided over more than a hundred witch trials, and who declared that witches, in their satanic rituals, kissed the anus of a goat and offered up their unbaptized children, who were then roasted and eaten with a draught of satanic piss— and this evil farrago was taken seriously by the church fathers. The massive tome called *The Hammer of Witches* (*Malleus Maleficarum* in the original Latin), written in 1486 by the "theologians" Heinrich Kramer and Jacob Sprenger, became the bible, if we can traduce that term, of the witch-hunters; it came with an encomium from the pope of the time, Innocent VIII, and was a bestseller for more than a century. Kramer, an experienced inquisitor, *knew* that women became witches because they were weak—more carnal than a man, "as is clear from her many carnal abominations. And it should be noted that there was a defect in the formation of the first woman, since she was formed from a bent rib, that is, a rib of the breast, which is bent as it were in a contrary direction to a man.... After all, the power of the devil lies in the privy parts of the man.... A woman is more bitter than death, and [even] good women subject to carnal lust."[13] (Kramer was oblivious as well as maleficent: his tome included the anecdote that witches commonly stole penises and kept them in a nest, feeding them oats to make them grow—a bawdy medieval joke that Kramer, in his humourlessness, took for reportage.[14])

On a similar misogynistic note, consider the reason, given in 1785, for Satan's nicknames of Old Nick and Old Scratch: "The angel first employed in forming women, had forgot to cut their parts of generation, which the devil undertook to do by the following contrivance, he placed himself in a kind of sawpit, with a scythe fixed to a stick, in his hand, and directed the women to straddle over it; the pit being too deep for the length of his instrument, he gave the tall women only a moderate scratch, but the little women by the shortness of their legs coming more within his reach, he maliciously gave them monstrous gashes, or nicks, whence he was called old scratch, and old nick."[15]

Which brings us to Pierre de l'Ancre, who, when he was not burning witches alive, was by all accounts a talented writer of bucolic country scenes; when he retired, "he turned all of his attention to writing and the construction of chapels, fountains, and grottos to beautify his lavish grounds."[16]

Retired from what? He was a magistrate who, by his own account, tortured and burned more than six hundred men and women for consorting with demons. In 1609, as a member of the Bordeaux *parlement*, l'Ancre was sent by Henry IV to administer justice to the sorcerers who were supposed to have infested the region. This he did with gusto, and the memoir he wrote afterwards, called *Tableau de l'Inconstance des mauvais Anges*, was, in the scholar Elspeth Whitney's words, "a lengthy, lurid, and sensationalized account of satanic practices among the population of the Labourd (Basque) region of France, [which] has been taken with varying degrees of seriousness since its publication in 1612."

It was, certainly, pornography of the most lurid kind. Much of it is taken up with the satanic Sabbath ritual itself, "down to the food eaten (cakes made of black millet and the liver of an unbaptized child) and the hierarchies of age, experience, and beauty imposed on the assembled witches."[17] He was obsessed with the details of his subjects' carnal encounters with demons—indeed, the more he tortured them, the more graphic their recountings became, so he tortured them some more. He also denounced a dozen or so clergy for participating in these rituals, two of whom were promptly executed. (The Bishop of Bayonne, who wasn't a fan, spirited the others away. Even so, the church as a body believed l'Ancre was admirably on message, and as Mark Twain once put it, the "church gathered up its halters, thumbscrews, and firebrands, and set about its holy work in earnest.")

Interestingly, in his view and the view of others of his ilk, devils never indulged in homosexual acts. More than three centuries earlier, Thomas Aquinas had suggested this was a kind of hangover from their days as angels, when they would never have contemplated "sins against nature." Sodomy with women was apparently fine in devil etiquette, but never with men—that would be unnatural.

Piquantly, l'Ancre had read an earlier account of witch trials in the neighbouring region of Franche-Comté, which suggested that the devil's penis was no longer than a finger, whereas *his* witches described it as covered with scales, as long as an alder bush, and twisted and wound up like a snake, or as long as a mule's or one-half iron or made out of horn—the accounts varied. This suggested to him that the female witches of his Labourd region were *much* better served by the devil than those of Franche-Comté.

Muhammad had his own encounterwith
the devil. He wasn't impressed.

MUHAMMAD, ALREADY FAVOURED of God, entered hell
and contended with the devil, whom he called Iblis. The
kingdom of Iblis, he reported, was so thick with demons
that he couldn't drop a pin.[18] To Muhammad, Iblis was
neither gorgeous Lucifer nor grotesque fiend, but an altogether lesser figure. He appeared to the Prophet and his
companions as an old man, cross-eyed and scant of beard,
with only six or seven long hairs hanging from his chin.
He had a very big head, his crossed eyes close to the top
of his head, high on his forehead, with big thick hanging
lips like those of a water buffalo. Despite this unprepossessing appearance, Iblis explained to Muhammad how
he was able to seduce and mislead all mankind.

CHAPTER 5

HELL'S UNRULY
BOARDROOM FRACAS

*The governors of hell sometimes just
seem ineffectual old kvetchers*

IN ALMOST ALL RECOUNTINGS, HELL IS RELIABLY
awful—"grim and braid" as Saint Hildegard of Bingen
once called it after a visit, sulphurous and dark, filled
with jostling demons and sinners wailing and lamenting and gnashing their teeth. But sometimes when you
eavesdrop on its management it seems less awful than
tiresomely quarrelsome, its leaders like an old married
couple, kvetching to each other and to whomever would
listen, boasting and whining in turn, less evil than ineffectual. Such is the state of affairs recounted by Nicodemus in his eponymous gospel, of a quarrel between
"Satan, the prince and captain of death," and the Prince
of Hell himself, Hades or Beelzebub. The occasion was
the "harrowing of hell" by Jesus.[1]

Here's the dialogue, overheard by Nicodemus.

Said Satan to Hades: "Prepare to receive Jesus of Nazareth himself, who boasted that he was the Son of God, and yet was a man afraid of death, and said, my soul is sorrowful even to death."

Asked Hades: "Who is that so-powerful prince, and yet a man who is afraid of death?"

Well, admitted Satan, it's true he's powerful. "He did many injuries to me and to many others; for those whom I made blind and lame and those also whom I tormented with several devils, he cured by his word; yea, and those whom I brought dead to thee, he by force takes away from thee."

Hades was immediately skeptical that Satan could deal with such a person, saying, he may be afraid of death, "but he is almighty in his divine power, and no man can resist his power. When he told you he was afraid of death, he designed to ensnare thee, and unhappy it will be to thee for everlasting ages." So why bring him here? Too big a risk.

Satan remained confident. "As for me, I tempted him and stirred up my old people . . . with zeal and anger against him. . . . I sharpened the spear for his suffering; I mixed the gall and vinegar, and commanded that he should drink it; I prepared the cross to crucify him, and the nails to pierce through his hands and feet; and now his death is near at hand, I will bring him hither, subject both to thee and me."

Hades didn't like this at all. Satan was being played for a fool. "They who have been kept here till they should live again upon earth, were taken away hence, not by their own power, but by prayers made to God, and their almighty God took them from me. Who then is that Jesus of Nazareth that by his word hath taken away the dead from me without prayer to God? Perhaps it is the same who took away from me Lazarus, after he had been four days dead, and did both stink and was rotten, and of whom I had possession as a dead person, yet he brought him to life again by his power."

Grudgingly, Satan agreed. "It is he."

So what are you doing, demanded Hades, bringing him here? "I adjure thee by the powers which belong to thee and me, that thou bring him not to me. . . . Bring not therefore this person hither, for he will set at liberty all those whom I hold in prison under unbelief, and bound with the fetters of their sins, and will conduct them to everlasting life."

He will, in short, ruin everything.

Too late, for Jesus showed up at hell's gate anyway, and "on a sudden there was a voice as of thunder and the rushing of winds, saying, Lift up your gates, O ye princes; and be ye lift up, O everlasting gates, and the King of Glory shall come in."

See? said Hades. Now you've done it! Get out of here and deal with it! "Depart from me, and begone out of my habitations; if thou art a powerful warrior, fight with the King of Glory. . . . And he cast him forth from his habitations."

Hades instructed his minions to keep Jesus out if they could. "Shut the brass gates of cruelty, and make them fast with iron bars, and fight courageously, lest we be taken captives." But it was no good. There was more rushing wind and thundering voices, "and the mighty Lord appeared in the form of a man, and enlightened those places which had ever before been in darkness, and broke asunder the fetters which before could not be broken; and with his invincible power visited those who sate in the deep darkness by iniquity, and the shadow of death by sin. . . . Then the King of Glory trampling upon death, seized the prince of hell, deprived him of all his power, and took our earthly father Adam with him to his glory."

All hell was in disarray, and Beelzebub (Hades) said, to paraphrase somewhat, *Jesus Christ, Satan! See what you have done!*

> THEN the Prince of Hell took Satan, and with great indignation said to him, O thou prince of destruction, author of Beelzebub's defeat and banishment, the scorn of God's angels and loathed by all righteous persons! What inclined thee to act thus? Thou wouldst crucify the King of Glory, and by his destruction, hast made us promises of very large advantages, but as a fool wert ignorant of what thou wast about. For behold now that Jesus of Nazareth, with the brightness of his glorious divinity, puts to flight all the horrid powers of darkness and death; he has broke down our prisons from top to bottom, dismissed all the captives, released all who were bound, and all who were wont formerly to groan under the weight of their torments have now insulted

us, and we are like to be defeated by their
prayers. Our impious dominions are sub-
dued, and no part of mankind is now left
in our subjection, but on the other hand,
they all boldly defy us; Though, before,
the dead never durst behave themselves
insolently towards us, nor, being prisoners,
could ever on any occasion be merry.

As the author of *The Testimony of Truth* (quoted above)
put it, "the son of humanity clothed himself . . . and went
down to Hades. There he performed many mighty deeds
and raised the dead. And the rulers of darkness became
envious of him for they did not find any sin in him." Envy
seems to be the least of it: before departing, Jesus took
Satan by the throat, told the angels to bind him and cast
him backwards into Tartarus. There, Beelzebub would
watch over him until the second coming, a thousand
years hence or more.

Bartholomew got the same sorry tale from Jesus himself

THIS CHATTY GOSPEL of *Nicodemus*, one of the "lost
books" of the Bible, never did make it into the canon;
early church fathers suspected that Nicodemus (a member of Jerusalem's Great Sanhedrin, after all, the ruling
body of the Pharisees) never had much to do with it, but
that a third-century forger simply attached his name to
add credibility to his own lurid work. Still, there were
other accounts of Christ's descent into hell, including the
one by Bartholomew in his self-aggrandizing *Questions*,

where he suggested that he had gotten the tale directly from Jesus himself. It shared many of the same aspects: an unseemly quarrel between the two oldsters, and useless boasting by Satan. Bartholomew's gospel was also rejected by the church powers that be, but it remained popular for centuries anyway.

It starts with Bartholomew in conversation with Jesus, location unspecified. "When thou wentest to be hanged upon the cross," he asked Jesus, what happened? I mean, I saw you hanging there, and the angels coming down and worshipping you, and then darkness came and you were gone. I heard a great wailing and gnashing of teeth in the "parts under the earth." Where did you go?

Jesus replied to "Bartholomew, my beloved" (as Bartholomew put it), I'll tell you everything. When I vanished I went down to Hades to bring up Adam and all that were with him. Michael the Archangel asked me to do so.

"What was that voice I heard?" asked Bart.

Oh, that was Hades talking to Belial. "As I perceive," he (Hades) said, "a God cometh hither." Then (my) angels demanded that Hades "remove the gates, remove the everlasting doors, for the King of Glory is coming down." That was me.

"And when I had descended five hundred steps, Hades was troubled, saying: I hear the breathing of the Most High, and I cannot endure it. But the devil answered and said: Submit not thyself, O Hades, but be strong: for God himself hath not descended upon the earth. But when I had descended yet [more] five hundred steps, the angels and the powers cried out: Take hold, remove the doors, for behold the King of Glory cometh down. And Hades said: O, woe unto me, for I hear the breath of God. . . . And he saith to the prince and captain of death [Satan], my belly is rent, and mine inward parts are pained: it cannot be but that God cometh hither. Alas, whither shall I flee before the face of the power of the great king?"

So, Jesus told Bartholomew, "then did I enter in and scourged him and bound him with chains that cannot be loosed, and brought forth thence all the patriarchs and came again unto the cross."

Yes, Bartholomew replied, I saw you there again, "and all the dead arising and worshipping thee, and going up again into their sepulchres. Tell me, Lord, who was he whom the angels bare up in their hands, even that man that was very great of stature? And what spakest thou unto him that he sighed so sore?"

"It was Adam the first-formed, for whose sake I came down from heaven upon earth. And I said unto him: I was hung upon the cross for thee and for thy children's sake. And he, when he heard it, groaned and said: So was thy good pleasure, O Lord."[2]

THE GOSPEL OF Peter, which did make it into the Bible, also mentions Christ's "harrowing" of hell, though in less colourful form and in more allusive words: 1 Peter 3:19–20 says that Jesus "went and made a proclamation to the spirits in prison [hell], who in former times did not obey, when God waited patiently in the days of Noah," and 1 Peter 4:6 says that the gospel was "preached also unto them that are dead." And both the Apostles' Creed, which was put together largely to counter the popularity of some of the soon-denounced gnostic gospels, and the Athanasian Creed (an anti-heresy formulation of the Trinity), still assert that Jesus descended into hell before being resurrected in order to save those who had come before his time on earth, and to bind Satan in chains until the second coming.

Many popular medieval commentaries on the event include some sort of tribunal to see if Christ's actions were justified—after all, hadn't God given Satan the governance of all sinning souls after the sin in Eden? Wasn't Jesus therefore trampling on the devil's privileges? In this version, Satan had an advocate in the person of the demon Belial (or Beliar), the patron saint of lust or pleasure, who was renowned as an orator. To no avail: God judged that Jesus had sufficient moral leverage—that he had paid sufficient ransom through his death to prevail.

There were Hindu hell-harrowers too

GENERALLY, CHRISTIANS BELIEVE that no one was able to enter hell before Christ because of Adam's original sin, which rather begs the question: are such harrowings unknown in other creeds—and other hells? (And the Gospel of Mary had the Virgin harrowing hell off her own bat.) Several of the prominent Hindu texts from well before the Christian era (ca. 600 BCE) describe how an unnamed king made his way into hell and refused to leave, preferring solidarity with the souls of the damned he found there (and by his presence soothing their torment). Naturally, as befits such an uplifting tale, his virtue won not only his own release but the souls he found in hell with him.

Several Hindu sources have tactlessly pointed out that *their* harrower prevailed through superior virtue, and not by trouncing the opposition and putting them in chains, as Christ apparently did. This is not a majority point of view.

CHAPTER 6

CAN THERE REALLY
BE ROMANCE IN THE
HEART OF HELL?

NOT VERY OFTEN, OF COURSE, WHICH IS WHY THIS chapter is so short. But still, setting a decently cheerful tone, consider Ereshkigal, Assyrian "Lady of the Great Earth," Mistress of the Underworld, Queen of the Dead, and her torrid romance with an above-ground god called Nergal, who might not seem the ideal mate because he is the God of War and Pestilence, but apparently even war gods have their softer moments. (Or maybe he just liked the mettle of his new love—this was a lass who hung her sister on a meat hook, after all.) Ereshkigal, as far as we know, is the only Governor of the Dead to be female—the Phoenicians' bisexual Astoreth, sometime consort to Baal, was Queen of Heaven, not Hell—ruling alone until she marries her guy, and even afterwards clearly in charge. Even more curiously for the realm of the dead, the story apparently has a happy, or at least happyish, ending.

We will meet Ereshkigal again when we follow the descent of her sister, Inanna (a.k.a. Ishtar), who came down for a visit but incurred her sister's rancour.

The story as we know it is from clay tablets dating to the seventh century BCE; there are many gaps (smeared patches in the clay), but the outline is clear enough. The gods were to hold a banquet, and everyone was invited except Ereshkigal, because according to the bureaucratic regulations of heaven, heavenly gods cannot descend to hell, nor could any underworld gods ascend to heaven. The solution, because they seemed to want Ereshkigal there, was to send her vizier in her stead. This personage, Mantar (whose name means "fate") duly ascended the long stairway to heaven, where he was cordially received with all the gods kneeling in his mistress's honour—except Nergal, God of War and Pestilence, who refused.

After exclamations of shock and horror at this violation of etiquette, the other gods overruled their own rules about hellish travel and sent him down below to make his apologies. In an early version, just a few clay lines long, he made only one trip, overpowered Ereshkigal, and seized the throne. In the fuller version, the story is more complicated. He took with him a throne, which was apparently a device to allow him to escape from hell when needed. He was warned by the "cunning god, Ea," as Persephone was in the later Greek story, not to accept any hospitality from hell's queen, lest he be trapped there forever; that meant that he was not to sit on a guest chair if offered one (hence the portable throne), not to eat bread or meat, not to drink beer or wash his feet, and, definitely "not to do with her that which men and women do."

Then there is a break in the text, perhaps the equivalent of a fade to black in the movies, but eventually Nergal spied the goddess preparing for her bath and slipping off her clothes. That was enough:

> He gave in to his heart's desire to do
> what men and women do,
> The two embraced each other
> And went passionately to bed

Six days they spent in bed before Nergal, doing what miscreant lovers so often do, crept away and won his way back to heaven, leaving Ereshkigal asleep. The goddess was not happy:

> Ereshkigal cried out aloud, grievously,
> Fell from the throne to the ground,
> Then straightened up from the ground.
> Her tears flowed down her cheeks:
> "Erra [Nergal], the lover of my delight—
> I did not have enough delight
> with him before he left!
> Erra, the lover of my delight—
> I did not have enough delight
> with him before he left!"

As an assertive chief executive, she did not take this lying down, either on the nuptial bed or her throne, but instead dispatched her vizier back to the top to argue her case. In heaven he complained on her behalf about her lonely childhood, about not having known of children's

play and fun as a young goddess, and about the respon-
sibilities she had taken upon her shoulders as the Great
Goddess of the Underworld from an early age. None of
this, it turned out, was necessary: the vizier didn't have
to plead and the gods had no need of a ruling, because
Nergal

> Went up to her and laughed.
> He seized her by her hair,
> And pulled her from the throne.
> He seized her by her tresses.
> The two embraced each other
> And went passionately to bed.
> They lay there, queen Ereshkigal
> and Erra, for a first day
> and a second day.
> They lay there, queen Ereshkigal
> and Erra, for a third day.
> They lay there, queen Ereshkigal
> and Erra, for a fourth day.
> They lay there, queen Ereshkigal
> and Erra, for a fifth day.
> They lay there, queen Ereshkigal
> and Erra, for a sixth day.
> When the seventh day arrived,
> Anu [chief of the gods] made his
> voice heard and spoke,
> Addressed his words to
> Kakka, his vizier,
> "Kakka, I shall send you to Kurnugi,

To the home of Ereshkigal who
    dwells within Erkalla,
To say, "That god, whom I sent you,
Forever . . . "

Forever? Happily ever after? Maybe. No sequels exist.[1]

III

WHAT'S THE
OPERATING
PLAN

?

CHAPTER 7

———◆X◆X◆———

ONCE YOU'RE IN, WHAT'S IT LIKE? A SURVEY OF A-LIST HELLS

TAKE IT FROM THOSE WHO LEARNED, SOMETIMES the hard way: you could either be devoured in hell, or tortured. Those seem to be the main choices. Oh, and in some versions you could get out. Eventually.

Egyptian sinners could get a cheater's guide to the afterlife

FROM THE EARLIEST days, the Egyptian upper classes would get a good reception in whatever afterlife there was. Here's what Teti, first Pharaoh of the Sixth Dynasty (2345 BCE) could reasonably expect:

> Oho! Oho! Rise up, O Teti!
> Take your head, collect your bones,

Gather your limbs, shake the
    earth from your flesh!
Take your bread that rots not,
    your beer that sours not,
Stand at the gates that bar
    the common people!
The gatekeeper comes out to
    you, he grasps your hand,
Takes you into heaven, to
    your father Geb.
He rejoices at your coming,
    gives you his hands,
Kisses you, caresses you,
Sets you before the spirits, the
    imperishable stars . . .
The hidden ones worship you,
The great ones surround you,
The watchers wait on you,
Barley is threshed for you,
Emmer is reaped for you,
Your monthly feasts are made with it,
Your half-month feasts are made with it,
As ordered done for you by
    Geb, your father,
Rise up, O Teti, you shall not die![1]

    Civilized Egypt, of course, goes back a very long way, long before Teti—the *Aegyptiaca* of the Egyptian priest Manetho, compiled somewhere in the third century BCE, lists all the Pharaohs of the first to thirtieth dynasties, but also a long list of "pre-dynastic" rulers who governed all or parts of Egypt before it was formally unified by Menes around 3050 BCE. It is hardly surprising, then, that Egyptian views of what happens after death changed, even over the eighteen "main" dynasties, covering almost two thousand years. There was no steady progression of belief, though; emendations made in one dynasty could easily be reversed in another, and often were. As discussed in chapter 2, during the five hundred years or so of the Old Kingdom (2686–2134 BCE) only the royal family (who were in any case gods themselves) survived death, and the afterlife had nothing to do with justice or punishment. By the time the Coffin Texts of the Middle Kingdom (2030–1640 BCE) were written, the notion of a soul that outlives the "corpus" had become common currency, along with the companion notion that anyone could dodge oblivion, with caution and good guidebooks.

Along the way, as the cult of Osiris grew in importance and popular acclaim, so did the democratization of beliefs concerning the afterlife. This didn't necessarily seep down to the worker-bee slaves building the pyramids, but according to the evidence, it did at least reach down to the bureaucracy and commercial classes. Judging from the few surviving texts and inscriptions from the period, known as the Pyramid Texts, the upper crust still had every reason to believe that life in the hereafter would be an extension, usually a pretty pleasant one, of life above ground. More or less everyone got to go below, but inequality in life was followed by inequality in death, which presumably seemed just and natural to the rulers. Teti would have approved.

For all classes, the corpus remained important. For full participation in the afterlife, bodily identity had to be preserved—hence the ongoing importance of sealed sarcophagi well stocked with the necessities of life, both material goods and food, and of mummification.

In due course the dead began to be sorted into the damned and the not-so-damned. There were criminals and rotters above ground, so why not below? So henceforth at death a person was obliged to face judgment in a ritual called the Balancing of the Souls; failure meant torment by the Devourer of Souls (or sometimes, more grimly, the Eater of Entrails). *The Book of Am-Tuat*, for example, explicitly exhorts the gods of the underworld, especially Ra, to annihilate the damned so they couldn't continue the journey on the River Tuat, which separated the afterlife from that which goes before.

You could evade judgment, even if you were unworthy, by trickery and magic. Many useful spells were recorded in *The Book of the Dead* (a poor title, because there really wasn't one book; each rich individual would have his or her own, an early version of print-on-demand; and in any case, it is not a book *of* the dead as much as a book *for* the dead. The original title, if there really was one, seems to have been *The Spells for Going Forth by Day*, a nicely utilitarian framing).

Spell 125 of *The Book of the Dead* is perhaps the most famous of them all. It serves as an instruction on how to deal with Osiris: "What should be said when arriving at this Hall of Justice, purging [insert person's name here] of all the evil which he has done and beholding the faces of the gods? Hail to you, Great God, Lord of Justice!

I have come to you, my lord, . . . so that I may see your beauty for I know you and I know your name and I know the names of the forty-two gods of those who are with you in this Hall of Justice, who live on those who cherish evil and who gulp down their blood on that day of the reckoning of characters in the presence of Wennefer [another name for Osiris]. Behold the double son of the Songstresses; Lord of Truth is your name . . . "

OSIRIS EMERGES IN these stories as a benign god, possibly because, like Jesus after him, he was sacrificed and resurrected and so had an unusual perspective on life. (He was killed by Set, the God of Chaos, reportedly in revenge for a kick, and cut into forty-two pieces. Various goddesses found the pieces and stitched him together again.) Even so, benign or not, it would seem from this text that cringing is one of the required techniques for dealing with Osiris, along with obsequiousness.

Early views of what actually happened to those who failed the balance test were inconclusive: mostly the souls mouldered away, sometimes depicted as upside down (this was the underworld, after all), but nothing much happened—rather like the Jewish Sheol. Oh, it was hazardous enough—plenty of fiery caves, lakes of hellfire, basins of hot lead, and so on—but it was survivable.

The Book of Gates, written during the Nineteenth Dynasty around 1315 BCE, was the first Egyptian text to describe, with apparent relish, the torments and horrors that await the unrighteous dead. By the time *The Book of the Earth* was compiled, somewhere around 1250 BCE, the torments that would become so familiar in the Christian era were amplified: the condemned are bound, dismembered, and decapitated before being cast into cauldrons of boiling oil and pits of fire; indeed, those pits of fire, along with wailings and gnashings of teeth, would become staples of early medieval visions of hell, having been picked up by the Christian Copts and then transmitted across Europe. (A small cultural sidelight: *The Book of Caverns*, written between 1186 and 1069 BCE, was the first ancient text to recognize that women, too, were just as worthy as men of being condemned and tortured.)

The point, though, was still to slaughter the sinful—to put an end to them. The notion that torment should be *eternal* had to wait for more "sophisticated" cultures.

As time went on, the Hebrews' boring hell became . . . more hellish

AS INDICATED IN chapter 2, the Jewish hell was dull stuff. In the earliest times the dead simply went to Sheol, all of them, without exception; and Sheol was not a place of punishment, unless you define darkness and eternal silence to be torment. Through this period there were few descriptions of what hell actually looked like, though there were suggestions that it seemed to resemble an elaborate family tomb. In other references there is mention of strong cords binding the spirits of the dead, and sometimes gates and iron bolts to keep them from straying, so it was not completely featureless.

But after the Babylonian captivity ended and the Jews of Babylon came home, views changed. Perhaps a more jaundiced outlook on religious affairs prevailed, and the whole notion of the righteous being ground down began to seem bitterly unfair, as it eventually did in most other cultures' views of hell. And so, a few centuries before the Christian era, Sheol was finally divided into a neighbourhood for the righteous and another for the wicked. As Carol Zaleski, in a scrupulous essay in the online *Encyclopaedia Britannica*, put it, "late prophetic books, concerned with the vindication of God's justice, warn of a coming 'Day of the Lord' in which . . . the corpses of God's enemies will suffer endless corruption (Isaiah 66:24), and evildoers who have died will be resurrected to 'shame and everlasting contempt' (Daniel 12:2) while the just enjoy the fulfillment of God's promises."[2] Later, as suggested, Gehenna became the preferred place for punishment. It was impressively big too: "The earth is one-sixtieth of the Garden [Paradise], the Garden one-sixtieth of Eden, Eden one-sixtieth of Gehenna; hence the whole world is like a lid for Gehenna. Some say that Gehenna can not be measured."[3]

The Book of Enoch, a rambling compilation of uncertain provenance (we'll revisit Enoch in chapter 10), describes the whole thing in vivid detail.

At first, this new Sheol/Gehenna hell was just a place to bind Azazel (a Satan precursor, chief of the fallen angels): "And again the Lord said to Raphael: Bind Azazel hand and foot, and cast him into the darkness: and make an opening in the desert, which is in Dudael, and cast him therein. And place upon him rough and jagged rocks, and cover him with darkness, and let him abide there for ever, and cover his face that he may not see light. And on the day of the great judgment he shall be cast into the fire. And heal the earth which the angels have corrupted, and proclaim the healing of the earth, that they may heal the plague, and that all the children of men may not perish through all the secret things that the Watchers have disclosed and have taught their sons." We will meet those Watchers again.

Not much of a hell that: rudimentary at best, just jagged rocks and not much else. In later elaborations, it became a place to stash all the other fallen angels, those who defiled themselves with women, as Enoch reports: "And I came to a river of fire in which the fire flows like water and discharges itself into the great sea towards the west. . . . And I saw there something horrible . . . a place chaotic and horrible. And there I saw seven stars of the heaven [fallen angels] bound together in it, like great mountains and burning with fire."[4]

On the sunny side, as Enoch points out, there will be no need for Gehenna, or hell, after Judgment Day, "for God will take the sun out of its case, and it will heal the pious with its rays and will punish the sinners."

As for resurrection of the righteous after death, the book of Daniel, written during the reign of Nebuchadnezzar, and added to the Jewish canon late in its evolution, contains the only verse in the Old Testament to testify on the subject: "And many of them that sleep in the dust of the earth shall awake, some to everlasting life and some to reproaches and everlasting abhorrence."[5]

There were Jewish sects, like the Sadducees, who believed in God, but denied any afterlife at all. The Pharisees, by contrast, maintained that an afterlife did exist, and that

God punished the wicked and rewarded the righteous in the world to come. They also believed in a future messiah who would herald permanent world peace—a view, obviously enough, adopted by those Jews who would become Christians.[6] (On the other hand, the Pharisees were dubious about Jesus when he did show up, and cast a skeptical eye on his demon-casting. Matthew 12:24 relates their dismissal as follows: "they said, this [fellow] doth not cast out devils, but by Beelzebub the prince of the devils.")

Jewish views, then, were evolving over the centuries.

The intricate geography of Hades

THE GREEKS OF antiquity had a quarrelsome, argumentative, opinionated, aggressive, interfering, lustful, jealous pantheon of gods above ground (and in the sky), under the more or less rambunctious tutelage of Zeus and his various consorts/sisters, but as indicated in an earlier chapter, only one god, Hades, in the underworld—though Hades is a place as well as a personage, so it can get confusing. Part of Hades-the-place was Tartarus, the most tormenting part reserved for the truly wicked. Tartarus is as far below Hades as Hades is below the earth, and was originally envisaged as a prison for the Titans. There is sometimes said to be a prince in charge, though he is seldom mentioned (like Hades, Tartarus can be both a person and a place). As already suggested, hell's queen, Persephone, is usually described as a prisoner or a hostage.

Hades (the place, not the person) isn't really hell, though. Much of it isn't even hellish, and its best *quartiers* can be positively idyllic (I offer you the Elysian Fields).

In Homer's recounting of hell, the earliest detailed Greek view, Hades rather resembled the dreariness of Mesopotamian hells. Hell was inhabited by the psyches (souls) of the dead (a.k.a. shades). All humans were infused with their personal psyche at birth, which leaves the body at death and goes directly to hell—all shades, of whatever rank or persuasion. Shades are witless, even stupid: they can't talk or communicate except by screeching, and they cease to exist completely when forgotten by the living, rather like African ancestors. When Odysseus shows up at the entrance to Hades to get advice from Tiresias, the late-lamented blind prophet of Apollo, the seer remains mute until Odysseus gives him a good slug of ram's blood, which does the trick. Odysseus did find some hierarchy in Hades—the shades of the "untimely dead" and the improperly buried were generally treated worse than the others, and there were a few celebrity sinners, but generally the place was dreary for all. (Odysseus also had a brief and sobering chat with Agamemnon in Hades, seeking guidance on how to get home. The old man warned Odysseus about the treachery of family; he himself, after all, died at the hands of his wife and her lover when he made it home.)

Later, things began to get more complicated for the dead. Adherents of the cult of Demeter, for example, were told that they would be granted immortality, while everyone else would still turn into witless shades—a dichotomy adopted and adapted by many later Middle Eastern cults, including Christianity: heaven for the saved, hell for everyone else. That in turn led to the developing notion of a place where those saved could be housed—a place for the blessed to revel in their blessedness, a verdant paradise that came to be called the Elysian Fields. There was, to be sure, another place reserved for the very-much-not-blessed.

IT IS ACROSS the Styx, the first of Hades's five rivers, that Charon carries all souls, good or bad, who had been properly buried. After which, everyone was decanted onto the Fields (or Meadows) of Asphodel, the virtuous, the evil, and the in-between; the *Odyssey* vividly described the shades of heroes wandering sadly about, pestered by the shades of lesser beings, occasionally and temporarily cheered up by libations of blood offered in the world of the still living, far above.

Beyond lay Erebus, home to the palace of Hades and his sometime wife Persephone. In the forecourt of the palace sat the Three Judges.

Those found neither virtuous nor particularly sinful were returned to the Fields of Asphodel to wait out eternity in everlasting labour—eternal boredom a fate to match their boring personalities. In a corner of Asphodel were the Mourning Fields, which Virgil describes as reserved for those souls who had wasted their lives in unrequited love.

The blessed and the blameless were then taken to drink the waters of the River Lethe, which made them forget all bad things, if they still had any to worry about, and were then sent on to Elysium, the equivalent of the Christian paradise, a place just as placid and tedious as extant descriptions of that same Paradise—or even of heaven.

Shady parks, mostly, with residents participating in athletic contests and music (thus the Theban poet Pindar). Or residing in groves and on mossy beds, as Aeneas put it: "by crystal streams, that murmur thro' the meads: But pass yon easy hill, and thence descend; The path conducts you to your journey's end . . . the shining fields below. They wind the hill, and thro' the blissful meadows go."

The rest of the judged, the worst of the sinners, the truly bad actors, were whipped by the Furies and driven to Tartarus. That is hell proper, in the modern view.

Which is where? Tartarus, like Hades itself and himself is both a god and a place. He was the primeval God of the Pit, beneath the foundations of the earth—but in all senses he also *was* the pit, the prison and jailer of the Titans, sealed with walls of bronze and with just two gates guarded by the hundred-handed Hecatoncheires. Pausanias, the Greek geographer, said of Tartarus that "it is so dark there that the night is poured around it in three rows like a collar round the neck, while above it grow the roots of the earth and of the unharvested sea."[7]

Aeneas, who was in Hades as a tourist, managed only one horrified look at Tartarus, a high cliff with a castle below it, surrounded by a torrent of flame. The sibyl pointed it out to him: "Here is the place, where the road parts: there to the right, as it runs under the walls of great Dis [Hades], is our way to Elysium, but the left wreaks the punishment of the wicked, and send them on to pitiless Tartarus." Suddenly Aeneas looks back, and under a cliff on the left sees a broad castle, "girt with triple walls and encircled with a rushing torrent of flames—Tartarean Phlegethon, that rolls along thundering rocks."

The landscape was dramatic, as you can plainly see from artists' renderings over the centuries: bottomless ravines, massive craggy mountains, and pits of fire.

In Plutarch's *Moralia* a youth called Timarchus had a closer look at Tartarus, seeing a great chasm filled with howling and the souls of the wicked leaping up and down like sparks. This was a constant motif in later imaginings of hell: the Venerable Bede, for example, himself saw frequent "globes of flame rising out of a pit, in which flared the sparks of human souls."

Rome's gloss on Hades

ROME ADOPTED MUCH of the Greeks' corpus of hell, alongside their prickly pantheon. But being a more orderly people, the Romans were sometimes much more precise about how the whole place was set up and its architecture. There were five "parts": the assembly point on the east, or up side, of the River Styx (sometimes referred to, rather opaquely, as the "previous region"); the Styx itself and its guardians; the pre-judgment region called Erebus (itself divided into multiple sub-parts, such as a gathering place for infants, one for those unjustly executed, a melancholy one for suicides, etc.); and the final two parts, Tartarus and Elysium, which fork off from Erebus. Rome also started the practice, commonplace later and greatly amplified in medieval Christianity, of reserving certain compartments for the punishment of specific sins.

Elysium was a delightful place with excellent weather. Virgil's contribution was to adopt the Greek notion of the

River Lethe (forgetfulness), in which the virtuous bathed to be restored and to forget their forgettable mortal lives. The other rivers of hell were often ignored by Roman tourists like Virgil. Tartarus is still the worst part of hell, where all the tormenting goes on—Virgil puts the vile and treacherous there. In Roman Hades, Tartarus has its own city and its own prince, though it consisted of the usual deep pit, with fiery smokes and boiling liquids of all kinds, all as black as a coal mine.

A few centuries later, Rome was overwhelmed by Christians, and that was that: Hades soon became Hell.

Zoroastrian hell was grim, but not eternal

ZOROASTRIANISM MAY BE the precursor for the Christian hell, or not—dating is problematic. The Prophet Zoroaster (that's the Greek rendering—Zarathustra, in various spellings, in the original) probably lived somewhere around 1200 BCE, though some theories place him much earlier and a few much later. In medieval Christian tracts, such as that of the notorious Heinrich Kramer, "quoting many learned authorities," Zoroaster was "the first to practice the arts of magic and of astrology." He was, according to this version, named Cham, the son of Noe, "and according to S. Augustine in his book *Of the City of God*, Cham laughed aloud when he was born, and thus showed that he was a servant of the devil."

Be that as it may, the religion he founded, probably the world's first poly-national religion, flourished for fourteen hundred years, from around 700 BCE to 700 CE. The earliest surviving manuscript that describes his world view dates from around the sixth to the ninth centuries CE, though its content is much older.

Zoroastrian texts are among the first to mention, for example, Satan, and to set up the transition of Satan from an emissary of God to his adversary. There were several other firsts too: Zoroastrianism was one of the first religions to introduce the notion that torment for the wicked might be never-ending. A Zoroastrian text, *The Book of Arda Viraf,* was one of the first to provide a guided tour of hell itself (replete with demons, fiends, vicious spiny hedgehogs inserted into bodily orifices, and damsels, both hideous and gorgeous—we'll follow Viraf's adventures in due course). Zoroastrianism was also one of the first religions to spell out that the punishment should be calibrated to the sin; to suggest that the dead had to cross a perilously narrow bridge after death; and that, when they did, they would face a resurrection (which it called "renovation") and a last judgment, in which the fiend perishes in a bath of molten metal; and it was possibly the first to suggest a future messiah.[8]

As Thomas Sheehan of Stanford University put it,

> Zoroaster had taught that the world was the scene of a dramatic cosmic struggle between the forces of Good and Evil, led by the gods Ormazd and Ahriman. But this conflict was not to continue forever because . . . history was not endless but finite and in fact dualistic, divided between the present age of darkness and the coming age of light. Time was devolving through four

(or in some accounts seven) progressively worsening periods toward an eschatological cataclysm when Good would finally annihilate Evil and the just would receive their otherworldly reward in an age of eternal bliss. Zoroastrianism's profound pessimism about present history was thus answered by its eschatological optimism about a future eternity.[9]

But what was the Zoroastrian hell actually like?

The *Religious Judgments* of Dastur Manuschihr, quoted earlier, provides questions and the sage's responses to ninety-two questions posed by his followers. A few of them deal with hell.

For example, questions 19 and 20 deal with where the righteous and the wicked go, and the sage's response was, "he who is of the wicked fall from the lower end of the bridge, or from the middle of the bridge; he falls head foremost to hell, and it precipitated unto that grade which is suitable for his wickedness." The crossing, he wrote, "becomes a broad bridge for the righteous, as much as the height of nine spears—and the length of those which they carry is each separately three reeds; and it becomes a narrow bridge for the wicked, even unto a resemblance to the edge of a razor."

On the nature of hell itself, question 26 receives this depressing answer:

> It is sunken, deep, and descending, most dark, most stinking, and most terrible, most

supplied with wretched existences and, worse, the place and cave of the demons and fiends. And in it is no comfort, pleasantness, or joy whatever; but in it are all stench, filth, pain, punishment, distress, profound evil, and discomfort; and there is no resemblance of it whatever to worldly stench, filthiness, pain, and evil. . . . And so much more grievous is the evil in hell than even the most grievous evil on earth, as the greatness of the spiritual existence is more than that of the world; and more grievous is the terror of the punishment on the soul than that of the vileness of the demons on the body. And the punishment on the soul is from those whose abode it has become, from the demons and darkness—a likeness of that evil to hell—the head of whom is Ahriman the deadly. And the words of the expressive utterance of the high-priests are these, that where there is a fear of every other thing it [the fear] is more than the thing itself but hell is a thing worse than the fear of it.[10]

Hell for oath-breakers, Valhalla for the valiant

OKAY, NOT EXACTLY an A-list hell, but Valhalla has taken its place in the Western imagination, and is worth a mention.

The Norse pantheon is different from those of the Middle East and Levant, and the obsession with battle and warriors shown therein is peculiarly Norse, but the structure of the afterlife is familiar.

Heaven, loosely, is Asgard, one of the Nine Worlds and home to a tribe of gods known as Aesir. Odin and his wife Frigg rule Asgard, and more specifically Odin presides over Valhalla, Hall of the Slain, where half the warriors who die in battle end up, feasting and drinking and having an uproarious good time. The other half of the slain end up in Fólkvangr, which is sort of like the Elysian Fields—a great meadow where good times rule (though apparently this cohort often pines for the baronial hall of Valhalla). Who gets to go where remains unclear—perhaps there are degrees of valour.

As in the Greek Hades, Hel (Norse for "the covered hall") is divided into two parts, one corresponding to the Fields of Asphodel, Náströnd (where those who were neither good nor bad go—boring people end up there), and Nifthel ("the dark hell"), which, like its counterparts from other cultures, is *down there*, below everything, where those who commit vile deeds (such as breaking oaths) are sent for punishment; this corresponds to Tartarus.

The eighty (and counting) hells of Hinduism

HINDU HELL IS largely self-policing—that is, the sinful "eat the fruit of their own acts," and therefore don't have to be whipped into self-loathing: no overlords are needed. In contrast to Hebrew tradition, Hindu hell was never merely a parking place for the dead, but rather a dark, putrid place for punishment. (Hindu theologians had an unseemly fascination with human waste and with the malfunctioning of the human body, especially the intestines and the "anal passages.") In some Hindu traditions, sharp-beaked birds are on duty for intestine-ripping if called upon.

The layout of Hindu hell, or Naraka, changed over time, and according to what *purana* was being consulted. (*Puranas* are generally regarded as exhortations and instructions for the laity.) There was only one hell at first, but hells were soon multiplying, and new spaces were accreted to accommodate new offences, often sins against religion— Hindu holy men were also prickly about self-image. In some of the texts, hell is described as a bottomless pit of darkness where souls are trapped and denied rebirth and where no one is in charge. No Satan to torment anyone; torments were inherent and endemic to the place.

Twenty-eight hells seems to be the majority opinion. In each of them messengers bring all the dead to the court of Yama, where they are judged, sending the virtuous to the exit and the rest to one of the hells suited to his character. Yama was also the ruler of the Southern Quarter (south of the earth, that is); his chronicler was called Chitragupt, and he kept a journal of all the deeds of all the beings on earth. No sin was too small for Chitragupt to note down. As time went on, the underworld hells became "as numerous and varied as the heavens"; just so, the listed punishments and tortures grew ever more grisly.[11] As Eileen Gardiner recounts in a piece included on her indispensable website Hell-On-Line, "the *Vamana Purana*, for example, assembled somewhere around 300

CE, mentions 21 hells, while the *Padma Purana*, several hundred years later, had 7, but each with 6 divisions, or 42 hells, each of those then halved again, for a grand total of 84. An assemblage from around 1500 CE, the *Agni Purana*, upped the ante a little: 5 major divisions, 28 subdivisions and 140 'others,' their purposes left unspecified."

Many of the sub-hells had names that indicated their purpose and their inhabitants. One was associated with the gut and the diseases thereof, another with suppurations and the anus—they were not supposed to be pleasant, after all.

Some of these hells were reserved for actions that were sinful only by the most liberal of definitions—urinating in front of a cow, for example, had its own hell, and awful it was. Hindu punishment is renowned for its ingenuity, even virtuosity.

On the other hand, hell was not forever, only a way station on the Great Journey.[12] *Samsara*, or reincarnation, means that eventually, after thousands or perhaps millions of years, the sinful soul re-enters the world, chastened no doubt, but once again intact. This was a notion picked up by Plato when he separated the soul from the body and made the soul immortal. The ultimate goal, obviously, is ending the cycles of rebirth by approaching perfection.

The plan of these hells is generally cursorily described (punishment was the issue, not architecture), but each hell generally contained at least one river—rivers are mentioned ninety-nine times in various texts, though are seldom given names. One named river was the Vaitarani, which is supposed to form a border around all hells, rather like the Egyptian Tuat and the Greek Styx, and it sometimes doubles as a hell itself. It is full of boiling ash, and crops up in various later Buddhist texts too.

Hinduism has no one "God" in the Christian and Islamic sense, nor is there a "Devil." As suggested earlier, Yama has come to do as the captain of hell, though he is not a punisher, only a dispenser of justice. After all, devils are only useful when there is an eternity to contemplate, and Hindus are more properly exercised in trying to improve themselves out of hell and into union with the Ultimate Reality. A boss-devil would just get in the way.

The ever-proliferating hells of Buddhism

IN THE VARIOUS Buddhist traditions, hell's edifices get ever more complicated and their architecture ever more baroque. Though it varies from text to text, in general seven rings of mountain ranges divided by seas surround an enormous mountain called Mount Sumeru. A vast ocean encompasses the outer, seventh range. This sea contains four continents—to the south is the one humans inhabit, called Jambudvīpa. Heaven is above, hell, obviously, below.

Some Buddhist traditions do have only one Great Hell, an enclosure of burning iron with flames bursting from the walls, floor, and ceiling, but others have far more. Most count 8 hells, each stacked above the next, each with 16 secondary hells, one at each corner, for the hells are generally cubes, 100 *voianas* square and tall, laid out in tidy grids and closed off with an iron wall—a vault of iron above, molten iron below. (And yes, a cube has 16 corners, if you count them the right way—maybe 24 if you want to be picky.) A *voiana* is around 11 kilometres, so these were hells of a considerable girth. In *The Sutra on the Eighteen Hells*, Buddha himself asserted that there were 8 fiery hells below the earth, and 10 cold hells beneath the sky. Each one is named and its tortures described.

As with the Hindus, there was no one in charge—no chief demon—but still, these hells are described as difficult to leave, populated by cruel fiends: "Their ceiling is fire, their sun is burning, sparkling fire, and they are filled with flames hundreds of voianas high."[13]

The Tibetan Buddhist tradition goes further. The Tibetans in their mountain fastnesses knew about cold, so they added another 8 major cold hells to the existing hot ones, and each of those had the usual 16 subsidiaries—or 272 hells altogether. The cold hells, which were beneath the realm of the living but above the hot hells, are vividly named, clearly by a people who were familiar with intense cold: Arbuda (hell of swelling); Nirarbuda (hell of shrinking); Atata (hell of chattering teeth); Hahava (hell of shivering tongue); Huhuva (hell of shuddering mouth); Utpala (hell of blue-lotus-coloured patches on the skin); Padma (hell of crimson-lotus-coloured patches on the skin); Mahapadma (hell of great-crimson-lotus-coloured patches on the skin).

The Tibetan Book of the Dead, which briefly became trendy in the West among mystics and the crystal-gazing set, is as misnamed as its Egyptian counterpart—its actual name is the *Bardo Thodol*, which roughly translates as "Great Liberation Through Hearing"; it is a collection of advisories to be read to the dying or newly dead, not to be used by them, as in the Egyptian case.[14]

Many Buddhist texts contain usefully comprehensive gazetteers to hell. In *The Sutra of the Past Vows of Earth Store Bodhisattva*, for example, the "Humane One," as the monk Ksitigarbha is often called, named many of the hells he had visited, their names indicating what is to be found there:

> East of Jambudvipa there is a mountain called Iron Ring, which is totally black and has neither sun nor moonlight. There is a great hell there called Uninterrupted, and another called the Great Avici. There is also a hell called Four Pointed, a hell called Flying Knives, a hell called Flying Arrows, and a hell called Squeezing Mountains; a hell called Piercing Spears, a hell called Iron Carts, a hell called Iron Beds, and a hell called Iron Ox; a hell called Iron Clothing, a hell called Thousand Blades, a hell called Iron Asses, and a hell called Molten Brass; a hell called Embracing Pillar, a hell called Flowing Fire, a hell called Plowing Tongues, and a hell called Head Chopping; a hell called Burning Feet, a hell called Eye Pecking, a hell called Iron Pellets, and a hell called Quarreling; a hell called Iron Ax, and a hell called Much Hatred.
>
> In addition there is the hell of Crying Out, the hell of Pulling Tongues, the hell of Dung and Urine, and the hell of Brazen Locks; the hell of Fire Elephants, the

hell of Fire Dogs, the hell of Fire Horses,
and the hell of Fire Oxen; the hell of Fire
Mountains, the hell of Fire Stones, the hell
of Fire Beds, and the hell of Fire Beams;
the hell of Fire Eagles, the hell of Sawing
Teeth, the hell of Flaying Skin, and the
hell of Drinking Blood; the hell of Burning
Hands, the hell of Burning Feet, the hell
of Hanging Thorns, and the hell of Fire
Houses; the hell of Iron Rooms, and the
hell of Fire Wolves.

Such are the hells, and within each of
them there are, one, two, three, four, or as
many as hundreds of thousands of smaller
hells, each with its own name.[15]

Ksitigarbha (also translated as Earth Matrix or Earth
Womb) is usually shown as a monk with a halo around
his shaved head, carrying a staff to force open the gates of
hell and a jewel to light up the darkness; he once vowed
not to achieve Buddhahood until all hells were emptied.

Of course, the point of Buddhist hell, no matter which
one, is not the punishment but the self-improvement
that unpleasantness can bring—good people, if they
are virtuous on earth or they repent in death, can either
escape hell altogether, or spend only a few cycles there,
before reaching the state of Nirvana, in which the self is
extinguished in the Altogether.

SINHALESE BUDDHISM HAS 136 hells, but the Burmese version has no fewer than 40,040, one for each particular sin—and as in certain Hindu hells, some of those are low-grade sins that hardly seem to warrant even a single minute's suffering, such as nosiness, chicken-selling, and eating sweets with rice.[16]

If anything, the Chinese Buddhist hells were ever more pedantic, ever more bureaucratic, and ever more frustrating. Most traditions divided the underworld into ten "courts." The first of these is called the Mirror of Sin, which allowed sinners to look back in anguish at their wasted lives. This being Buddhism, the last of the ten courts is the Wheel of Fortune, which selects one of the six paths of incarnation for each sinner, who is given a draught of oblivion so the soul can get on with its new incarnation without lamentation or remorse. In the remaining eight courts, you can find the usual piercings and flayings and swamps of disgusting fluids, but as Eileen Gardiner points out at Hell-On-Line, more impressive than even the punishments . . . are the lists of sins punished in each court. Here we find people who keep other people's books, pretending to have lost them, people who lie about their ages when they get married, people who throw broken pottery over fences, those who write anonymous placards (the Chinese hells should have lots of room, then, for Internet trolls), those who allow their mules to be a nuisance, and people who complain about the weather. In Chinese Buddhism, though, hell often seems to mostly consist of endlessly waiting in anterooms, with no one paying the sinner any attention at all— hell as a multiplicity of petty paper-pushers, resembling nothing so much as the afterlife in Paul Simon's song of the same name:

> Well it seems like our fate to suffer
> And wait for the knowledge we seek
> It's all his design, no one cuts in the line
> No one here likes a sneak
>
> You got to fill out a form first
> And then you wait in the line
> You got to fill out a form first
> And then you wait in the line

Of course, Simon was writing about heaven. But it serves just fine for the passage through hell. Designed by the same people, after all.

The New Testament has little to say about hell itself

IT IS IN Christian and Muslim eschatology that the notions of hell are most fully developed, but not so much in scripture—the Bible itself doesn't have much to say on the subject (there are 622 verses in the Bible that mention heaven, and a mere fifteen that mention hell), though it is true that Gehenna, "where the worm never dies and the fire is never quenched," appears twelve times, and there are many hints of fiery pits and so forth, along with multiple wailings and gnashings of teeth. (More on these gnashings later.)

It is worth remembering that the Christian/Hebrew version of hell began before there were sinners to put into it—indeed, before there were people to sin at all. As per the Hebrews, hell started merely as a hole in the ground into which the Lord stuffed the recalcitrant Azazel (the Lucifer-that-was), and grew from there. By the time Milton caught up with it, in *Paradise Lost* (set in a period before Adam and Eve), hell had grown to a sprawling country, replete with palaces and towns, and ruled strictly but more or less benevolently by Hades with Satan as his unwilling guest.

Eastern (Orthodox) Christians, it should be noted, never shared their Western counterparts' obsession with hell. In their view, there is no place God is not, therefore God is also in hell. They actually go further, and suggest that for those who hate God, being in his presence is hell enough. Torture is a Western idea; and even in the West the doctrine of perpetual torment was only propounded by the Lateran Council in 1215, just a century before Dante.

Modern biblical scholars maintain that Jesus himself, and even Saint Paul, made no mention of "hell" or "damnation" in the New Testament. In this view, the Greek words mistranslated as hell meant only "judgment" and "condemnation"; and these conditions were to last only for "a long time," not forever. The New Testament contains not a single chapter devoted to hellishness—or even the afterlife, for that matter. Original sin, however, was basic to the creed. God created man pristine and guiltless, but that didn't last: it was Adam (and of course Eve) who polluted the future and thus made punishment necessary. Hence, there must be a final Day of Judgment, in which Christ will return for a final, thousand-day battle with Satan, which will end with Satan's defeat. After that, well, the day of reckoning. Which means hell for some, forever.

Jesus famously said that a man should forgive his sinning brother not seven times, but "seventy times seven." And even grumpy Paul suggested that God would eventually have mercy on everyone. Modern Christian commentators cling, rather wanly, to this notion—it is impossible for God to be cruel, after all, because cruelty is unjust, and God is surely incapable of inflicting an unjust punishment.

On the other hand, Jesus also said, at least according to Matthew, "you that are accursed, depart from me into the eternal fire prepared for the devil and his angels; for I was hungry and you gave me no food, I was thirsty and you gave me nothing to drink, I was a stranger and you did not welcome me, naked and you did not give me clothing, sick and in prison and you did not visit me." And at another time he lashed out at those who disagreed with him: "Ye serpents, ye generation of vipers, how can ye escape the damnation of hell?" That doesn't sound too forgiving.

Islam is only a little more explicit

THE QUR'AN IS more forthcoming than the Bible about hell, with ninety-eight direct mentions, and many more allusions.

Jahannam is the Islamic hell, probably derived from Gehenna. Predictably, given the geographic provenance of the Qur'an, it was a fiery pit where the lost struggle for water amid everlasting thirst. It was located underneath al-Sirat, a path leading to paradise; hell has seven ordered gates; the path crosses a bridge that gives safe passage only on the say-so of Allah.

Like Christianity (and later versions of Judaism), on which much of Islam is based, there is some slippage between the notions of God's sovereignty on the one hand, with its attendant justice and mercy, and the notion of hellfire on the other, with its inherent cruelty. That is, between the notion of God's omnipotent authority and goodness and god-awful punishment. Theologians of both persuasions have long wrestled with this notion of evil in the world—if God is omnipotent, the question goes, why does evil exist?

The soul of the pious Muslim, it seems, "will experience an easy death and a pleasant sojourn in the grave. The infidel's soul, violently torn from the body and failing interrogation by the angels Munkar and Nakīr, will suffer torment in the grave until the day when it will take up its place in hell, there to dine on bitter fruit and pus and to be roasted and boiled with all the usual infernal devices for as long as God sees fit."[17]

The hells of Dante's precursors

DANTE HAD A rich literature to choose from when constructing his poem and his architecture of hell.

There was Virgil's *Aeneid*, of course. Arda Viraf. The poetizing Tundale. The Irish monk Adamnán. *The Apocalypse of Peter*, which focused "on the terrors of the last judgment . . . [offering] a ghastly picture of a brutal underworld where each specific sin garners a corresponding punishment. For every offence against God there is a particular torture, described with great relish."[18]

Then there were the many medieval writers, building on Christian texts such as *The Apocalypses of Peter and Paul*, *The Apocalypse of Mary* and *The Gospel of Nicodemus*, who competed with each other in lurid depictions of the afterlife—see, for example, the *Elucidarium*, by the eleventh-century mystic called Honorious of Autun, a Q&A intended as a handbook for the lower clergy, a kind of cheater's guide for sermon preparation. (As its title modestly put it, it sought to "elucidate the obscurity of various things.") The tract is divided into three books, the last of which deals with the Antichrist, the last judgment, purgatory, and the pains of hell. The author described, with evident delight, how the underworld is divided into two sections, an upper section for lesser offences, and a lower one where the usual torments await: fire and ice, stench, worms and serpents, demons, darkness, and confinement in burning shackles.[19]

In the late seventh century, the Spanish monk Bonellus described hell as a series of steep precipices; on his visit he is shown the devil, the deepest pit, bad angel giants, and arrows shot from a lake of fire (Bonellus escapes by giving the sign of the cross and vows thereafter, as well he might, to lead a virtuous life).

Much earlier was the *Pistis Sophia* (roughly, the Faith of Sophia), a gnostic text from the third century hastily suppressed by the early church (you can see why: it considered the crucifixion pointless, since mankind could just as easily have been redeemed by the incarnation itself, and has Jesus hanging around on earth for eleven years after he rose from the dead, to teach his disciples the lesser mysteries). The *Pistis* also has Jesus telling his mother about hell, describing it as a huge dragon that encompasses the material world and whose body houses twelve dungeons of horrible torment.[20] Satan himself described hell as extending for 160,000 kilometres.[21]

The Vision of Paul (usually known as *The Apocalypse of Paul*, which was itself but an elaboration of *The Apocalypse of Peter*), was definitely used by Dante as source material—Dante mentions the "Chosen Vessel's visit to Hell," said vessel being Paul himself. (For our purposes, *The Vision of Paul* is mostly interesting because in it Paul and the Virgin manage to persuade God to give everyone in hell Sundays off, a notion not met with anywhere else.[22])

Pope Innocent III was another who wrote eagerly of hell's punishments. He didn't describe hell, exactly, but he did note that the conventional wisdom of his time (he died in 1216) listed nine levels of sinners, which may be where Dante got his number.

> Now the first punishment of hell is for those of unbridled appetite; the second, for those of malicious will; the third for the lecherous; the fourth for the envious and those who hate; the fifth is for those who in this world did not deserve to be beaten with scourges, because "the sinner hath provoked the Lord, according to the multitude of His wrath he will not seek him"; the sixth is for those walking in darkness who disdainfully refuse to come to the true light, namely, Christ; the seventh for

those who confess their sins and despite repentance; the eighth is for those who freely see the evils in this world and [yet] do them; and the ninth is for those who have wallowed in every vice, who travel the road of their own desires and follow only their own appetites."

Dante doesn't follow these exactly, but his own version was very similar.

In her tract *The Book of Divine Works*, Saint Hildegard of Bingen (1099–1179), a grim abbess and noted killjoy (although also a talented composer and inventor), described the Land of Bad Things as "grim and braid, full of boiling pitch and sulphur, and around it were wasps and scorpions, who created but did not injure the souls therein; which were the souls of those who had slain in order not to be slain. . . . Near a pond of clear water I saw a great fire. In this some souls were burned and others were girdled with snakes, and others drew in and again exhaled the firelike breath, while malignant spirits cast lighted stones at them. . . . And I saw a great swamp, over which hung a black cloud of smoke, which was issuing from it. And in the swamp there swarmed a mass of little worms. Here were the souls of those who in the world delighted in foolish merriment." Ah, yes! Foolish merriment, not to be tolerated. Pretty much sums up monastic traditions.

CHAPTER 8

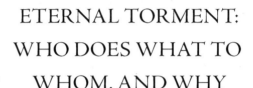

ETERNAL TORMENT: WHO DOES WHAT TO WHOM, AND WHY

A SINNER'S JOB IN HELL IS TO HANG AROUND TO BE flayed and dismembered and boiled in noxious liquids, over and over, often forever, though not always.

A full catalogue of the tortures of hell would make for dispiriting reading. One can only take so many piercings and flayings and boilings and immersions in disgusting fluids before shutting down . . . So this is just a quick overview of hellish torment, showing that the inventiveness of human nastiness cuts across cultures and religions, and showing, too, the purely pornographic delight that the medieval mind found in ever more grotesque punishment—this was the period in Europe, after all, when women accused of being witches were burned at the stake, but periodically removed from the flames for revival, lest they perish too quickly and the cheering crowds be cheated. Just so, there was a medieval game that entailed nailing a cat to a tree and allowing contestants to attempt to head-butt it to death without getting their eyes scratched out. What fun!

The forever files

THE NOTION THAT hellish torment was forever dates from the medieval period—there were earlier approving hints but, as noted above, the Lateran Council of 1215 made it official church doctrine. Before that, in most religions torment was pretty bad, but almost always finite. The Egyptians, we'll remember, liked to burn and maim the departed, but only until they were *really* dead—after that, they were gone. Early Christian texts were generally silent on the matter of eternity; even Lucifer was to be imprisoned and tortured, but only until Judgment Day, when he was cast again into the fires of hell, his post-judgment fate generally undisclosed.

Only Western Christianity even considered the open-endedness of punishment. Most non-Christian versions of hell were pretty bad, but there was always an out—eventually.

All this was necessary, you understand. *Pace* Saint Ignatius of Loyola, a Jesuit novice is supposed to pray for an intimate sense of the pain that the damned suffer: to feel the fire, hear the lamentations, smell the brimstone, taste the tears. Saint Bernardino of Siena put the case perfectly: "There can be no perfect sweetness of song in heaven if there were no infernal descant from God's justice,"[1] meaning that everlasting celestial joy depends on a contrast of everlasting horror. You should be able to listen, as John Bunyan put it, to the crying of the damned, who shall be ever whining, pining, weeping, mourning, ever tormented without ease.[2] Otherwise, what's the point of being good?

"If we regard hell as a divine overreaction to sin, we deny that God has the moral right to inflict ongoing punishment on any humans. By denying hell, we deny the extent of God's holiness. When we minimize sin's seriousness, we minimize God's grace in Christ's blood, shed for us. For if the evils he died for aren't significant enough to warrant eternal punishment, perhaps the grace displayed on the cross isn't significant enough to warrant eternal praise." (Thus the sophist argument, made by Randy Alcorn in his book *Heaven*.)

In consequence, you get screeds like that of the firebrand cleric John Shower, in his resoundingly named *Heaven and Hell, or, The unchangeable state of happiness or misery for all mankind in another world occasion'd by the repentance and death of Mr. Shetterden Thomas, who departed this life April 7, 1700: preach'd and publish'd at the desire and direction of the deceased.* Shower writes approvingly that "we have heard of some who have endured breaking on the Wheel, ripping up of the Bowels, fleaing alive, racking of Joynts, burning of Flesh, pounding in a Mortar, tearing in piece with Flesh-hooks, boyling in Oyl, roasting on hot fiery Grid-irons, etc. And yet all these, tho' you should superad thereto all Diseases, such as the Plague, Stone, Gout, Stragury, or whatever else you can name most torturing to the Body . . . that would all come short . . . of that Wrath, the Horror, that unconceivable Anguish, which the dammed must inevitably suffer every Moment, without any intermission of their Pains, in hellish Flames."[3]

But it is not just Christians who think god's grace can be soothed with such savagery. Most faiths have an inventive, if alarming, litany of punishments, including torture by ropes and knives, swords, chains, bamboo, tridents, brushes, needles, iron pincers, thorns, and axes; dogs, birds, snakes, and maggots, even a hedgehog; hail and sleet, snow and ice, fire, burning oil, burning rivers, and putrid stuff of all sorts. All manner of cutting, trampling, force-feeding, dismemberment, drowning, burning, and crushing are also gainfully employed.[4] There will be stinking dungeons, and a loathsome lake that burns with fire and brimstone forever . . . And so on and so on.

Explications of torture by Srosh the Pious and Adar the Angel

SO WHERE TO start? Perhaps with the Zoroastrian scholar and traveller Arda Viraf, whose actual picaresque journey to hell will be described in a subsequent chapter—here just to give a sampling of what he found *down there*. (Charles Horne's 1917 translation gives the flavour, but not all of it, for as he wrote in his introduction, "Most of the brief book is given here, except where the details of hell become too bestial, too coarsely sordid for modern taste.")

Here, then, are a few punishments, presumably just on the decent side of coarsely sordid:

I came to a place, and I saw the soul of a man, through the fundament of which soul, as it were a snake, like a beam, went in, and came forth out of the mouth; and many other snakes ever seized all the limbs.

And I inquired of Srosh the pious, and Adar the angel, thus: "What sin was committed by this body, whose soul suffers so severe a punishment?"

Srosh the pious, and Adar the angel, said thus: "This is the soul of that wicked man, who, in the world, committed sodomy, and allowed a man to come on his body; now the soul suffers so severe a punishment."

I also saw the soul of a woman who was suspended, by the breasts, to hell, and its noxious creatures seized her whole body.

And I asked thus: "What sin was committed by this body, whose soul suffers such a punishment?"

Srosh the pious, and Adar the angel, said thus: "This is the soul of that wicked woman who, in the world, left her own husband, and gave herself to other men, and committed adultery."

This question-and-response format goes on for many pages, and there is no need to repeat it here. But among the other punishments Viraf watched were these: women hanging head downwards, and something like a hedgehog with iron spikes growing from it introduced into their bodies, and from it, a finger dropping the semen of the demons and demonesses, which is stench and corruption, into the inside of their jaws and noses—this for women who refused their husbands sex; and women tied by one leg, head downwards, into whose eyes a wooden peg was driven while frogs, scorpions, snakes, ants, flies, worms, and other noxious creatures went and came inside their jaws, noses, ears, posteriors, and sexual parts—this for women who granted other men the favour of sex, and who thus defiled their husbands.

Viraf also saw a man boiling in a cauldron, but his right foot remained outside. Why? As the Pious One and the Angel explain, he was a wicked man in life who "lustfully and improperly went out" to married women, but his right foot was spared because he had used it to stomp on frogs, ants, snakes, scorpions, and other noxious creatures, therefore that foot deserved not to be harmed.

In common with many other versions of hell, Viraf's seems occasionally to mete out punishment somewhat disproportionate to the sin. For example, he saw a number of women who "ever shed and sucked and ate the flood and filth of their fingers," and who had worms in their eyes, and his guides explained that in life they had used makeup and "kept the hair of others as ornament" and thereby "captivated the eyes of the men of god."[5] Zoroastrian men of god easily had their heads turned by a little mascara, it seems.

For the Christians, plenty of wailings
and gnashings of teeth

IN THE CHRISTIAN tradition, Jesus didn't have much to say about the actual torments of hell. He was big on threats, but (except for fire) sketchy on the actual punishments. But he did make some pretty potent threats: "The son of man," he declared, referring to himself, "shall send forth his angels, and they shall gather out of his kingdom all things that offend, and them which do iniquity, and shall cast them into a furnace of fire; and there shall be wailing and gnashing of teeth"[6]—those same wailings and teeth-gnashings occur frequently in the New Testament.

The disciples, too, didn't have much to say, but hell does come up a few times, almost always with fire in mind. Matthew, for example, said, "every tree that bringeth not forth good fruit is hewn down, and cast into the fire." (Matthew also suggested, quoting Jesus, that the Jews are all going to hell, except that in their case it would be weepings and gnashings of teeth, not wailings.)

The pre-Christian prophet Isaiah, for his part, was keen to show that the inhabitants of heaven, the holy angels themselves, would rather enjoy the spectacle of all this pain: "And they shall go forth, and look upon the carcasses of the men that have transgressed against Me: for their worm shall not die, neither shall their fire be quenched; and they shall be an abhorring unto all flesh."[7] Fire-and-brimstone preachers have long been fond of quoting this passage: as a 1741 sermon called *Sinners in the Hands of an Angry God* put it, "you shall be tormented in the Presence of the Holy Angels, of an angry God and in the Presence of the Lamb; and when you shall be in this State of Suffering, the glorious Inhabitants of Heaven shall go forth and look on the awful Spectacle, that they may see what the Wrath and Fierceness of the Almighty is, and when they have seen it, they will fall down and adore that great Power and Majesty."

Jesus shows Peter how torment is done

ONE OF THE earliest Christian texts to catalogue hell's torments was *The Apocalypse of Peter* (a.k.a. the *Revelation to Peter*), which purports to be a conversation between Jesus and his apostle; it dates to somewhere around the early second century CE, and seems to have lifted long passages from some of the "Orphic sources" (from the cult of Orpheus), thereby introducing Hellenistic and pre-Christian ideas of heaven and hell into Christianity. The apocalypse was disavowed by the early church fathers, but remained popular.

It starts with Peter questioning Jesus about torment-ing sinners—surely it would have been better for them not to have been born at all? Jesus demurs. God created the sinners, after all, and they disobeyed—that should be justification enough for damnation. "Now because thou hast seen the lamentation which shall come upon the sinners in the last days, therefore is thine heart trou-bled; but I will show thee their works, whereby they have sinned against the Most High."

And show Peter he does. Here's a sampling:

> Then shall men and women come unto the
> place prepared for them. By their tongues

wherewith they have blasphemed the way
of righteousness shall they be hanged up.
There is spread under them unquenchable
fire, that they escape it not.

. . . Behold corrupt women: they hang
them up by their neck and by their hair;
they shall cast them into the pit. These
are they which plaited their hair, not for
good but to turn them to fornication, that
they might ensnare the souls of men unto
perdition. And the men that lay with them
in fornication shall be hung by their loins
in that place of fire. . . .

And near this flame shall be a pit, great
and very deep, and into it floweth from
above all manner of torment, foulness,
and issue. And women are swallowed up
therein up to their necks and tormented
with great pain. These are they that have
caused their children to be born untimely.

Children and maidens are not spared:

"Furthermore the angel Ezrael shall bring children
and maidens. . . . They shall be chastised with pains,
with hanging up and with a multitude of wounds which
flesh-devouring birds shall inflict upon them. These are
they that boast themselves in their sins, and obey not their
parents and follow not the instruction of their fathers,
and honor not them that are more aged than they."

And so on and so on. No sins go unpunished. Hell
is ever vigilant.[8]

Paul is not to be outshone, torment-wise

THE APOCALYPSE OF *Paul* was another early Christian fabrication, this time dating to the fourth century. It is similar in structure to Peter's, but considerably more self-satisfied. Still, while there was a similar catalogue of sins matched with punishment, Paul had many cross things to say about errant church fathers.

One passage concerned a priest who had failed to fulfill his mission ("for when he was eating and drinking and whoring he offered the sacrifice unto the Lord at his holy altar . . .") who had his entrails pierced with iron hooks by three agents of Tartarus. Another dealt with a bishop who had no compassion for orphans and widows; God "sank him up to his knees in the river of fire, and smote him with stones and wounded his face like a tempest." A deacon, said to have "devoured the offerings and committed fornication and did not right in the sight of God," was punished by being sunk up to his knees in the river of fire, his hands stretched out and bloody; worms issued out of his mouth and his nostrils, and he was groaning and lamenting and crying out . . .

Like Peter, Paul didn't neglect sins committed by common people either: usury (he really hated that one, its practitioners endlessly devoured by worms), adultery, fornication, and the rest: "And again I beheld men and women with their hands and feet cut off and naked, in a place of ice and snow, and worms devoured them. And when I saw it I wept and asked: Who are these, Lord? And he said unto me: These are they that injured the fatherless and widows and the poor, and trusted not in the Lord: wherefore without ceasing they pay the due penalty."[9]

The Qur'an appreciates the therapeutic value of fire—and of a bad diet

THE QUR'AN, WHILE only slightly more explicit than Jesus in the Bible, is just as keen on fire: "On the day when it will [all] be heated in the fire of hell, and their foreheads and their flanks and their backs will be branded therewith." And again: "Hell is before him, and he is made to drink a festering water, which he sippeth but can hardly swallow, and death cometh unto him from every side while yet he cannot die, and before him is a harsh doom . . . hell, where they will burn, an evil resting-place. Here is a boiling and an ice-cold draught, so let them taste it. . . . Take him and drag him to the midst of hell, then pour upon his head the torment of boiling water. . . . On the day when they are dragged into the Fire upon their faces (it is said unto them): Feel the touch of hell. . . . Then the welcome will be boiling water and roasting at hell-fire."[10]

Imam Kamil Mufti has identified several variants of hellfire in Islamic texts: *jaheem* (fire); *jahannam* (hell, because of the depth of its pit); *ladthaa* (blazing fire, because of its flames); *sa'eer* (blazing flame, because it is kindled and ignited); *saqar* (because of the intensity of its heat); *hatamah* (broken pieces or debris, because it breaks and crushes everything that is thrown into it); *haawiyah* (chasm or abyss, because the one who is thrown into it is thrown from top to bottom).[11]

To eat there is only "a bitter, thorny plant which neither nourishes nor avails against hunger." This is the *zaqqum* tree, reprised several times in the Qur'an (see, for example, 17:60 and 44:43), a repulsive thing, with roots to the bottom of hell, its fruit like the heads of the devils. And Allah says, "And indeed, they will eat from it and fill with it their bellies. Then, indeed, they will have after it a mixture of scalding water. Then, indeed, their return will be to the hellfire." The stuff was so bad that Muhammad himself said that "if a drop from *zaqqum* were to land in this world, the people of earth and all their means of sustenance would rot. So how must it be for one who must eat it?"

Other authorities, such as Imam Kamil Mufti, suggest that "another food served to the people of hell will be festering pus that oozes out of their skin, the discharge that flows from the private parts of adulterers and the decaying skin and flesh of those being burnt. It is the 'juice' of the people of hell."

The ungentle visions of the monk Adamnán

THE GREAT IRISH monk Adamnán (whose bridge to hell was described in an earlier chapter) entered the Iona monastery in the year 650 as a novice, but soon became its abbot. He is recognized as the foremost Irish cleric of his time, a period in which the Irish church had reached its greatest wealth and its widest influence on Western culture. He is widely regarded as a precursor to Dante; his writings, especially his vision of the torments of hell, were the most-copied volumes in the monasteries of the period. His views were unbending: if the Lord receive the soul, and "if he be an unrighteous and unprofitable soul, harsh and ungentle is the reception of him by the Mighty Lord. For He saith to the heavenly Angels, 'Take, O heavenly Angels, this unprofitable soul, and deliver him into the hand of Lucifer, that he may plunge him and utterly extinguish him in hell's profound, through ages everlasting.'"[12]

Adamnán was pleased to find in hell, or at least purgatory, vast multitudes, feeble and powerless, in the land of utter darkness, whose souls had not yet received final judgment. "Every other hour the pain ebbs away from them, and the next hour it returns upon them again. Now these are they in whom good and evil were equally balanced, and on the Day of Doom, judgment shall be passed between them, and their good shall quench their evil on that day; and then shall they be brought to the Haven of Life, in God's own presence, through ages everlasting."

That was just hell's anteroom. Real sinners had it much worse. They were fettered to fiery columns, surrounded by a sea of fire, with fiery chains about their middles. Who were these unfortunates? "They who are tormented thus are sinners, fratricides, ravagers of God's Church, and merciless Erenachs, who, in presence of the relics of the Saints, had been set over the Church's tithes and oblations, and had alienated these riches to their private store."

What they got was therefore only just. "Demon hosts surround them, with fiery clubs in their hands, striking them over the head, though they struggle against them continually. Red showers of fire are raining on them, every night and every day, and they cannot ward them off, but must needs endure them throughout all ages, wailing and making moan. . . . An unspeakable throng of demons is throttling them, holding in leash the while raw-hided, stinking hounds, which they incite to devour and consume them. Red glowing chains are constantly ablaze about their necks. Every alternate hour they are borne up to the firmament, and the next hour they are dashed down into Hell's profound."

A few other Christian visions of what happens in the pit

IN THE MEDIEVAL *Vision of Merlino*, a "wicked man of Bohemia" is shown how the seven deadly sins are punished by the insertion of snakes and adders into various bodily parts. But the text is most interesting for its description of the Lake of Pains, of whose waters "one single drop . . . would destroy all the creatures on the surface of the earth by the bitterness of its chill."[13]

Another prolific commentator on hellish matters was Pope Innocent III, the masterly politician (he had consolidated papal power in the teeth of stiff opposition from emperors and kings, and had waged war on the Cathars in the Albigensian Crusade). Innocent was another who attempted to match sin to torment. But he was more specific than most, even going so far as to match the body part to the punishment: "For it is written, by what things a man sins, by the same also shall he be tormented. So he who has sinned with his tongue was tortured in the tongue, for which he cried out, Father Abraham, have mercy on me and send Lazarus that he may dip the tip of his finger in water to cool my tongue, for I am tormented by this flame. The finger signified work, for we work with our fingers. It is as if to say, If I had the least work of Lazarus I would experience less punishment."

The worse the sin the worse the punishment: "There will indeed be order in the quantity of punishment, because with what measure you mete, it shall be measured to you again. So he who has sinned more grievously will be punished more grievously, for the mighty shall be mightily tormented. But here will be no order in quality: they will all be plunged from icy water into unbearable heat, so that the sudden extremes will inflict a more dread torment. For I have found from experience that if one who has been burnt applies cold, he feels a more burning pain."

Innocent also provided a useful explanation of this business of wailings (weepings) and gnashings of teeth. "There are various punishment in hell for various kinds of sins. The first punishment is fire, the second cold. Of these the Lord says, 'there will be weeping and gnashing of teeth,' weeping because of the smoke, gnashing of teeth because of the cold. The third punishment will be stench."[14]

Sword-leaf trees and other Buddhist devices

FOR A RELIGION without a god (not even a benevolent one, never mind one filled with malice), and certainly without a devil, Buddhism has an unseemly preoccupation with torture. Buddhist hells—and as we saw earlier, there are many of them—are filled with pain, and Buddhist writings (including the collected sayings of the Buddha himself) have left us graphic descriptions of the torments suffered by those who have not yet expunged the evils that they did in life.

Take the hell of the sword-leaf trees. The trees in this hell are 65 kilometres tall, with thorns 40 centimetres long. The wardens of hell drag sinners up the trees and throw them down, shearing their flesh and piercing their bodies. Those who in life ignored their families and had affairs, leaving their spouses to suffer, are all sent here. In another variant, when (presumably male) offenders look up to the top of the trees they see there "seductive and soft-bodied" women. Mesmerized, they rush up the tree, its leaves cutting their flesh and tendons, shearing their bones, shredding their bodies into pieces. Revived by the winds of karma, they look down and see the seductive, soft bodies on the ground. Deceived by karma, they let desire control their actions, and rush down the trees, again being cut into pieces. This goes on for many thousands of cycles.[15]

The Buddha himself wasn't shy about recounting tales of this sort. In *The Middle-Length Discourses of the Buddha*, he describes what happens when a man first goes to hell—namely, he gets the "five-fold transfixing."

"They drive a red-hot iron stake through one hand, they drive a red-hot iron stake through the other hand, they drive a red-hot iron stake through one foot, they drive a red-hot iron stake through the other foot, they drive a red-hot iron stake through his belly. There he feels painful, racking, piercing feelings. Yet he does not die so long as that evil action has not exhausted its result. Next the wardens of hell throw him down and pare him with axes. There he feels painful, racking, piercing feelings. Yet he does not die so long as that evil action has not exhausted its result. Then he is harnessed to a chariot and driven across burning ground, after which he is made to climb a massive hill of coals, then he is cooked in a cauldron in a swirl of froth." Only then is he pushed into hell proper, a great hall, with a door at each corner, "Walled up with iron and all around, and shut in with an iron roof. Its floor as well is made of iron, heated till it glows with fire." The whole thing was a hundred leagues in size.

Each time the sinner tries to get out at one of the corners, the door slams in his face, and his outer skin burns, his inner skin burns, his flesh burns, his sinews burn, his bones turn to smoke . . . Eventually he gets out the eastern door, only to find himself in the vast Hell of Excrement, where needle-mouthed creatures "bore through his outer skin and bore through his inner skin and bore through his flesh and bore through his sinews and bore through his bones and devour his marrow," after which he is shifted to the Hell of Hot Embers, where he experiences those familiar painful racking, piercing feelings. Only after that does he get to the vast Wood of Simbali Trees, a league high, with thorns sixteen finger-breadths long, burning, glowing, and blazing, which the wardens of hell make him climb over and over. Thence, to the self-same vast Wood of Sword-Leaf Trees . . . and after that, "immediately next to the Wood of Sword-Leaf Trees is a great river of caustic water. He falls into that. There he is swept upstream and he is swept downstream and he is swept upstream and downstream."

Once again he feels those painful racking, piercing feelings.

As well he might.[16]

The monk Genshin's runaway
bestselling guide to torment

JAPANESE BUDDHISM IS well represented in the torture chronicles by the monk Genshin, who died in 1017; he mostly argued for the Pure Land movement, but he listed the various hells as instructive contrast. The book was a bestseller for centuries. Perhaps Genshin was his monastery's cook, for many of the tortures he describes sound as though they were written by a former chef, what with boiling cauldrons, mincemeat, and pounded flesh . . .

In Genshin's view the shallowest of hells is called the Hell of Revival, reserved for those who have harmed others: they attack each other with iron fingernails, tearing each other apart, and then climb the by-now-familiar sword-leaf trees.

Next down is the Hell of Black Ropes, reserved for those who killed and stole: they are marked by demons with black burning ropes, then forced to lie down on the scorching ground, where they are dismembered by axes or saws.

The third hell is for people who killed, stole, or committed adultery; it is called the Hell of Assembly, and has a complicated set of tortures: the damned are driven by demons into a crevice between two of the many iron mountains found here. These mountains crash into each other, crushing the people between them, then other iron mountains fall down from the sky, grinding the damned to mincemeat. Demons also throw the damned into a river of molten copper; place them on stone slabs and pound them with rocks; or place them in iron mortars and mince them with iron pestles. Finally, their bodies are devoured by demons, beasts, and birds of hell. Then they are revived to do it all over again.

Beneath all this, "at the very bottom of the Realm of Desire," is the worst hell of all, the Hell of No Interval:

> There is nothing but flames.
> They fill the sky and there is no
>   space between the flames.
> In the four directions, in the four
>   intermediate directions
> And on the ground, there is no
>   place which is free of flame.
> Every place on the ground
> Is filled with evil people.
> I can't rely on anything.
> I am alone, with no companion.
> I am within the darkness
>   of this evil realm
> And will soon enter the mass of flames.
> In the sky, I can
> See neither the sun, the
>   moon nor the stars.[17]

For Hindu sinners, the hell of the River of Semen and other delights

THE EARLIEST VIVID description of hell in classical Hindu literature is found in the last part of the epic called the *Mahābhārata*. It was pretty rudimentary. When the poem's protagonist, King Yudhisthira, went down to hell to find his brothers and his wife (who were there for no obvious reason) he found that hell was shrouded in darkness and inhabited by a massive bird with an iron beak, a copper pot for boiling, a tree whose branches were like blades, and the "difficult-to-cross Vaitarani River."

As the number of Hindu hells multiplied, so did the sins and their punishments. There is no point cataloguing the full dreary list, but a few stand out. For example, hell #15 is called *Puyodakam* (the Well of Hell), and consists of a well filled with feces, urine, blood, and phlegm, reserved for men who have intercourse and cheat women with no intention of marrying them. Hell #17 is *Visasanam* (the Hell of Bashing from Clubs), for those rich people who in life looked down at the poor and spent excessively just to display their wealth and splendour. Then there is hell #18, *Lalabhaksam* (the Hell of the River of Semen), which is reserved "for lustful men and the lascivious fellow who makes his wife swallow his semen." This is actually a sea, not a river, of semen, in which the sinner lies "until his time is up," feeding upon semen alone. The final hell, #28, is *Sucimukham* (the Hell of Torture by Needles), where those who do not repay the money they have borrowed will be constantly pricked and pierced by needles.[18]

When you ask whether these punishments aren't, well, a little extreme, practitioners just shrug. The sinners brought it on themselves, and can do better next time. This will no doubt teach them a valuable lesson.

Which is surely true enough.

CHAPTER 9

—◆)(◆—

THE PECULIAR PHYSICS
OF HELL: HOW LONG
IS FOREVER?

THE QUESTIONS WITH WHICH THIS BRIEF CHAPTER
is occupied are as follows: If crows are to draw out your
entrails through your anus, as they are standing by to do
in many versions of hell, how long before you, well, *run
short*? If you are to be boiled in oil, how long before you
are done? If you are consigned to the Hindu hell called
Vinmutra, where you are submerged in an endless lake of
feces and urine, how long before you drown? The answer,
at least according to the physics of the standard hellish
texts, is . . . never. Hell's matter, like heaven's, is endlessly
self-renewing—radioactive decay is greased lightning by
comparison.

Three issues of physics are in play here. Firstly, the
fires of hell need no fuel and do not consume what they
burn—that would rather defeat the purpose, for it would
have ended sinners' torment too soon, which would not

do. So hell's designers saw to it that hellfire could burn but not damage, hurt but not destroy.

The second issue is one of time, which needed to be stretched in ways the scribes of hell tried very hard to grasp: hell does seem to teeter on the very edge of time. As early as twenty-five hundred years ago Hesiod thought that all beginnings and all ends contended just beyond hell's gate, a very quantum idea. In the sword-leaf-tree hell, sinners are condemned to strive for those soft-bodied women for as long as necessary, until the evil they have done in life is thoroughly scrubbed. Genshin, the monk who yearned for the Pure Life Land, but who seems to have had only a hazy view of cosmological time, estimated at one point that ten trillion years would be about right.

The third issue seems more mundane, but is not: can hell ever fill up?

The matter of matter

SOMETIMES THE FIRES of hell don't seem to actually "burn" at all—that is, they burn but do not consume. Pope Innocent III asserted that "the fire of hell is not fed by wood nor kindled by wind, but was created unquench-able by God from the beginning of the world. Thus is it written, A fire that is not kindled shall devour him [the sinner]. The fire of hell, however, will always blaze and never give light, always burn and never consume, always afflict and never go out. For there is in hell the profoundest obscurity of darkness, an immense harshness of punishment, an eternity of misery. Bind his hands and feet and cast him into the exterior darkness: there shall be weeping and gnashing of teeth." In this he was just echoing Saint Augustine, who pointed out, in his *City of God*, that if God is all-powerful, as he surely is, he is therefore perfectly capable of creating a body that can endure eternal torment—a great miracle, as Augustine declared, in obvious admiration.

But sometimes the fires of hell do actually consume, if only temporarily. Like the Prophet, Imam Kamil Mufti described how hellfire would burn off a sinner's skin, which would then be renewed, to be burned off again, in endless cycles. "The Fire kindled by God will burn the skin of the people of hell. The skin is the largest organ of the body and the site of sensation where the pain of burning is felt. God will replace the burnt skin with a new one to be burnt again, and this will keep on repeating." He quotes the Qur'an: "Indeed, those who disbelieve in Our verses—We will drive them into a Fire. Every time their skins are roasted through We will replace them with other skins so they may taste the punishment. Indeed, God is ever Exalted in Might and Wise." The Prophet added a gloss: "Super-heated water will be poured onto their heads and will dissolve through it until it cuts up their innards, expelling them; until it comes out of their feet, and everything is melted. Then they will be restored as they were."

How long before parole?

JAMES JOYCE, IN *A Portrait of the Artist as a Young Man*, recalled how as a teenager he had been burdened with the knowledge of souls in torment, while a mountain of sand a million miles high, a million miles wide, and a million miles deep, would diminish by the efforts of a little bird, which would carry away a single grain of sand every million years . . . after which, not a single instant of eternity would have ended. (This notion of the grains of sand and the little bird was cribbed directly from certain Buddhist texts, although they tended to use sesame seeds instead of sand—see below.) In this longish interim the souls had "ever to be eaten with flames, gnawed by vermin, goaded with burning spikes, never to be free from those pains; ever to have the conscience upbraid one, the memory enrage . . . ever to curse and revile the foul demons who gloat fiendishly over the misery of their dupes."

Islam, whose hell is every bit as fierce as its Christian predecessor, nevertheless recognizes the awkwardness of a merciful god imposing unmerciful torture, and most Islamic scholars argue that evildoers will be punished in hell for an appropriate period and then cease to exist, so their suffering (which is graphically described in the Qur'an and therefore must happen) will not be eternal, but justly measured. Only one Quranic verse (22:47) actually mentions duration: it asserts that one day in the hereafter (in this context, hell) is the equivalent of a thousand years in life ("And they will bid thee hasten on the Doom, and Allah faileth not His promise, but lo! A day with Allah is as a thousand years of what ye reckon").

Both the Hindu and the Buddhist traditions wrestle with the measurement of eternity, perhaps because in their view souls get multiple chances of redemption, not just the one shot envisioned by Christianity and Islam. They are often quite precise on how long a soul must wait.

For the Hindus, it would be hundreds of thousands, and perhaps millions, of years. For all practical purposes this sounds pretty eternal, but a soul must wait, after all, while it works its way through the deeds (or karma) of previous incarnations. The long-term goal is to seek release from the cycle of rebirths and attain union with the Ultimate Reality. This may take a long time, but it is not an eternity.

The Buddhists are more precise, sometimes hilariously so. In the Blister Hell, for example, which is a frozen plain surrounded by mountains and pounded by blizzards, sinners spend the amount of time it would take a little bird to empty a barrel of sesame seeds by taking a single seed every hundred years; and the time spent in each of the seven subsequent hells is twenty times the length spent in the one before it. Other descriptions escalate the quantity of sesame seeds to be removed at the one-a-century rate to 10,240 quarts; again, increasing this twenty-fold through the remaining hells, the final amount would be 510 billion quarts.

The hot hells are worse: in the first, the Reviving Hell, in which people attack each other with iron claws, sinners must stay for 1.62×10^{12} years, or 1.62 trillion years, give or take an eon (earlier for good behaviour). The final hell, Uninterrupted Hell, is much longer, 3.39×10^{19}, which comes out well into the quintillions of years.[1]

Some of the Chinese Buddhist texts suggest that hell's torments last a mere 432 million years, whereas a Japanese text from the tenth century maintains that the duration of the first hell is 9,125,000 years, and increases four-fold for each succeeding hell. The dour Irish priests

who so terrified the young James Joyce would have nod-
ded approvingly.

IN THE WESTERN tradition, what arguments have been
raised against this notion of eternal torment are not really
physical at all, but philosophical: because humans have a
finite lifespan they can commit only a finite number of sins
worth punishing, and so isn't eternity a little . . . disproportionate? Eighty years or so on earth, living according
to confusing instructions and generally bad advice, draws
an infinity in hell? Isn't there, asked physicist Sean Carroll
in an acerbic essay in *Discover* magazine, any notion of
parole? "Is a god who threatens eternal punishment for
temporal disobedience any different than an abusive
husband?"—thus a pop feminist view from Crystal St.
Marie Lewis.

Jorge Luis Borges took up this theme in his *La dura-
ción del infierno*. "No transgression can warrant an infinite
punishment, for there is no such thing as an infinite
transgression," wrote Borges, thereby putting the case for
heavenly sentence mitigation. Immanuel Kant took the
opposite view, in an argument only an eminent philosopher could make with a straight face: since morality lies
ultimately in a person's disposition, and as disposition is
concerned with the adoption of universal principles, or
"maxims," every human being is guilty of, in one sense,
an infinite number of violations of the law, and so consequently an infinite punishment is not unjustified (this
from *Religion Within the Boundaries of Mere Reason*).[2]

How big is big enough?

DANTE AND OTHERS have agreed that, at the base of hell where Satan is kept, hell has frozen over. Yet the massive hellish rivers, Acheron and Cocytus, pour endlessly into the pit, never filling it up. And then there is this observation, from *The Apocalypse of Paul*:

> I beheld and saw pits exceeding deep, and in them many souls together, and the depth of that place was as it were three thousand cubits; and I saw them groaning and weeping and saying: Have mercy on us, Lord. And no man had mercy on them.
>
> And I asked the angel and said: Who are these, Lord? And the angel answered and said unto me: These are they that trusted not in the Lord that they could have him for their helper.
>
> And I inquired and said: Lord, if these souls continue thus, thirty or forty generations being cast one upon another, if (unless) they be cast down yet deeper, I trow the pits would not contain them.
>
> And he said to me; The abyss hath no measure: for beneath it there followeth also that which is beneath: and so it is that if a strong man took a stone and cast it into an exceeding deep well and after many hours it reacheth the earth, so also is the abyss. For when the souls are cast

therein, hardly after five hundred years
do they come at the bottom.

Abyss upon abyss, down into the Deep . . .

How's the weather? Stormy, with a chance of acid rain

NOT YOUR NAMBY-PAMBY forecast here, no "mix of
sun and cloud with a chance of showers . . ." Instead,
hellfire, boiling oil, molten-metal libations, acid baths,
scorching lakes, demons belching fire, icy blizzards, and
scorching winds—pretty rugged stuff.

Pace Vulcan, hell was almost certainly hot. As volcanoes showed, such temperatures were achieved at the
centre of the earth, so that's where hell was probably to
be found, and if you peered past the sulphurous vents
and steaming pools of any volcano at all, that's where
you'll find an entrance. There were some dissenters. As
mentioned before, William Whiston argued in 1696 that
hell must be located in a comet, "ascending from the Hot
Regions near the Sun, and going into the Cold Regions
beyond Saturn, with its long smoking Tail arising up
from it," and Tobias Swinden's 1727 tract *An Enquiry into
the Nature and Place of Hell* put hell in the sun itself, the
hottest place imaginable. Milton, in *Paradise Lost*, didn't
say where hell was, but he agreed that its meteorology
was pretty bad, with boiling oceans breaking on black
shores and glossie scurff lying on the griesly hills, and
everywhere caves, beaches, and bogs of fire. Dante has
a river of boiling blood for people guilty of bloodshed,

tombs of fire for heretics, and a desert where it rains flakes of fire on blasphemers, usurers, and homosexuals.

Still, there are pockets of variant weather. Many of Dante's circles aren't fiery. In the second circle, the lustful are blown about by strong winds, while the gluttons in the third are subjected to sleet and sludge. Occasionally, sinners just trudge around in apparently benign weather— their heads may be on backwards, sure, or they are pushing stuff in circles, but the weather doesn't seem to be a crucial factor. Even for Milton, beyond the fire plains of hell there are regions of ice, hail, snow, and wind, where the damned are taken on forced excursions. The change in temperature offers no respite, as "cold performs th' effect of fire," and in fact the variation only makes things worse (a notion he cribbed from Innocent iii).

Dante's ninth circle was the innermost pit, reserved in its four sub-circles for the worst sinners of all; this is where Lucifer is encased in his ice tomb, eternally gnawing away at the other traitors. So hell really does freeze over in places, and for the devil, it really is a cold day in hell.

EYEWITNESS
ACCOUNTS

CHAPTER 10

THE WATCHERS AND
THE ORIGIN OF HELL

The Nephilim. The Titans. The Watchers.
Whatever they were called, there was hell to pay

WE KNOW THAT JEHOVAH OF THE OLD TESTAMENT
waxed wroth on many an occasion—indeed, it sometimes
seems that wrath was his dominant operating mode. (As
the grim eighteenth-century preacher Jonathan Edwards
described it in a sermon, "the Wrath of God is like great
Waters that are dammed for the present; they increase
more and more, & rise higher and higher, till an Outlet
is given, and the longer the Stream is stop'd, the more
rapid and mighty is its Course, when once it is let loose.")
Sometimes the cause of this volcanic anger remains obscure,
but in some cases it is obvious—and, from the evidence
presented, somewhat justified. Such was Jehovah's reac-
tion to the activities of the Nephilim, sometimes known
in the Bible as the Watchers, or Children of the Watchers,

and occasionally described as giants, and less often as the Titans, a title borrowed from the Greeks. Their goings-on brought on a Jehovah tantrum that was thought to be one reason why he created hell in the first place. And it was definitely the prime reason that he sent the Flood to destroy his creation. That's what Enoch tells us, anyway.

These giants were popular villains, employed by many ancient fabulists. Ovid mentions them in his opening books of the *Metamorphoses*. Hesiod wrote about them with evident relish. Porphyry of Tyre, the neo-Platonic philosopher, declared that yes of course, everyone believed that "these [demons] were hostile to god and man." Plutarch wheeled them into play too, "on the authority," as he says, "of Empedocles," the Sicilian philosopher and poet. And the orator Pherecydes of Syros referred to the giants' chief as Ophioneus, "that old serpent, which is called the devil."

In any case, the events that led to the mass drowning of early humankind began, indeed, with the Watchers, variously defined as "those who are awake" or "those who do not sleep." In the most common version, there were several hundred of them, a special order of angels sent by God to supervise the development of early human-kind—mistrusted in heaven after Adam and Eve abused God's hospitality in Eden. In other versions of the story, these Watchers were not just sent by God as stewards but were fallen angels that had displeased God. (Lucifer, known in this context as Azazel, is sometimes associated with their fall, although the chronology is confusing—hadn't he fallen out with God before Adam and Eve?) In yet another view, these Sons of God (another of their names) were not angels at all, but pious men who lived on a mountaintop; this is a minority position, mostly held by preachers who don't like the idea of angels doing the nasty with human women. New-agey people have suggested that these Watchers were extraterrestrials, a notion derided by the religious as impious and implausible—and they should know.

Then they set about defiling the comely daughters

INSTEAD OF THE hands-off supervisory approach God had apparently wanted, these Watchers interfered ceaselessly. The third-century-BCE *Book of Enoch*, our prime source for all this (its first thirty-six chapters are called, in fact, *The Book of the Watchers*), says that Lucifer and his confreres taught men to forge swords and make shields and breastplates, and taught them metalworking and mining. To the women (sexism began early) they taught the art of making bracelets, ornaments, rings, and necklaces from precious metals and stones, and how to beautify their eyelids with kohl and other tricks of seduction, including letting their hair flow free (covering hair is an injunction that lives on, lamentably, to our day).

But there was worse, as *Enoch* tells us:

> And it came to pass when the children of men had multiplied that in those days were born unto them beautiful and comely daughters.
>
> And the angels, the children of the heaven, saw and lusted after them, and

said to one another: "Come, let us choose us wives from among the children of men and beget us children."

And Semjâzâ, who was their leader, said unto them: "I fear ye will not indeed agree to do this deed, and I alone shall have to pay the penalty of a great sin."

And they all answered him and said: "Let us all swear an oath, and all bind ourselves by mutual imprecations not to abandon this plan but to do this thing." Then sware they all together and bound themselves by mutual imprecations upon it.

And they were in all two hundred; who descended in the days of Jared on the summit of Mount Hermon, and they called it Mount Hermon, because they had sworn and bound themselves by mutual imprecations upon it.[1]

Well, they sware together, and then they did as promised—they "took unto themselves wives, and each chose for himself one, and they began to go into them and defile themselves with them" (or as Mark Twain put it, "the sweeter sex, the dearer sex, the lovelier sex was manifestly at its very best, then, for it was even able to attract gods. Real gods. They came down out of heaven and had wonderful times with those hot young blossoms"[2]). Having "gone into them," the Nephilim taught them charms and enchantments, and the cutting of roots, and made them acquainted with plants, and they became pregnant, and bore great giants, whose height was three thousand ells. Great giants indeed: an ell is about a third of a metre, so these giants were not far short of a kilometre tall. (By way of comparison, the Goliath of the Bible, brought down by David's slingshot, was estimated at between 1.9 and 2.7 metres, depending on the text. That's between 6 feet 6 inches and 9 feet, if you prefer the imperial system.)

The Book of Genesis is, at first, more circumspect than this, avoiding the pejorative language ("defile"): "And it came to pass, when men began to multiply on the face of the earth, and daughters were born unto them, that the Sons of God saw the daughters of men that they were fair; and they took them wives of all which they chose. And the Lord said, my spirit shall not always strive with man, for that he also is flesh: yet his days shall be an hundred and twenty years. There were giants in the earth in those days; and also after that, when the Sons of God came in unto the daughters of men, and they bare children to them, the same became mighty men which were of old, men of renown."

God's views, expressed in this paragraph, remain a puzzle. But whatever he meant, these giants, these "men of renown," became known as the Nephilim, or fallen ones.

At first, they were fed on manna, but they were giants, after all, and soon took to hunting the beasts of the field and the fowl of the air, and after that, according to some traditions, they added humans to their diet too. As Enoch lamented, they "consumed all the acquisitions of men; and when men could no longer sustain them, the giants turned against them and devoured mankind; and they began to sin against birds, and beasts, and reptiles, and fish, and to devour one another's flesh, and drink the blood. . . . The whole earth has thereby been filled with blood and unrighteousness."

Well, this would not do. To hell with them, literally. So Jehovah issued his marching orders, instructing the angel Raphael to make a hole in the ground for Azazel (Lucifer) and his crew, as reported in an earlier chapter, and then to blame Azazel for the whole thing: "the whole earth has been corrupted through the works that were taught by Azazel: to him ascribe all sin."

Then, as Enoch recorded,

> The Great Holy One will come forth
>   from his dwelling,
> And the eternal God will tread from
>   thence upon Mount Sinai.
> He will appear with his army,
> He will appear with his mighty
>   host from the heaven of
> heavens.
> All the Watchers will fear and quake
> And those who are hiding in all
>   the ends of the earth will
> sing.
> All the ends of the earth will be shaken,
> And trembling and great
>   fear will seize them
> Unto the ends of the earth.

And so Raphael went to work, but seems to have been a bit of an overachiever, even by these standards, and did better than a mere hole in the ground. Enoch, in a later trip to the netherworld, saw what he had wrought: a deep valley with burning fire, and mighty smiths preparing chains. He asked what they were for, and Raphael answered him: they are "for the hosts of Azazel, so that they may take them and cast them into the abyss of complete condemnation, and they shall cover their jaws with rough stones as the Lord of Spirits commanded. And Michael, and Gabriel, and Phanuel shall take hold of them on that great day, and cast them on that day into the burning furnace, that the Lord of Spirits may take vengeance on them for their unrighteousness in becoming subject to Satan and leading astray those who dwell on the earth."

But perhaps some of them escaped? Some tales from the outer reaches of Irish folklore suggest some connection between the Watchers and the not-quite-divine magicians of Irish legend, the Tuatha De-Danaan, "who descended to earth on the sacred hill of Tara." When Christianity, in turn, descended on Ireland, the Tuatha De-Danaan were banished into the "hollow hills" and became the Sidhe, or Shining Ones, the elves and fairies of Irish folklore. Christian O'Brien, oil geologist turned speculative historian (who's written books on where the Garden of Eden really was—hint, in Lebanon), wrote that there has always been a strong belief among the peasantry in Ireland that the Good People or fairies were originally the fallen angels who sided with Lucifer in the Battle of Heaven.[3] Perhaps, then, it was the fate of these giants to be reduced to Little People because of their disobedience?

Thus, the Flood

IN ANY CASE, with Azazel and his host now buried in rocks, God could have rested, but he was not quite done. To Gabriel he said: "Proceed against the bastards and the reprobates, and against the children of fornication: and destroy the children of fornication and the children of the Watchers from amongst men and cause them to go forth: send them one against the other that they may destroy each other in battle: for length of days shall they not have." And so Gabriel did.

Even that wasn't the end. The Book of Jubilees indicates that God *still* wasn't quite done. Ridding the earth of these Nephilim (evil giants, as *Jubilees* put it) was one thing, but not enough—the Creator was by this time repenting of his creation altogether, and therefore decided on a do-over. Genesis has a go at this too, though by now the Nephilim seem to have dropped out of the narrative:

> And God saw that the wickedness of man was great in the earth, and that every imagination of the thoughts of his heart was only evil continually. And it repented the Lord that he had made man on the earth, and it grieved him at his heart. And the Lord said, I will destroy man whom I have created from the face of the earth; both man, and beast, and the creeping thing, and the fowls of the air; for it repenteth me that I have made them.
>
> But Noah found grace in the eyes of the Lord.

"And God said unto Noah, The end of all flesh is come before me; for the earth is filled with violence through them and behold, I will destroy them with the earth."

Well, he didn't, quite. But he did have a crack at it.

CHAPTER 11

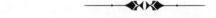

HELL'S EARLIEST TOURISTS

Gilgamesh and Enkidu, his BFF.
Enkidu goes to hell. Dies

GILGAMESH WAS KING OF URUK, A POWERFUL SUMErian trading city state (in what is now Iran), who ruled around 2700 BCE. There are hints in the saga that he was a demigod as well as a king, but this was probably royalist propaganda, developed as an excuse for Gilgamesh's having behaved badly, which he seems to have done pretty much as a matter of routine. As the story has it, he developed a reputation as an arrogant bully (among other things, asserting his "right of kings" to bed brides before their husbands did), and the local citizenry, fed up, finally appealed to the gods to do something about it. Anu, the father of the gods, therefore had Aruru, his consort, create "a wild man," Enkidu, to deal with the errant king.

Aruru did her job well: a right piece of work this Enkidu was, a mighty savage who ran with the gazelles and whose whole body was shaggy with hair, "billowing in profusion."

This hairy fellow one day confronted a famous trapper at a watering hole, and frightened him half to death. When he (the trapper) fled home and told his father what he had seen, the old man suggested he go to Uruk to consult with Gilgamesh himself to see what could be done. This he did, to good effect. Gilgamesh, never at a loss, told the trapper to return and take with him Shamhat, a renowned harlot, who would surely overcome the wild creature. Tell her, Gilgamesh urged, to take off her robe and expose her sex; Enkidu will surely fall upon her, his gazelles will thereafter find him alien, and he will thus be tamed. All of which seemed to the trapper sensible advice; he returned to his trapping grounds, Shamhat in tow.

For three days they waited at Enkidu's watering hole, and then, sure enough, he showed up with his companion gazelles.

And Shamhat did what was asked of her, and more: "She unclutched her bosom, exposed her sex, and Enkidu took in her voluptuousness. / She was not restrained, but took his energy. / She spread out her robe and he lay upon her, / and she performed the primitive task of womankind. / His lust groaned over her; / for six days and seven nights Enkidu stayed aroused, / and had intercourse with the harlot / until he was sated with her charms."

Sure enough, as Gilgamesh had suggested it would, that did the trick: thereafter Enkidu's animal companions fled at his sight, and he was tamed. The trapper and Shamhat gave him food and drink, and he got thoroughly soused ("his spirit was loosened, he became hilarious"), after which he was carefully shaved and taken to Uruk. Almost at once, he intercepted Gilgamesh entering the wedding chamber of a newly married couple and grabbed him. That was a fight! "They grappled with each other like bulls at the entry to the marital chamber, they broke the doorposts and the walls shook, in the street they attacked each other, the public square of the land. . . . Gilgamesh bent his knee with his foot planted on the ground and with a turn Enkidu was thrown. Then immediately his fury died. When Enkidu was thrown he said to Gilgamesh, 'There is not another like you in the world . . . who is as strong as a wild ox in the byre, she was the mother who bore you, and now you are raised above all men, and Enlil has given you the kingship, for your strength surpasses the strength of men.' So they kissed each other and became friends."

After some years Gilgamesh, ever restless, decided on a quest and a trial. He would go with Enkidu to destroy the monster Humbaba, "he of the visage that looks like coiled intestines . . . whose roar is a Flood, his mouth is Fire, his breath Death! He can hear any movement in his sacred forest 100 leagues away!" Long story short, through trickery and treachery they succeeded in their task, dragged the monster's entrails out by pulling on his tongue, then severed his head and cut down some of the sacred cedars to take home. When they arrived in Uruk, Gilgamesh washed his hair, cleaned his weapons,

> flung back his hair from his shoulders; he
> threw off his stained clothes and changed
> them for new. He put on his royal robes and

made them fast. When Gilgamesh had put
on the crown, glorious Ishtar [the Goddess
Ishtar, for whom see next section] lifted her
eyes, seeing the beauty of Gilgamesh. She
said, "Come to me Gilgamesh, and be my
bridegroom; grant me seed of your body,
let me be your bride and you shall be my
husband."

Alas, the arrogant Gilgamesh spurned her, and she
went in a rage to Anu, her father and father of the gods,
demanding that he give her the Bull of Heaven [a.k.a.
the constellation Taurus] to take down to Uruk to kill
the wretch. Otherwise, she threatened, she would break
down the doors of the netherworld and unleash the dead
upon earth.

When Anu heard her words, he placed
the nose rope of the Bull of Heaven in
her hand.
Ishtar led the Bull of Heaven down
to the earth.
When it reached Uruk it climbed down
to the Euphrates. . . .
At the snort of the Bull of Heaven a
huge pit opened up, and a hundred young
men of Uruk fell in.
At his second snort a huge pit opened
up, and two hundred young men of Uruk
fell in.

At his third snort a huge pit opened up,
and Enkidu fell in up to his waist.
    Then Enkidu jumped out and seized
the Bull of Heaven by its horns.

Together Enkidu and Gilgamesh destroyed the beast,
and further insulted Ishtar by wrenching off the bull's
hindquarters and flinging the offal in her face.

That was enough for the gods. Either Gilgamesh or
Enkidu had to die, and Gilgamesh, a demigod after all,
was spared. This is where hell enters the tale. Said Enkidu
to Gilgamesh, as he lay on his bed, already critically ill:

> Listen, my friend, this is the dream I
> dreamed last night. The heavens roared,
> and earth [a.k.a. hell] rumbled back an
> answer; between them stood I before an
> awful being, the somber man-bird; he had
> directed on me his purpose. His was a vam-
> pire face, his foot was a lion's foot, his hand
> was an eagle's talon. He fell on me and his
> claws were in my hair, he held me fast and
> I smothered; then he transformed me so
> that my arms became wings covered with
> feathers. He turned his stare towards me,
> and he led me away to the palace of Irkalla
> [Ereshkigal], the Queen of Darkness, to
> the house from which none who enters
> ever returns, down the road from which
> there is no coming back.

There is the house whose people sit in darkness; dust is their food and clay their meat. They are clothed with wings for covering, they see no light, they sit in darkness. I entered the house of dust and I saw the kings of the earth, their crowns put away for ever; rulers and princes, all those who once wore kingly crowns and ruled the world in the days of old. They who had stood in the place of the gods like Ann and Enlil stood now like servants to fetch baked meats in the house of dust, to carry cooked meat and cold water from the water-skin. In the house of dust which I entered were high priests and acolytes, priests of the incantation and of ecstasy; there were servers of the temple, and there was Etana, that king of Dish whom the eagle carried to heaven in the days of old. I saw also Samuqan, god of cattle, and there was Ereshkigal the Queen of the Underworld; and Befit-Sheri squatted in front of her, she who is recorder of the gods and keeps the book of death. She held a tablet from which she read. She raised her head, she saw me and spoke: "Who has brought this one here?" Then I awoke like a man drained of blood who wanders alone in a waste of rashes; like one whom the bailiff has seized and his heart pounds with terror.

His last words were a plea to his friend: "I who went through every difficulty with you, / remember me and forget not all that I went through with you."

Then he died, and went to hell for real.

Gilgamesh mourned, "six days and seven nights I mourned over him / and would not allow him to be buried / until a maggot fell out of his nose. / I was terrified by his appearance, / I began to fear death, and so [began to] roam the wilderness."

Only then do we get to the real point of the saga: a meditation on the futile wish for immortality. After many trials in the wilderness, Gilgamesh made his way to Utanapishtim, from whom he sought the secret to everlasting life, so he would never have to spend eternity in the grey dust of the netherworld. There he got short shrift, and was lectured instead of the inevitability of death and of the proper duties of a king. "No one can see death, / no one can see the face of death, / no one can hear the voice of death, / yet there is savage death that snaps off mankind. . . . How alike are the sleeping and the dead! / The image of Death cannot be depicted . . . the Great Gods . . . established Death and Life, / but they did not make known the days of death."

After which, he returns home to rebuild Uruk and—though this is never spelled out—to reign again, sadder but a little wiser, before eventually succumbing to death itself, and helping to rule the shades in hell.

THIS PICARESQUE TALE dates from the third millennium BCE; it is recognized as one of the great literary epics of human history, and is possibly the earliest surviving work of literature. How much of it does survive is remarkable; and how lucky we are that it was uncovered in modern times but before the barbarians of ISIS began demolishing the remains of the great civilization in which it was created.

The very earliest version, titled *Surpassing All Other Kings*, is known as the Old Babylonian version, and dates to the eighteenth century BCE. Only fragments of this version survive. The "standard" version dates to between the thirteenth and the tenth centuries BCE, and is titled *He Who Saw The Deep*. About a third of this version is still missing. The eleven clay tablets on which the story was scribed have survived only because multiple fragments of multiple copies existed—clay survives in dry climates better than wax, and the story was widely copied in the royal libraries of the time, including that of King Ashurbanapal (668–626 BC) in his palace at Nineveh, and it seems to have been a favourite entertainment of ships' captains on long voyages, and of caravan masters on extended long-distance trade trips. Curiously, the story survives at least partly because schoolmasters of the time filed the copying exercises of their pupils ("apprentice scribes"), complete with scratchings-out, errors, and false starts. The standard version is really a compilation by generations of clever scholars piecing together fragments of Sumerian and later Akkadian versions.[1]

Dozens of translations are extant—some of them more picaresque than others (translator fastidiousness has sometimes intervened; in some versions Shamhat's "sex" is primly described as her "parts," while Enkidu's "lust groaning over her" becomes the more genteel "love").

There was a coda to the story, a "twelfth tablet"—perhaps a contemporary addendum, perhaps a later editor, feeling the story incomplete and insufficiently hellish, added his own interpolation. In it, Enkidu visited the netherworld (earth) in person on Gilgamesh's behalf (to recover a drum and drumstick that had dropped into it) and was captured by the Queen of the Dead, Ereshkigal.

> And so the Cry of the Dead seized him
>   and held him
> Naked the goddess mother lies in hell;
> Naked Ninazu's mother lies exposed,
> The holy garment fallen
>   from her shoulder,
> Bare are the breasts of the
>   mother, Ereshkigal.
> The Cry of the Dead seized him
>   and held him fast.[2]

His spirit had to be pried out of hell by the intervention of Ea (Anu), and he gives Gilgamesh a quick summary:

> Your wife whom you touched and your heart was glad vermin eat like an old garment. Your son whom you touched and your heart was glad sits in a crevice full of dust. "Woe!" she said and groveled in the dust. "Woe!" he said and groveled in the dust.
>
> I saw him, whom you saw at the poles [of the tent?], now he cries for his mother

and tears out the pegs. I saw him who you saw die a sudden death. He lies in bed and drinks pure water. I saw him whom you killed in battle. His father and mother honored him and his wife weeps over him. I saw him whose corpse you abandoned in the open country. His ghost does not sleep in the earth. I saw him whom you saw, whose ghost has nobody to supply it. He feeds on dregs from dishes and bits of bread that lie abandoned in the streets.[3]

Ishtar visits her sister in hell. It does not go well

WE MET ISHTAR before, most recently in the Gilgamesh chronicle described above. She was the Mesopotamian Goddess of Fertility, Love, War, Sex, and Power, and the patron saint of agriculture, brothels, and whores, and from her association with the planet Venus she was often called the Brilliant Goddess. From the record, she was easily angered, "a raging goddess who smites those who disobey her commands with wasting disease."[4] In any case, Gilgamesh spurned her advances, setting off the chain of events that led to the death of his friend Enkidu. Even so, revenge turned out to be a bitter draught for Ishtar. After all, for a goddess of love she hadn't much luck with love herself: her husband, Tammuz, the great passion of her youth, had died very young (killed by a pig, if you must know) and had been taken down to the dark and dusty abode of Ishtar's sister, Ereshkigal, Queen of the Dead.

Tammuz is sometimes known as a solar god, the God of Spring, but also of Death and Destruction.

After the Gilgamesh debacle, Ishtar decided to descend to the underworld herself, to demand the water of life to bring Tammuz back to the living. She dressed in her finest garments and jewels, placed a crown on her head, and off she went.

She set the wrong tone from the start, banging on the first of the seven gates, demanding entry:

> "Gatekeeper, ho! open thy gate!
>   Open thy gate that I may enter!
>   If thou openest not the gate
>   to let me enter,
>   I will break the door, I will
>   wrench the lock,
>   I will smash the door-posts, I
>   will force the doors.
>   I will bring up the dead to eat the living.
>   And the dead will outnumber
>   the living."
> The gatekeeper opened his
>   mouth and spoke,
>   Spoke to the lady Ishtar:
> "Desist, O lady, do not destroy it.
>   I will go and announce thy name
>   to my queen Ereshkigal."

"Ho!" said Ereshkigal (who in this version of the saga has the head of a lioness and the body of a woman, and carries a deadly serpent as her pet), "What has moved her heart [to do this], what has moved her liver? Ho there! Does this one wish to live with me? Go let her in, and deal with her according to the ancient decree."

So the gatekeeper went up through the seven gates to fetch Ishtar. At the first gate he removed her crown, at the second her earrings, at the third her necklace, at the fourth "the ornaments of her breast," at the fifth "the girdle of her body studded with birthstones," at the sixth "the spangles off her hands and feet," and at the seventh her last garment, her loincloth, and naked she entered her sister's realm.

Really annoyed by now, Ishtar flew at her sister in a rage. But her sister wasn't having any.

> To Namtar, her messenger, she
> addressed herself:
> "Go Namtar, imprison her in my palace.
> Send against her sixty diseases,
> to punish Ishtar.
> Eye-disease against her eyes,
> Disease of the side against her side,
> Foot-disease against her foot,
> Heart-disease against her heart,
> Head-disease against her head,
> Against her whole being,
> against her entire body."

Namtar, the demon of the plague, a human body with a viper's head, naked under a cloak of bones, did as he was told: he spread plague over her whole body. "Feathers grew on her, and the light disappeared from her eyes.

She tasted dust and ate mud. All memory of her past existence, of her great love Tammuz, disappeared with the light." Then, according to some versions, Ereshkigal hung her sister on a hook as a piece of rotting meat, and left her in the dark. "You may be the Lady of the Gods, but you are in my place now, and nobody returns from this place of darkness, magistrate or warrior, king or shepherd, milkmaid or goddess, whoever enters here has no more need of light. The gates are already bolted behind you, lady!"

Back on earth, things were not going well either. In the absence of the Goddess of Fertility, the rains stopped, the crops failed, "the bull did not mount the cow, the ass approached not the she-ass, to the maid in the street no man drew near, the man slept in his apartment, the maid slept by herself, the women in the brothels had no customers, there was no music in the temples" . . . and so on. Affairs of state were going downhill fast. The gods in conclave decided something had to be done, so Ea the Earth God created a eunuch, Asu-shu-namir, who would be impervious to Ereshkigal's insults and curses, and dispatched him, armed with the power of the gods, to bring Ishtar back. Descending, the eunuch demanded the water of life from the Queen of the Dead and for her to give it to Ishtar. She did not, it seems, take this well. Indeed, she "cursed Asu-shu-namir with a great curse," declaring that the sweepings of the gutter would be his only food and the sewers of the city his drink, and that drunkards and sots would strike him with impunity.[5]

To no avail. She had no power to defy the collective gods, and sent Namtar to fetch Ishtar off her hook, sprinkle her with the water of life, and get her out of there. And so Ishtar left, regaining her clothing and her personal ornaments as she went.

But wait—it was not so simple. Even the gods couldn't altogether defy death. No one ascends from the underworld unmarked. If Inanna (Ishtar) really wishes to return from *down there*, she must provide someone in her place. As she walked up the staircase from hell, the Galla, the demons of the underworld, clung to her side.

> "Walk on, Inanna, we will take Ninshubur in your place."
> Inanna cried: "No! Ninshubur is my constant support . . . .
> "Walk on to your city, Inanna, We will take Shara in your place."
> Inanna cried: "No! Not Shara! He is my son who sings hymns to me."
> "Walk on to your city, Inanna, We will take Lulal in your place."
> "Not Lulal! He is my son. He is a leader among men. . . . "
> "Walk on to your city, Inanna. We will go with you to the big apple tree in Uruk." In Uruk, by the big apple tree, Dumuzi [a.k.a. Tammuz, now once again safely above ground], the husband of Inanna, was dressed in his shining garments. He sat on his magnificent throne; he did not move.
> Inanna fastened on Dumuzi the eye of death. She spoke against him the word

of wrath. She uttered against him the cry
of guilt: "Take him! Take Dumuzi away!"

The Galla, who know no food, who
know no drink, who eat no offerings, who
drink no libations, who accept no gifts,
seized Dumuzi.

They made him stand up; they made
him sit down. They beat the husband of
Inanna. They gashed him with axes.[6]

And so, by permission of the gods, Ishtar returned
to the world, by betraying the husband she had gone to
hell to rescue.

The Crown Prince of Ninevah pesters
Ereshkigal and Nergal, to his peril

KUMAYA (OR KUMMAY, the transliterations vary) was
an heir to the throne of Ninevah in the seventh century
BCE. He was unable to rest, fretting constantly about the
time of his death and his fate thereafter, and so, though
he was surrounded by luxury, he never seemed to get
anything done. The chronicler is not impressed: he was
a wastrel and a layabout, obsessed with glitter and glitz,
all the tawdry bling of the earth: "What he [should have]
held in awe, he held in contempt, what he [should have]
feared, and thought evil, he did not; he reckoned his
accounts day and night, he would shower his treasuries
with jewels fit for a king, as if with a bucket from a well."

Wastrel or not, he really wanted to know the hour of his death, so decided to visit the netherworld. He set up an incense burner with juniper, and prayed for revelation.

Sure enough, the Queen of the Dead appeared to him, and said she heard his prayer, but she refused to tell him the hour of his death. Kumaya tried again, and this time he got to visit hell itself, and was confronted with fifteen terrifying demons, each more ghastly than the last. At least he had the presence of mind to take good notes: "I saw Namtar, courier of the netherworld, who issues decrees. A man stood before him, he was holding his hair in his left hand, he was holding a sword in his right hand. Namtartu, his female counterpart, had the head of a protective spirit, her hands and feet were human. Death had the head of a dragon, his hands were human, Evil Spirit had a human head and hands, it was wearing a crown, its feet were those of an eagle, with its left foot it trod upon a crocodile." And so on, quick pen sketches of them all. "Fifteen gods were in attendance. When I saw them I prayed to them." As well he might.

But then he was seized by Nergal himself, consort to Ereshkigal. His first instinct, sensibly, was to cringe.

> When I raised my eyes, there was valiant Nergal sitting on his royal throne wearing the royal crown, he held two terrible maces with both hands, each with two heads . . . lightning was flashing, the great netherworld gods were kneeling. . . . The netherworld was full of terror. . . . He seized me by the forelock and drew me towards

him. My legs shook, his wrathful splendor
overwhelmed me, I kissed the feet of his
great divinity, I knelt. When I stood up,
he was looking at me, shaking his head.
He gave me a fierce cry and shrieked at me
wrathfully, like a raging storm. He drew
up his scepter, his divine symbol, ghastly
as a serpent, to kill me!

Nergal's counsellor, Ishum, intervened. "Do not
kill this young man, O mighty king of the vast netherworld! Let the subjects of the land all and always hear
your praises!" So Nergal relented, and sent the prince up
above, albeit with dire warnings: "I will not sentence you
to death. [But] by the command of Shamash there shall
gust upon you want, violence, and revolts, all at once. You
shall have no sleep because of their fierce clamor."

And so it ends. The prince, knowing his fate would be
turmoil and chaos, sings the praises of Ereshkigal and
Nergal anyway, and (presumably) goes on with his life,
for there is no more.[7]

Baal takes on Death and wins, sort of . . . or at least his sister does

THE CLUTCH OF Canaanite gods that includes Baal seem
as quarrelsome and cantankerous as the Greek pantheon,
constantly warring with each other and uttering threats.
Much of the Baal saga has to do with this godly politics
and only a small portion to do with hell. Nevertheless,
Baal does visit the underworld to deal with death, and

so does his unruly sister, who seems a little like Ishtar, but much more violent.

There are three parts to this tale, each scribed on double-sided clay tablets, six columns per side, "copied by Ilimilku, the master," a functionary in the court of Niqmad (or Niqmat, as Genesis would have it, and some-times Nqmd) king of Ugarit from 1380 to 1346 BCE; how much earlier the tales were first written down is unknown. In any case, Ugarit's ruins, the so-called Mound of Ras Shamra, can still be seen on Syria's northern Mediterranean coast—or could, before the civil war wrecked the region.

The whole thing started when the chief god, El, called for a cessation of the constant familial fighting, and announced plans to crown Yamm-Nahar, the God of the Chaotic Seas, as the God of Earth as well. Soon enough, Yamm ruled like a tyrant and Baal, the God of Storms, resolved to put an end to him with the help of a divine craftsman who made two magical war clubs for him to use.

After that, it was easy: "And the club swoops in the hands of Baal, like an eagle in his fingers; it strikes the head of Prince Yamm, between the eyes of Judge Nahar; Yamm collapses, he falls to the earth; his joints tremble, his body is spent; Baal draws and drinks Yamm, he finishes off Judge Nahar. . . . Victorious Baal! Yamm is dead! Baal shall reign!"

El, confronted with a *fait accompli*, acquiesced and Baal became the God of Earth. However, it turned out that Yamm was not really dead, he was just sent back sulking to the sea. But his part in the saga was now over.

The second sequence of the three seems largely a digres-sion, and involves a rancorous discussion about whether

Baal would be allowed to build a palace as big as those his brothers already owned, with a bizarre subplot about whether Baal would have to include windows, which he feared would be used by his enemies (Yamm?) to enter his home and wound him. In the end, he agreed to open windows in the clouds, and the palace was hastily built with silver and gold bricks, in seven days (on the seventh day Baal rested, his work done), and he was thereafter free to "peal his thunder in the clouds, flash his lightnings to the earth," doing generally what storm gods do.

At the end of part 2, Baal issued an invitation to all the other gods to a feast to celebrate his new palace. He sent messengers to the underworld to invite Mot (Death) to come up for the occasion.

As part 3 opens, it becomes clear that the invitation had been spurned. Word came from Mot in hell as follows:

> Have you then forgotten, Baal, that I
>   can surely transfix you
> for all that you smote Leviathan
>   the slippery serpent [Yamm]
> (and) made an end of the
>   wriggling serpent,
> the tyrant with seven heads?
> The heavens will burn up
>   (and) droop (helpless),
> for I myself will crush you in pieces,
> I will eat (you) . . . (and) forearms.
> Indeed you must come down into
>   the throat of divine Mot,

> into the miry depths of the
> hero beloved of El.[8]

All in all, a sorry litany of threats.

Well, that would not do. A messenger (from whom is not clear) advises Baal to take his storm clouds and his attendants down to hell to deal with his arrogant brother. "As for you," the messenger declares, "take your clouds, your winds, your thunderbolts, your rains, take with you your seven pages and your eight boars, take with you Pidray daughter of mist, take with you Tallay daughter of showers, then of a truth do you set your face towards the rocks at the entrance. . . . Lift up a rock on your two hands, a wooded height on to your two palms, and go down into . . . the earth, and be counted among those who go down into the earth [hell], and know inanition like mortal men."

Okay, but then it gets a little weird.

Baal set off for battle in hell, but got sidetracked along the way, smitten by a heifer in a field.

> He loved a heifer in the pasture,
> a cow in the fields by the shore
> of the realm of death;
> he did lie with her seven
> and seventy times,
> she allowed him to mount
> eight and eighty times;
> and she conceived and gave
> birth to a boy.

    Mightiest Baal did clothe
       him with his robe,
    [given] him as a gift for the beloved one
    to his breast . . .

Then there is an abrupt cut, and the next thing we
know the gods are mourning the death of the mighty
Baal. It is possible, but not certain, that Baal clothed his
heifer-born son to look like him and sent him to hell to
deal with Mot, and that it was the son who died in his
stead. In any case, great mourning and lamentation followed, because the gods, at least, believe Baal dead. And
none more than his sister, Anath, a personage every bit as
energetic as her brother and even more aggressive. (She is
also, like Ishtar, the Goddess of War and Sex, and, also
like Ishtar, is described as beautiful and seductive.) She
was not, however, a nice person. Elsewhere in the sagas
she boasted of multiple killings "in bloody slaughter" of
sundry enemies, and she is the villain in another tale,
The Story of Aquat, in which she kills Aquat, a young boy,
in order to steal his magical bow. It was she who came
across Baal's dead body, and mourned him, in her fashion: "For clothing she covered herself with sackcloth of
Baal; she scraped her skin with a stone with a flint for a
razor; she cut her cheek she cut her chin, she harrowed
her collar-bone; she ploughed her chest like a garden
she harrowed her waist like a valley, saying Baal is dead!"
    Then she took him home to Mount Zephon, and
"slew seventy wild oxen for mightiest Baal, she slew seventy sheep for mightiest Baal, she slew seventy harts
for mightiest Baal, she slew seventy mountain-goats for

mightiest Baal, she slew seventy asses for mightiest Baal," then she put him in a hole reserved for the earth gods, and then she had more slaying to do: she descended into hell to deal with Death.

And deal with him she did. Mot was a match for Baal, but not for his sister:

> She seized divine Mot,
> with a sword she split him,
> with a sieve she winnowed him,
> with fire she burnt him,
> with mill-stones she ground him
> in a field she scattered him;
> his flesh indeed the birds ate,
> his limbs indeed the
>   sparrows consumed.
> Flesh cried out to flesh
> for Mot has perished!

But it was all a mistake. Baal was not dead after all. Baal was back, better than ever and understandably angry, and Mot was not dead after all—the saga seems to have missed out on decent editing. Mot (now called Mavet) threatens Baal; Baal threatens Mot; "they shake each other like Gemar-beasts, / Mavet is strong, Baal is strong, they gore each other like buffaloes, / Mavet is strong, Baal is strong, they bite like serpents, Mavet is strong, Baal is strong, they kick like racing beasts, / Mavet is down, Baal is down." Finally, El takes charge, puts a stop to the nonsense, sends Mot back to Sheol, and Baal resumes rule of earth.

And so it ends. Or it would have, except for Baal's sister Anath, who is still *really* annoyed:

"And lo, Anath . . . smites the people of the seashore, / destroys mankind of the sunrise, / under her are heads like vultures, / she piles up heads on her back, / she ties up hands in her bundle, knee-deep she plunges in the blood of soldiery, / up to the neck in the gore of troops, with a stick she drives out foes . . . "

She "washes her hands in the blood of soldiers." That will teach them to mess with brother![9]

CHAPTER 12

---◆✕◆✕◆---

SOME BUDDHISTS
GO TO HELL FOR THE
DAMNEDEST REASONS

BUDDHISTS WERE OFTEN INDEFATIGABLE TRAVEL-
lers, and many of them visited the infernal regions, sometimes out of sheer curiosity, sometimes out of piety, and
sometimes apparently just for the hell of it. Here's a
small sampling.

Governor Kwoh visits hell and is politely given some tea

KWOH, THE GOVERNOR of Sichuan province, once heard
wailings and shriekings coming from the entrance to hell.
This could hardly have surprised him: it was late in the
reign of the Ming emperor Wang-Lih (1573–1620 CE), and
the entrepreneurs of Fengdu had long been notorious
for supplying the netherworld with their implements
of torture—a most profitable trade—and they knew
perfectly well how hell was to be reached. Still, instead

of prudently retreating and visiting a temple, Kwoh had the door forced open, provided himself with a torch, and strode into Fengdu mountain. After some distance, he saw a shaft going deep into the earth. Still undaunted, he put together an iron box, and had his fellows lower him away on ropes; he later calculated that he hit bottom about 200 feet down.

With his torch blazing, he set out to explore. Hell's borderlands, a landscape covered with lush vegetation, rather resembled the luxurious farmlands in the province above. Across a plain, he saw a massive portal, with a nail-studded gate. He banged on the gate and, somewhat to his surprise, was greeted by the God of War and Justice, Yama, hell's chief administrator, who offered to show him around. First they toured Yama's palace, then proceeded to the Second Court of Hell, and then to all the others, all the way to the Tenth.

They paused at the Fifth Court, where Yama (sometimes described as the president of that court, and not the ruler of the whole place) invited him to sit down for a nice cup of tea, while the structure of hell's government was explained to him. "We, the judges of hell, have to punish all the souls of the dead, without distinction of position or rank while they lived in the world above," Yama told his visitor. "These souls, after death, wander throughout the world, but are seized by our lictors, and brought to this dismal region."

Instead of the eight hot hells and eight cold ones fondly imagined by earthly storytellers, he said, hell is divided into just ten courts, in mimicry of the aboveground empire's administrative structure. Of these ten, only eight are real hells. The First Court is the reception desk, where the president keeps a register of the living and the dead, and measures their lives, and the Tenth Court is the checkout counter, leaving the remaining eight to deal with sinners. Truly virtuous people, if they are so assessed at reception, can go straight to the Tenth Court, where they are given permission to leave right away, to be reborn in a lower or higher state of existence among the six classes of created being (gods, men, demons, animals, hungry ghosts, and beings undergoing torment). The not-so-virtuous are not so lucky. They are taken first to the Mirror Tower, in which they can see a mirror image of their past transgressions. After that, the wardens take them to the Second Court, where their tortures begin.

As in other aspects of Buddhism, torture is not forever—a long time, yes, but not eternal. "Just enough," Yama told Kwoh.

As part of its bureaucracy, each of the ten courts has its own judicial apparatus, complete with police, judges, recording officials, jailers, and housekeepers. Annually, court officials tour the premises to check up on their charges, and to note down the bad versus the good of their actions.

All this was duly explained, then Yama cordially led his visitor back to the main gate, where he re-entered his iron box and was hauled up to the surface. There, he told of all he had seen, and a plaque was erected on the spot.

Fengdu, where the commemorative slab was erected, really does have a two-thousand-year history of hellish associations. More than a millennium ago its artisans were already described as experts in torture, and as indicated above, notoriously became prosperous by selling devices of pain to the demons of hell.

At the turn of the twenty-first century, the town of Fengdu was drowned by the rising waters of the Three Gorges Dam, but the nearby hillside theme park is still there, with its monuments to ghosts and the afterlife (and the putative entryway to hell). It has, alas, become a repository of hellish kitsch, a Disneyland of the Dismal, where tourists can surmount the three challenges intended to winnow people into groups of evildoers and the virtuous: the Nothing-To-Be-Done Bridge (virtuous people will pass over the bridge without obstacle; villainous people will fall into the pools below); Ghost-Torturing Pass (this is where the damned report to Yama—there are eighteen oversized and garishly painted stone demons as an honour guard); and the Tianzi (Son of Heaven) Palace, which is actually the oldest structure in the theme park, having been put together during the Ming Dynasty (here the waiting-to-be-damned must stand on one foot for three minutes without falling over, which visitors often find surprisingly hard to do). As though this weren't enough, the Communist authorities added a further attraction in 1985, the Last-Glance-at-Home Tower (sometimes just called the Tower of Viewing), from which spirits consigned to hell could take one last look at their families.

A good accounting of Fengdu can be found in the ancient text called *Voyage to the Western Sea of the Chief Eunuch San-Pao*, written by Luo Moudeng in 1597, copies of which are sometimes for sale at a kiosk just inside the main gate to the park, in multiple languages. Notable sites (covered by the cost of the entrance ticket) are stations called Blazing Fire Mountain, Lance and Knife Mountain, and the Dam of Despondency, which is supposedly haunted by a motley group of sinners, including spendthrifts and misers and those with irregular teeth. A little further on, the River of Blood is full of creatures that devour those who fall from its bridge, which, like almost all other infernal bridges, is broad and easy for the virtuous but razor-thin and perilous for the wicked. These days most of the wicked seem to make it across okay, and afterwards converge on the concession stands for bowls of noodles and plastic take-home demons.

As the park's website puts it, in typically artless prose, "visitors coming here will marvel at the artisanship of ancient craftsmen, the unique styles of architecture and the culture of the ghost. Whatever your beliefs, you are constantly reminded that 'Good will be rewarded with good, and evil with evil.' A major highlight is the annual temple fair every March 3–5 featuring all kinds of folk activities and performances."[1]

Mu-lien's mother was a bad lot, but he rescued her from hell anyway

IN SOME VERSIONS, hell seems easier to enter and to exit than in others, albeit with a little expert help. Take the story of Mu-lien (Maudgalyayana in its Hindu version) who was able to extract his mother from hell without too much difficulty, though not without the help of the Most Honoured One, the Buddha himself.

The story goes that Mu-lien, a deeply pious man decided to visit an unspecified foreign country in search of new adventures. Before he left, he divided his worldly possessions and left instructions for his mother to make the proper offerings, and to give food and alms to wandering Buddhists and other mendicants. But after Mu-lien left "his mother became stingy and selfish," and instead squirrelled away the money that had been entrusted to her. When her son returned, she lied and said she had "given alms and built up our blessings." Not good: "Because she had deceived both the secular and the holy community, she dropped straight down to the Avichi hell to suffer innumerable torments after she died; the Avichi hell being the last and deepest of the eight hot hells, the place where the condemned go through endless cycles of suffering, death and rebirth without intermission."

A bit harsh, but there it is.

Mu-lien was still clueless at this point. His mother having disappeared, he went into mourning for three years, but finally asked the Buddha, the Most Honoured One, where his mother was housed while enjoying her eternal bliss? The Buddha, ever truthful, was obliged to answer.

Mu-lien, hearing the response, went north several paces, where he saw a triple-layered gate, into which strong men could be seen herding and prodding numberless sinners. Mu-lien went looking for this mother, and, not being able to find her (she was already inside, after all), stood by the side of the road and cried loudly. Afterwards he dried his tears and marched up to the gate, banging loudly. When he had explained his purpose to the gatekeeper, he was granted an audience with the king, who, when he saw

Mu-lien come in, expressed his shock and dismay. He clasped his hands, shrank back, and nearly stood. "Your reverence, you couldn't have any business here!"

Still, in the face of Mu-lien's obvious virtue, the king summoned the keeper of karma, the commissioner of fate, and the custodian of records, who all came to his call.

"This monk's mother is Lady Ch'ing-t'i. How long ago did she die?"

"The lady has been dead three years. The record of her penance is filed with the Recorder of the Heavenly Court as well as the Commandant of the T'ai Mountains."

She was, indeed, in the Avichi hell, in the Seventh Cell, nailed down on a platform with forty-nine spikes. (Paperwork all in order, then—bureaucrats!)

Said the king to Mu-lien: "It appears we *do* have a Lady Ch'ing-t'i here, though I can't completely confirm that report. Bodies of new arrivals are strewn about. Please take my advice and go home. To look for someone here is to look in vain. You better go quickly to see the Tathagata. What use is there beating your breast in despair?"

Having come this far, Mu-lien was not daunted. He threw his magic begging bowl in the air and sat down across from the Buddha. After humble supplications, Buddha granted him the right to visit whatever part of hell he wanted. In a wink, he returned to the Avichi hell. Still in the sky, he saw fifty ox heads, horse-brained *rakshas* and *yakshas*, with teeth like jagged stumps, mouths like bowls of blood, voices like thunderclaps, all of whom yelled at him to go away lest he turn to ashes and dust.

Yet he persisted, ever the dutiful son. He went exploring—and at times was so overcome with fire and smoke that he almost fainted; this part of the hell had iron walls so tall they reached the sky, and the horrors within were beyond description. All the lictors had either ox heads or horse faces, before which "even hearts of stone would quake with fear."

But Mu-lien, still persistent, came at last to that part of the Avichi hell where his mother was nailed to the flogging platform with forty-nine spikes.

The bureaucrats asked her if she had a son.

"If he was called Lo-pu when he was small, then he is my son, my precious offspring, this sinner's own flesh and blood!"

Mu-lien was, understandably, distraught.

> The shackles around her, as full of
>   pricks as fish scales,
> A thousand years of punishment
>   that cannot be imagined.
> From the seven apertures,
>   blood spurted forth;
> Fire flared out from the woman's mouth.
> Ox-heads held the cangue
>   [stocks] on both sides
> Stepping and stumbling
>   she came forwards.
> Mu-lien embraced his mother,
>   bursting into tears,
>   And crying, "This comes from my not
> being a devoted son!"

Which seems a little . . . overly self-critical?

That wasn't the end of it. The lady was taken back to her cell and nailed down again, and so Mu-lien interceded with the Buddha once more, who sighed and said he would have to go down himself to effect the rescue. Even then, the lady's sins were not yet expiated, so she was first turned into a hungry ghost, and when that wasn't enough, a black dog destined to eat offal and scrounge for food scraps. "For seven days and seven nights" Mu-lien, whose devotion knew no bounds, "chanted the Mahayana sutras, made his confession, and recited the abstinences." His mother, having benefited from all this devotion, was finally able to shed her dog skin and hang it on a tree, once again assuming the body of a woman.

The last stage in her release was for the Buddha to check out her karma, to see if there was any sin left. (There wasn't.) Mu-lien, when he saw that his mother's sins were expiated, was overjoyed. He said, "Mother, you should go where you belong. The world of Jambudvipa is no place for you. Birth and death, there is no end to it. But in the west, the Land of the Buddha is most perfect." Then, Mu-lien's mother felt herself spirited away by the *devas* and the dragons and escorted by the heavenly maidens, and taken to the Trayastrinsha heaven, there to enjoy everlasting bliss.

There exists no record of whether she ever bothered to thank her son. Or of what the managers of hell had to say.

As for Mu-lien, he went back to his devotions.[2]

Miao-shen goes to hell, but they can't stand her there and so push her out

THE ESSENCE OF the story is that Miao-shen's relentless piety grated on hell's managers, and they couldn't wait to get rid of her. Early Buddhists really liked this story, so much so that Miao-shen became a true Buddha in her own right.

The story is very long, running to better than sixteen thousand words, but the essence of it is simple.

In the eleventh year of the Epoch of the Golden Heaven (that is, 2587 BCE) a young king known as P'o-kiah defeated a host of enemies and ascended to the throne. As the years went by, the king began to complain that while he had three daughters—and very nice they were—he had no male heir. Nothing would serve but for the king to make a pilgrimage to the God of the Sacred Mountain of the West, who would surely grant him a male child. His retinue didn't stint on the arrangements: the king sent over "the two Presidents of the Board of Rites and . . . assembled fifty Buddhist and as many Taoist priests, who would supplicate the god for seven days and seven nights, from the 13th to the 19th of the second month." After that, the king and queen would show up personally, and burn incense to the god. They took along a lot of good stuff too—ten pieces of the best Chengdu silk, fifty pounds of first-quality incense, five boxes of Korean paper, four Lingchi whole hogs, eight pairs of hens, ten fishes, a large quantity of marine plants, fragrant herbs, and an abundant supply of cakes.

But it was not to be: the God of the Sacred Mountain consulted the ledgers and became aware that the king would never have a male child, in punishment for the massacres committed in the many wars he had waged during his early struggle for the throne. That seemed to be that.

Still, the king was consoled by his three marriageable daughters, one of whom, he assumed, would surely marry a suitable heir.

The first two didn't do well, the one marrying the son of a high court official (not quite good enough) and the other a military officer whose rank was not high enough. So it was left to Miao-shen to do the right thing. But she refused. She wanted to be a nun.

The story tos and fros a lot after this. The king banishes Miao-shen to a secluded garden, expecting that she would soon repent, but she loved the solitude instead. Her mother tried to bring her to her senses by offering the lure of silken gowns and pearls, but predictably that didn't work. The king tried several more times, and so did his consort, but it was no use. By this time the king was furious. A Buddhist nun! "A child that disobeys her father is un-filial, and lacks the most necessary of all virtues. I consider that all those who become Buddhist or Taoist priests are lazy folks, miserable and starving wretches, the dregs of humanity, people seeking some kind of a livelihood; dear daughter, do not imitate such sorry knaves."

There was clearly nothing left for the king to do but to order Miao-shen's execution, which he did, more in sorrow than in anger. But that didn't go well either. The Pearly Emperor, apprised of all this, intervened, telling the local God of the Soil, "There is not in the whole Western world, with the exception of Buddha, a more virtuous person than this noble princess. Tomorrow, you will proceed to the place where the damsel is to be executed, and there shiver to pieces the swords of the executioners, so that they will be unable to put her to death. She must not feel even the least bodily pain. At the last moment, you will appear in the form of a tiger, and, seizing her body, bear it away to the pine-clad hills; there, you will lay it down respectfully, and place in her mouth a magic pill, which will preserve the corpse from corruption."

Still, after the swords were duly rendered unworkable, Miao-shen was strangled with a silken cord, her corpse carried away by the tiger, and her soul sent straight to hell, where she got a courteous reception. A blue-clad youth, waving a banner, arrived to escort her. He explained that he had been "ordered by Yen-wang, the ruler of hell, to take you through the eighteen departments of his dismal realm." When she demurred, he told her to fear not: "[This is] the nether world, the land of hell. Your refusal to enter the married state, and the magnanimity which made you prefer death rather than swerve from your purpose, have ingratiated you with the Pearly Emperor, Yuh-hwang, [and] all the ten presidents of hell . . . who have dispatched me to you; fear not and follow me." So she appeared before the assembled dignitaries of hell, who offered her their congratulations.

> "Who am I," said she, "that I should deserve
> to be complimented by you?"
> "We have heard," said the officers, "that
> when you recited your Sutras, all evils

vanished as if by enchantment; we would, therefore, be pleased to hear you praying."

"I accept," replied Miao-shen, "on condition that all the imprisoned souls of the ten infernal regions be set free, in order to listen to me."

Forthwith, Buffalo-head, and Horse-face set to liberating the legions of imprisoned souls, and Miao-shen commenced reciting the praises of Amitabha, O-mi-t'o-fuli. Scarcely had she ended, when hell was suddenly transformed into a paradise; all the instruments of torture were changed into lotus-flowers, and the suffering victims enjoyed unbounded happiness.

Clearly, this would not do. The point of hell, after all, was not lotus-flowers and eternal bliss. And so . . . paperwork again . . . The proper forms must be filled.

P'an-fcwan, registrar of the underworld, presented a petition to Yama Yen-wang, stating that since the arrival of Miao-shen in the Land of Shades all suffering had disappeared, the tortured victims now filled with joy. "As it has been eternally established, and as justice requires, there must be in the world a place of punishment, and a place of reward. You must, therefore, have Miao-shen sent back to earth without delay, or else there will be no further hell here."

"Since such is the case," replied Yama, "let forty-eight standard-bearers escort the princess across the bridge over the river, Nai-ho-k'iao, and let her soul return to the world above, and re-enter her body."

The ruler of hell, accompanied by his ten underlings, bade Miao-shen farewell beneath the bower of Mother Meng, at which point the blue-clad youth escorted the soul of the princess back to earth, where, finding its body in the dark forest, it re-entered it forthwith, and animated it anew. Miao-shen was thus again breathing mortal air, and heaving a sigh, exclaimed: "The memory of Hades, and all that I have seen there, is still fresh in my mind. I sighed for the day when I would be released, and here I am back again in my own body. Around me, is there no secluded place where I may lead a life of perfection; whither am I going to dwell?"

By this point, her father has disappeared from the story (except for a rambling digression, a subplot in which Miao-shen cures her father of a series of painful ulcers inflicted by the God of Epidemics). Then she visits the Sacred Isle, where she becomes a Buddha and mistress of the universe.

And hell, greatly relieved, resumes its torturing.[3]

CHAPTER 13

HELLISH TRAVELLERS IN CLASSICAL ANTIQUITY

THE "CLASSICAL WORLD" IS GENERALLY THOUGHT to mean Greece and Rome—"the glory that was Greece, the grandeur that was Rome," as the later Romantics put it. But for convenience sake I include here a quick in-and-out jaunt to hell described by the Norse god Odin, from the same period, and also the great classical poets' Zoroastrian contemporary, the traveller called Arda Viraf (yes, we have seen him before, but here we recount his actual journey).

First, the Greeks and Romans.

Only one person ever melted Hades's stone-cold heart

AS WELL AS being gorgeous to look upon, the Greek god Apollo had an extensive portfolio of duties. He was the God of Poetry, Art, Archery, Medicine, Light, and Knowledge, and, bizarrely, of Plague, as well as serving as the director of the Choir of the Muses, and thus acting God of Music too. His son, Orpheus, apparently inherited his father's musical talents and even improved on them; the myths say he had no rivals, and when he played his lyre and sang his songs "in the deep still woods upon the Thracian mountains, Orpheus with his singing lyre led the trees, led the wild beasts of the wilderness. Everything animate and inanimate followed him. He moved the rocks on the hillside and turned the courses of the rivers."[1]

The stories are silent on how he met and wooed the maiden he loved, Eurydice; we are told only that they married, and that after the wedding, as the bride walked in a meadow with her bridesmaids, she was bitten by a viper and died. Disconsolate, Orpheus determined to go down to Hades himself and plead with "Demeter's daughter" (Persephone) and Hades himself to let her go. And so he did: "He took the fearsome journey to the underworld; there he struck his lyre, and at the sound, all the vast multitude were charmed to stillness." So he sang his song to the rulers of the dead:

> O Gods who rule the dark and silent
>   world,
> To you all born of a woman
>   needs must come.
> All lovely things at last go down to you.
> You are the debtor who is always paid.
> A little while we tarry up on earth.
> Then we are yours forever and forever.
> But I seek one who came
>   to you too soon.

The bud was plucked before
    the flower bloomed.
I tried to bear my loss. I
    could not bear it. . . .

Weave again for sweet Eurydice
Life's pattern that was taken
    from the loom
Too quick. See, I ask a little thing,
Only that you will lend, not
    give, her to me.
She shall be yours when her
    years' span is full.

Even the gods could not resist such sweet song. Hades wept, and so did Persephone. Even Cerberus, the snarling hellhound, covered his many ears with his paws and howled in despair.[2]

"He drew iron tears down Pluto's cheek, and made Hell grant what Love did seek." So Hades and Proserpine (Persephone) gave Eurydice back to her husband. But on one condition (there is always a catch in hell, it seems): she would follow him up the long stairway to the earth above, but he was not to look back to see if she was there. One glimpse, and she would be lost to him forever. So they passed in small procession through the great gates of Hades to the path that would take them out of darkness. Finally, Orpheus joyfully reached the sunlight, and turned back to make sure Eurydice was there. But alas, she had not yet crossed the threshold, and was still under Hades's edict. In an instant, she was gone, back into the darkness; all he heard was one faint word, "Farewell!"

You can see why the story has inspired poets and painters and the composers of operas over the centuries. But it has a grimmer ending. As Orpheus wandered through the woods, shrunken with grief, a band of Maenads came upon him. This was bad luck: the Maenads were women who followed Dionysius, and their name translates as the "raving ones." And indeed, they seized the lost lover, cut him into pieces, and tossed the bits, along with his lyre, into a river.

Perhaps that was what he wanted. On this, the myths are silent.

Aeneas only went to hell to see his dad

IN THE GREEK and Roman telling, Hades wasn't necessarily inaccessible; you just needed the proper determination and the passcodes (and getting in was easier than getting out). It was toured by several Greek heroes at various times. By Hercules, who captured Cerberus as the last of his twelve labours and dragged the hellhound above ground, stashing the creature in "Hermione, Demeter's sacred grove," Demeter being Hades's mother-in-law, after all); by Odysseus seeking the counsel of wise Tiresias; by Orpheus to find Eurydice, as per the above; and by Pirithoüs, accompanied by Theseus, who wanted to re-kidnap Persephone in order to marry her. (This didn't work too well: Hades tied them to rocks and only Theseus escaped, rescued by Hercules.) And then there was Aeneas, the loser of Troy but the founder of Rome.

In Virgil's *Aeneid*, Hades was not much more than a digression, really, but then Virgil wrote so many digressions into *The Aeneid* that one more hardly seems to distract from the main story. Which was this: Aeneas and his fellow Trojans, fleeing from their home city of Troy after the Greeks had snuck in by means of the wooden horse and sacked the place, sailed for Italy, where the gods had told him he was to found a great city called Rome, which he did, after warring on the hapless Latins, losers all.

The Aeneid, therefore, was the founding myth of Rome, told by Rome's greatest poet at the height of his powers. Some of Aeneas's wanderings recall those of Odysseus (especially the shipwrecks, the lovelorn goddesses, and the harpies, as well as the quick trip down to Hades), which was not so surprising, since Homer was taught to every Roman schoolboy from the earliest years. The character Aeneas would also have been familiar: he was a player in *The Iliad*, after all. Nor is it so surprising that the structure Virgil employed, using one of the sibyls to show him around Hades, was later mimicked by Dante, who paid Virgil the supreme compliment of enlisting Virgil as his tour guide to the underworld.

The plot summary goes like this: after escaping Troy with a few of his retainers, Aeneas, his father Anchises, and his son Ascanius (plus sundry hearth gods) set sail for Italy. Twice they landed and attempted to build their new city before being driven away by cursing harpies, plagues, and bad omens. In one of these adventures, Anchises was killed; a great storm subsequently blew the little fleet to Carthage, where it was welcomed by the city's founder, Dido.

Dido was herself a Phoenician princess, driven from her home after her brother murdered her husband. Hearing Aeneas's tales, she falls in love, and invites him into her palace and her bed. Putting aside his quest, Aeneas gratefully accepts, and for a time they live together as lovers.

But this is, after all, a saga, and Aeneas has a duty to perform and a great city to found, as the nagging gods keep reminding him, so he sets sail once again, eventually winding up, as he was supposed to, on the "Cumean shore," on the Italian mainland near the "lone mystery of the awful Cumean Sibyl's cavern depth." Aeneas means to enlist the sibyl as his tour guide to Hades. Why would he want to go there in the first place? Mostly, it seems, to consult the shade of his father, who would tell him his fate; perhaps he believed the gods lied, and wanted his father to reassure him—Virgil is vague on this point. First, though, he has to sacrifice "seven unbroken bullocks of the herd, as many fitly chosen sheep of two years old," which he promptly does. After a lot of foofaraw about Daedalus and his fate (another digression), the sibyl emerges from her grotto, and Aeneas makes his pitch:

> One thing I pray; since here is the gate
> named of the infernal king, and the dark-
> ling marsh of Acheron's overflow, be it given
> me to go to my beloved father, to see him
> face to face; teach thou the way, and open
> the consecrated portals. Him on these
> shoulders I rescued from encircling flames
> and a thousand pursuing weapons, and
> brought him safe from amid the enemy; he

accompanied my way over all the seas, and bore with me all the threats of ocean and sky, in weakness, beyond his age's strength and due. Nay, he it was who besought and enjoined me to seek thy grace and draw nigh thy courts. Have pity, I beseech thee, on son and father, O gracious one! for thou art all-powerful, nor in vain hath Hecate given thee rule in the groves of Avernus.

The sibyl agrees to act as tour guide, but in order to win passage to hell—and even more importantly, to win passage back—Aeneas must first pluck the golden bough: "In the neighb'ring grove there stands a tree; the queen of Stygian Jove claims it her own; thick woods and gloomy night conceal the happy plant from human sight. One bough it bears; but (wondrous to behold!) the ductile rind and leaves of radiant gold: this from the vulgar branches must be torn, and to fair Proserpine the present borne, 'ere leave be giv'n to tempt the nether skies."

Bearing the bough, they plunge into the jaws of hell itself, where "Grief and avenging Cares have made their bed; there dwell wan Sicknesses and gloomy Eld, and Fear, and ill-counselling Hunger, and loathly Want, shapes terrible to see; and Death and Travail, and thereby Sleep, Death's kinsman, and the Soul's guilty Joys, and death-dealing War full in the gateway, and the Furies in their iron cells, and mad Discord with bloodstained fillets enwreathing her serpent locks." Plus many monstrous creatures, centaurs and cyllas, and the beast of Lerna hissing horribly, and the chimera armed with flame, gorgons and harpies, and more—the "empty dwellings and bodiless realm of Dis."

The hellhound Cerberus having been overcome with drugged honey cake, they begin their tour, passing wailing babies "torn from the breast and portionless in life's sweetness," and then those unjustly condemned in life, now waiting the judgment of Minos. Soon they reach the Wailing Fields, where Aeneas sees his former lover Dido, newly dead, but she spurns his conversation, fleeing "wrathfully into the shadowy woodland." The next few hundred lines recount the sad fates of a multiplicity of heroes of old, including the son of Priam, mourning the duplicity of the "Laconian woman and her treacherous guilt," for it was she who freed the Greeks from the wooden horse and doomed the city to its fate.[3]

A little later they passed the gate to Tartarus itself, "huge and pillared with solid adamant, that no warring force of men nor the very habitants of heaven may avail to overthrow; it stands up a tower of iron, and Tisiphone sitting girt in bloodstained pall keeps sleepless watch at the entry by night and day. Hence moans are heard and fierce lashes resound, with the clank of iron and dragging chains." Here, the sibyl says, "are earth's ancient children, the Titans' brood, hurled down by thunderbolt, and awful Tityos, fosterling of Earth the mother of all, whose body stretches over nine full acres, and a monstrous vulture with crooked beak eats away the imperishable liver and the entrails that breed in suffering, and plunges deep into the breast that gives it food and dwelling; nor is any rest given to the fibres that ever grow anew." Beyond that were the adulterers, the cheats, those who slighted the gods in life, traitors, those who forced their daughters' bridal chambers, and other perpetrators of wickedness.

Be that as it may, the golden bough gains them entrance to the Fortunate Woodlands, and at last Aeneas meets his father, Anchises, who bursts into tears at the sight of his son: "Art thou come at last, and hath thy love, O child of my desire, conquered the difficult road? Is it granted, O my son, to gaze on thy face and hear and answer in familiar tones? Thus indeed I forecast in spirit, counting the days between; nor hath my care misled me. What lands, what space of seas hast thou traversed to reach me, through what surge of perils, O my son! How I dreaded the realm of Libya might work thee harm!"

Pressed for time (the sibyl is by this point growing impatient), Anchises tells his son what awaits: war, and doom for a while, but then victory, for "Rome the Renowned will fill earth with her empire and heaven with her pride, and gird about seven fortresses with her single wall, prosperous mother of men. . . . Behold the people, the Romans that are thine." And he foretells the glorious future, after Aeneas himself is dead: "Here is he, he of whose promise once and again thou hearest, Caesar Augustus, a god's son, who shall again establish the ages of gold in Latium over the fields that once were Saturn's realm, and carry his empire afar to Garamant and Indian, to the land that lies beyond our stars, beyond the sun's yearlong ways, where Atlas the sky-bearer wheels on his shoulder the glittering star-spangled pole. Before his coming even now the kingdoms of the Caspian shudder at oracular answers, and the Maeotic land and the mouths of sevenfold Nile flutter in alarm."

. If you discount the sucking up to Caesar Augustus, that proved to be good news. And good news was rather the point, after all. Aeneas and his father embrace, then Anchises follows his son and the sibyl and dismisses them at the Ivory Gate. Without further poetizing, Aeneas regains his ships and his comrades, draws up the anchors, and sails for glory on the shores of what will one day be the Roman heartland.[4]

Arda Viraf tours hell, the Pious Ones as guides

THE ZOROASTRIAN AUTHOR of *The Book of Arda Viraf* cast his journey as a voyage to hell in the spirit, not the body, sent thither by a conclave of ecclesiastics to test the veracity of their faith—for this was in difficult times, following the destruction of Iran by Alexander the Great (dismissed in the text derisively as "Alexander the Roman"). It was probably written sometime during the Sassanid Empire—that is, somewhere between 220 and 651 CE— and was constructed in the same fashion as Virgil's *Aeneid*, but though Virgil was a few centuries earlier (he died in 19 BCE) there is no evidence that the Zoroastrian had heard of the Roman. In any case, just as Virgil did and as Dante did later, Viraf employed the pious-soul-as-guide-and-explicator literary device.

Most of the book is a catalogue of sins, eighty-five to be precise, each meticulously described, and the result-ing punishments; these, too, are also meticulously, even chillingly, described, each sin matched to a punishment, the punishments given in graphic detail. (Some of the more baroque tortures have already been described.) The very scrupulousness of these hellish descriptions were for centuries regarded as evidence that the belief in hell was both rational and reasonable. (The "Arda" in the title can roughly be translated as "truthful" or "righteous.")

Viraf has sometimes been associated with a scholar who wrote commentaries on the Avesta (the corpus of Zoroastrian works) in the Sassanid period, but in fact we know virtually nothing about the man; what little detail we have comes from the introductory section of his book. The first chapter provides some background: "The pious Zartosht [a.k.a. Zarathustra or Zoroaster] made the religion which he had received current in the world, and for 300 years the religion [lived] in purity, and men were without doubts." Thereafter, however, the Accursed Evil Spirit prompted Alexander, who was then in Egypt, to invade Iran, which he did "with severe cruelty and war and devastation," killing the emperor and destroying the metropolis and the empire. Among the war's casualties were the archives in Stakhar Papakan (the capital, Persopolis, founded by Darius the Great in 518 BCE), which contained the complete records of Zoroastrian life and thought, written on cow hide in gold ink, as well as all the custodians of the archive and its associated holy men, including the "competent of Iran and the wise." After sowing hatred and causing strife, Alexander returns to Egypt, and vanishes from the story ("self-destroyed," the book says piously, "he fled to hell").

In the years that followed, many cults and religions emerged, and "different fashions of belief, and various codes of law were promulgated," and the Zoroastrians were mired in doubt and confusion. Eventually, what

Zoroastrian leaders still existed called a conclave, and after days of speechifying it was decided to send an emissary to the spirits so that, as the record says, "people in this age shall know whether these . . . ceremonies and prayers and ablutions and purifications which we bring into operation attain unto god, or the demons, and come to the relief of our souls, or not."

This was a heavy task. Who to send? The priests summoned all the believers they could find to a general assembly, from which they winnowed seven who were believed to be exceptionally pious—"seven men who had not the slightest doubt of god and the religion, and whose own thoughts and words and deeds were most orderly and proper; and they were told thus: 'Seat yourselves down, and select one from among you, who is best for this duty, and the most innocent and respected.'" This one, it turned out, was Viraf, who won the three drawings of lots, one for pure thoughts, one for pure words, the last for pure deeds.

"And afterward . . . Viraf washed his head and body, and put on new clothes; he fumigated himself with sweet scent and spread a carpet, new and clean, on a prepared couch. He sat down on the clean carpet of the couch, and consecrated the Dron [the ceremonial cake], and remembered the departed souls, and ate food. And then those Dasturs of the religion filled three golden cups with wine and narcotic of Vishtasp; and they gave one cup over to Viraf with the word 'well-thought,' and the second cup with the word 'well-said,' and the third cup with the word 'well-done'; and he swallowed the wine and narcotic, and said grace whilst conscious, and slept upon the carpet."

And off he went, high as a kite on the wine and the narcotic.

His first stop is the Chinvât Bridge, which all souls must cross en route either to heaven (in which case the bridge is nicely broad) or to hell (very narrow, and extremely perilous). Here he is met by his guides, Srosh the Pious and Adar the Angel, who were a little astonished that he had come before his time, so to speak, but who were willing to show him around.

First he sees a virtuous soul who is destined for the sweet perfumes of heaven; he is conducted across the bridge by a damsel, the personification of his good life, who was therefore of a "beautiful appearance, that is, grown up in virtue; with prominent breasts, that is, her breasts swelled downward, which is charming to the heart and soul; whose form was as brilliant, as the sight of it was the more well-pleasing, the observation of it more desirable."

The damsel explained that she was who she was "on account of thy will and actions . . . that I am as great and good and sweet-scented and triumphant and undistressed as appears to thee." And off the soul goes to heaven.

Since heaven is not our concern here, we will pass over the next few chapters, except to say that when he arrived, the soul in question met archangels and guardian angels of all stripes; the brilliant and elevated souls of monarchs and good rulers in golden trousers; those of eloquent speakers; those of women of good thought and deeds in clothing embroidered with gold and silver threads; warriors whose weapons were made of gold and studded with jewels; good farmers and good artisans and good shepherds there in "the pre-eminent world of the pious, which is the all-glorious light of space, much perfumed with sweet basil, all-bedecked, all-admired, and splendid, full of glory and every joy and every pleasure, with which no one is satiated."

Viraf and his guides then returned to the Chinvât Bridge on their way into darkness. As in the entrance to heaven, a soul was waiting there to be taken across. And there was a damsel there too, but one of quite a different stripe. She stood in "a stinking cold wind . . . from the northern quarter, from the quarter of the demons, a more stinking wind than which he had not perceived in the world. And in that wind he saw his own religion and deeds as a profligate woman, naked, decayed, gapping, bandy-legged, lean-hipped, and unlimitedly spotted so that spot was joined to spot, like the most hideous, noxious creature (*khrafstar*), most filthy and most stinking." None of the pleasing, pendulous, eye-catching breasts of the heavenly damsel here. It is all his fault, she tells the doomed soul: "It is on account of thy will and actions that I am hideous and vile, iniquitous and diseased, rotten and foul-smelling, unfortunate and distressed, as appears to thee. Afterward, that soul of the wicked advanced the first footstep on Dush-humat and the second footstep on Dush-hukt, and the third on Dush-huvarsht; and with the fourth footstep he ran to hell."

And what was hell like? "Cold and heat, drought and stench, to such a degree as I never saw, or heard of, in the world." The greedy jaws of hell were like the most frightful pit, a narrow stair descending into the dark, "and in such stench that every one whose nose inhales that air will struggle and stagger and fall." Even the lesser noxious creatures are as tall as mountains, seizing and tearing and worrying at the souls of the wicked, "as would be unworthy of a dog."

After that, Viraf sets out on his tour of the eighty-five categories of sins and their associated punishments, carefully cataloguing the implements of torture (remember that spiny hedgehog wedged into bodily orifices?) as well as the methods of their employ, before eventually encountering Ahriman, the devil, the world-destroyer, whose religion is evil, who ever ridiculed and mocked the wicked in hell, and said thus: "Why did you ever eat the bread of Ohrmazd [the Creator], and do my work? And thought not of your own creator, but practiced my will? So he ever shouted to the wicked very mockingly."

Back in the real world, coming out from the hallucinations of the drugs and the booze, Viraf fancies he hears the somewhat cheerless words of Ohrmazd: "be ye aware of this, that cattle are dust, and the horse is dust, and gold and silver are dust, and the body of man is dust; he alone mingles not with the dust, who, in the world, praises piety and performs duties and good works."[5]

Odin, the Norse god, once visited hell, mostly to check on his son

OR SO THE sagas say: "Then Othin [Odin] rose, the enchanter old, and the saddle he laid on Sleipnir's back; thence rode he down to Niflhel deep, and the hound he met that came from hell."

Odin already knew hell was accessible, because he had once spoken to the giant Vafthruthnir, who had been there, and everywhere else too:

> Vafthruthnir spake: "Of the runes
>   of the gods and the giants' race
> The truth indeed can I tell, (For
>   to every world have I won);
> To nine worlds came I, to Niflhel
>   beneath, The home where
> dead men dwell."

Odin found his son there too. He was doing all right, apparently. So he left.

CHAPTER 14

INQUISITIVE CHRISTIANS
GO TO HELL

ONCE YOU START LOOKING, IT SEEMS THAT FROM the early Christian period to the Renaissance every monkish or nunnish literate went to hell, either in spirit, in person, or in a dream. There is no point in trying to catalogue them all, partly because they cribbed shamelessly from each other, but also because the indefatigable Eileen Gardiner has already done so. Some of them we have already met: *The Apocalypses of Peter* and *Paul*, the book of Daniel, and more. Some of them we skipped, mostly because they were redundant: *The Apocalypse of Zephaniah*, for example, which dates from somewhere around 100 BCE; *The Apocalypse of Ezra*, about a hundred and fifty years after Christ; and the famous *Discourse on Saint Michael the Archangel*, by the Archbishop of Alexandria, from somewhere around the late fourth century. (Even so, there are a few oddities worth noting—see for example Wetti, below. And the twelfth-century monk Edmund, who was astonished to find in the compartment of hell reserved for homosexuals a large number of women. "He was surprised because he had not suspected women to be capable of such a deed. But there they were, suspended in woe and pain."[1])

As time went on, the Christian visions of hell grew grimmer, and the devil grew ever larger, ever blacker, ever more grotesque, ever more horrific.

But first . . . what about the Virgin? Didn't she go to hell too?

IT SEEMS SO, at least if you believe *The Apocalypse of the Virgin*, more properly known as *The Apocalypse of the All-Holy Theotokos Concerning the Punishments*, in which Mary insists that the archangel Michael allow her to visit, mostly it seems out of curiosity. First she summons Michael down from heaven, demanding that he "tell me of all the things on earth."

"Whatever you ask me, Highly Favored One, I will tell you."

"How many punishments are there, by which the human race is punished?"

Clearly considering that it was better to show than to tell, Michael gave the order, Hades opened, and the Virgin saw those who were being punished there, a multitude of wailing and tooth-gnashing men and women, the souls of those who did not believe in the Father and the Son and the Holy Spirit. "And she saw in another place a great darkness, and there lay a multitude of men and women. And she said, 'What is this darkness and who are those being punished in it?' The commander-in-chief said, 'Lady, many souls lie in this darkness.'"

The All-Holy-One said, "Let the darkness be taken away so that I may see this punishment also."

But that was a request too far. Indeed, Michael denied it, pointing out that a command from what he called "the Invisible Father" insisted that they would not see the light until some unspecified time when Mary's "blessed Son shines forth on the earth."

But that would not do—this was the Virgin, after all, the All-Holy-One, so, as the apocalypse put it, "she lifted up her eyes to the Undefiled Throne of the Father and said, In the name of the Father and the Son and the Holy Spirit, let the darkness be taken away, that I may see this punishment also." And immediately that darkness was lifted up "so that it covered the seven heavens."

A peremptory tone works, apparently, even with God.

What she saw matched, sort of, the visions of others who had preceded her and others who came later: sinners covered in boiling pitch; sinners, "some up to the waist, some up to the neck, and others to the top of the head," in the river of fire; hanging people being devoured by worms (those who swore falsely by the cross); burning people on fiery benches (those who dissed priests); sinners hanging by their tongues from an iron tree (blasphemers and slanderers); a hanging man with blood pouring from his nails (who stole from the Temple), and more . . .

"The All-Holy-One went forth and saw priests hanging from their twenty nails, and fire was coming out from their heads and flowing over them. Seeing them the All-Holy-One wept and asked the commander-in-chief,

saying, 'Who are these and what are their sins?' The angel
said, 'These, All-Holy-One, are those who were standing
before the altar of God, and when they were breaking the
body of our Lord Jesus Christ, the stars fell down, and
the dreadful throne in heaven shook and the footstool
of our Lord trembled, and they did not realize it, nor
did they understand the mystery of God, but they were
thinking little of his immaculate body and blood without
fear of God. And because of this they are punished thus
here.'" How they were "breaking the body of our Lord
Jesus Christ" while Mary was still alive, the apocalypse
leaves unresolved.

For all of these, Mary asks for succour, but the angels
demurred.

God just won't listen! Michael says, sniffily: "As the
Lord God lives, seven times a day and seven times a night,
when we offer up the hymn of the Master, we, the angels,
intercede on behalf of them all, and the Lord God does
not hear us."

He heard Mary, though, after a fashion, and after she
called for relief for all sinners, God/Jesus addressed the
multitude of sinners (sounding here more than a little
testy) . . .

> Listen, all of you: I made Paradise and
> formed humankind according to my own
> image. But humankind transgressed, and
> by its own sins it was handed over to death.
> But I would not suffer the works of my
> hands to be tyrannized by the serpent, on

account of which I was born of the immaculate Virgin Mary.

I was nailed to the cross, in order to free you from the ancient curse. I asked for water, and you gave me vinegar with gall. I was placed in the tomb by the Jews; I trampled down the enemy; I raised up my elect. And you would not listen to me, but you bound yourself to the present age, and falling into sins, you became playthings of the demons, and you have received what is due according to your deeds.

But now, because of the supplication of my mother, and because of Michael my archangel and the multitude of the holy angels, and because of all the saints of the ages who are pleasing to me, you will have rest for the days of the holy Resurrection, until the day of Pentecost.[2]

Two thousand years later, the Virgin, by now an old hand at this hellish travel business, showed three children of Fatima, in Portugal, what the place was like. It wasn't pretty. They saw the usual vast sea of fire, the demons, the souls of the damned. These damned souls were transparent, like burning embers, blackened and bronzed, rising and falling like sparks, shrieking and groaning in despair, which no doubt horrified the kids. Why the Virgin wanted to scare the bejeezus out of the children with a vast sea of fire and torment, only to comfort them later, remains inscrutable. Never mind: in 2017, the kids were declared saints by the church, so there must have been something to it.

To the monk Wetti's great surprise, there was Charlemagne, in hell's waiting room

IN THE YEAR 824, a mere decade after the death of Charlemagne, the monkish schoolmaster Wetti, of the Benedictine monastery of Reichanau, had a vision, and then, a few days later, a new and embellished one. Ill, he had taken to his bed, where he was administered a potion, presumably a physic of some kind. Instead of helping, the potion caused him violent pain and to throw up his food (or a refusal to eat—the eyewitness accounts differ). After three days of this, his first vision presented itself. By his own account, a demon entered his bedchamber dressed as a fellow monk, carrying a basket of torture devices to punish him for his multiple sins. But before the torment could begin, his room was swarmed by a host of other demons, who were pushed away by a countervailing crowd of monks and an angel dressed in scarlet (or in some accounts purple) robes.

What did this mean? Wetti wasn't sure, but in an attempt to find out he had his fellows read aloud passages from Pope Gregory's *Dialogues* that dealt rather loosely with the afterlife.[3] This may or may not have helped. A night or so later Wetti was again asleep when the same angel, this time garbed in white, led him through to purgatory, then a fairly new idea—anteroom to the afterlife.

Wetti was shocked—*shocked!*—at what he saw. Oh, sure, there were the expected sights: priests with their concubines bound to stakes, standing hip deep in a river of fire, their genitals being flogged every third day. Wetti was *au courant* with this—*contrapasso* punishment (punishment that matched the sin) was already commonplace in visions of hell. Later he watched the flogging of those lay and ecclesiastical officials who had lusted for wealth and prestige, those who did not heed the prayers of the penitent, those who neglected people in need, and those who were indulgent, guilty of concealing wealth, adultery, concubinage, and sodomy—and so on and so on. So much, so commonplace. But suddenly he came upon the newly dead emperor, Charlemagne, Charles the Great, standing in a river, bound but unharmed—except for an animal (Wetti was unable to say what it was, exactly) tearing at his genitals.

How could this be? Charlemagne, the founder of the Carolingian Dynasty, the warrior who saved Christendom from the infidels (or Moors, or Saracens, or whatever they were called) after turning them back at Roncesvalles hard by the Pyrenees, who had seen his beloved Roland slain in battle, a turning point in the history of the West—how could he, the great king, be bound in hell, or even purgatory?

Wetti recounted his vision to his disciple Walahfrid Strabo, who put it this way: "He also observed among illuminated fields one who once had held imperial sway over the West and the exalted Roman people. He was rooted to the spot, and in front of him an animal was tearing at his genitals as he stood there. The limbs on the rest of his body were blessedly free from laceration."

When Wetti saw this depressing sight, he became numb with fear; but prolix as ever, he offered the following: "This man's destiny made him the defender of justice while he lived in the body, and in our new age he has caused the flourishing of great teaching on the Lord's behalf and provided the faithful with the shield of his pious protection, and, as it were, reached a new summit in this world, upholding the right and borne from land to land the sweet wings of popular favor. But here he is caught in this awful plight, enduring the dire punishment of this grim affliction. Please explain."[4]

This last—Wetti curtly demanding an explanation from an angel—was a bit rich, but clearly he was agitated enough not to curb his tongue.

Sure, the angel told Wetti, Charlemagne had been a good and pious king, at first. But in later years, as his paunch grew and the lines on his face became more pronounced, as his hold on the stories of the True Path waned, he descended into the lust and debauchery that dominated his later life. Never mind, though, he would eventually be forgiven because of his heroism in battle.

As Strabo wrote,

> He remains in this tortured state because
> he sullied his good actions with shame-
> ful debauchery, thinking his sins would
> be buried under the great quantity of his
> virtuous acts, and chose to end his life in
> a squalor to which he became habituated:
> yet even so he will attain a blessed life, and

joyfully assume the office that the Lord has
set aside for him.⁵

Disconcertingly, the angel also told Wetti that he
would die the following day, and that he would be punished eternally because he had become "smothered in lazi-
ness, had neglected his duties as a teacher and debauched
his students."

Well, he did die the following day, probably from the
potion he was given: that much, at least, we know.

THE WHOLE THING was buttressed by another vision
of the period, "the vision of the poor woman of Laon,"
whose name is never specified. She, too, saw "a prince of
Italy" (Charlemagne) in torment, and many other famous
people, some also in torment, some in glory. She asked
her guide if "that prince would return to eternal life," and
he said that indeed he would, "for if his offspring the
emperor Louis [Louis the Pious, a.k.a. Louis the Deb-
onair, Charlemagne's son] were to give seven memorial
agapes for him he should be set free."

She also saw a companion of Charlemagne's, Bego,
lying flat nearby, in torment as two black spirits melted
gold and poured it into his mouth, saying, "You thirsted
for this in the world and could not be satisfied, now drink
to saturation." A little further on, she saw Irmingard (or
Ermingard), the wife of Louis the Pious and daughter-
in-law of Charles the Great, lying in torment with three
molars above her—one over her head, one over her breast,
and one over her back, who "drowned her in the deep."

It remains unclear what set off such punishment, or indeed what "molars" may be.[6]

But the context, clearly enough, is political. Louis may have been pious, but his destiny, as David Ganz points out in an essay for the journal *Florilegium*, was the loss of certainty as regards his own celestial reward, since he is subject to a crescendo of criticism rising in the empire, its epicentre in the diocese of Rheims (Reims).

And so to the Venerable Bede's Drythelm and Tundale (again)

THE IRISH MONK Adamnán we have seen before; he seems to have been an exceedingly pious and sober person, and a careful administrator of his charges; his vision of hell is in this sense an aberration, being far more apocalyptic than his usual discourses; it is important mostly because it was later popularized by writers such as Tundale, and in that sense was a direct precursor of Dante's poem.

Tundale also borrowed liberally from the discourses of the Venerable Bede, especially Bede's recounting of the vision of a pious layman called Drythelm, who lived with his wife and children in Cunningham, near the Scottish border. Drythelm's story is worth a quick sketch. One night he takes ill and dies, but at dawn he revives, causing the mourners to flee in panic. He promptly divides his property into three portions (for his wife, his children, and the poor) and spends the rest of his days in the isolated monastery of Melrose, where he lives a life of scourging and repentance. At some point, he dictates his adventures in the afterworld to a scribe. While there, he is mostly shown souls still in purgatory, waiting for judgment, but Drythelm's guide, described only as "a person dressed in shining white," also leads him to the yawning pit of hell itself. From here, writes Bede,

> Drythelm can see nothing but the bright shape of his guide. Suddenly, masses of dusky flame shoot up out of a great pit and fall back into it. Drythelm finds himself alone. Souls rise and fall like sparks in the midst of this flame, accompanied by inhuman cries and laughter, and a terrible stench. Drythelm pays particular attention to the torment inflicted on five souls, including a clergyman, recognizable by his partly shaved pate, a layman and a woman, and two others who remain in the shadows. Devils surround him and threaten to grab him with glowing tongs, but all at once a light appears, like a brilliant star, that grows in size and sends the devils fleeing.

And that is pretty much that. The pilgrim and his white-robed guide then come to a wall so high and long that the eye cannot encompass it, beyond which is a vast fragrant meadow full of flowers and happy frolickers—in other words, heaven.[7]

Tundale (the happy plagiarizer) and his many editors (the happy embellishers) adapted and recalibrated many precursor stories. We have already seen his vision of the awful devil, and little more might be said, except for this: unlike many of the visions recounted here, Tundale self-identified as a most serious sinner (guilty of all eight of the deadly sins—the Irish added treachery to the traditional seven), and he not only visits hell, but is personally tormented there as well, unlike most other tourists, who are usually given a *laissez-passer* to keep out of the demons' clutches.

The story begins with Tundale's death. He perishes at the home of an aggrieved debtor, who has kindly (that's the debtor's word) given him dinner, at which point he is stricken with a violent fit and dies forthwith; could the dinner have been . . . off? His soul finds itself in a grim and dark place, where it is confronted with his guardian angel, who accuses Tundale of ignoring him while he was alive, a charge to which the sinner readily admits. The vision is recounted in ten *passus* (steps), and by *passus* 5 Tundale begins his personal punishment, which includes torment with fire and ice and being bitten by lions and adders "within the belly of Acheron." *Passus* 6 is where Tundale must cross the bridge with a wild cow, the reason given being that he had stolen his neighbour's cow in life. After that he is tormented for his many sexual sins, and is hacked into small pieces by fiends (only to be restored by his irrepressible guardian angel). After that he is infested with vermin and beaten by infernal blacksmiths in the Forge of Vulcan.

In the end Tundale is once again restored to what passes for health. It is here that his guardian angel asks him the awkward question: why, without the threat of punishment, would man do God's will?

To this, Tundale has no answer.[8]

After this, the torments of Teresa of Ávila seem modest enough, if rather more literary

THEN THERE WAS Saint Teresa of Ávila, born Teresa Ali Fatim Corella Sanchez de Capeda y Ahumada in Ávila in 1515, a prolific commentator on all matters spiritual (and the heroine of a splendid *bande desinée* by the French satirist Claire Bretécher). And sure enough, she was taken to hell for a visit:

> A long time after the Lord had already granted me many of the favors I've mentioned and other very lofty ones, while I was in prayer one day, I suddenly found that, without knowing how, I had seemingly been put in hell. I understood that the Lord wanted me to see the place the devils had prepared there for me and which I merited because of my sins. . . . The entrance it seems to me was similar to a very long and narrow alleyway, like an oven, low and dark and confined; the floor seemed to me to consist of dirty, muddy water emitting foul stench and swarming with putrid vermin. At the end of the alleyway a hole that looked like a small cupboard was hollowed out in the wall; there I found I was placed in a cramped condition.

As she put it in her copious memoirs,

What I felt . . . cannot even begin to be exaggerated; nor can it be understood. I experienced a fire in the soul that I don't know how I could describe. The bodily pains were so unbearable that though I had suffered excruciating ones in this life and according to what doctors say, the worst that can be suffered on earth for all my nerves were shrunken when I was paralyzed, plus many other sufferings of many kinds that I endured and even some as I said, caused by the devil, these were all nothing in comparison with the ones I experienced there.

This, however, was nothing next to the soul's agonizing: a constriction, a suffocation, an affliction so keenly felt and with such a despairing and tormenting unhappiness that I don't know how to word it strongly enough. [It was an] interior fire and despair, coming in addition to such extreme torments and pains. I didn't see who inflicted them on me, but . . . I felt myself burning and crumbling.

Satan appeared to her personally several times, and once in an oratory, "a high flame seemed to issue out of his body, perfectly bright, without any shadow, and [he] threatened, though I had escaped from his hands, [that] he would lay hold of me again."[9]

On a more cheerful note, and to her evident satisfaction, she said that she had seen many Lutherans in hell.

CHAPTER 15

THE GREAT POETS
AS TOUR GUIDES

DANTE TOURED HELL, MILTON DID NOT (BUT HE clearly had good sources and took copious notes).

Dante's tattle-tale chronicles

IT'S TRUE THAT the *Divina Commedia* is one of the greatest narrative poems in world literature, it's true that it helped establish the Tuscan dialect as the national language of Italy, and it is, truly, a magnificent allegory for man's approach to god. But for the historian of hell its pickings are somewhat more meagre.

Dante's geography of hell (a funnel or inverted cone, with nine subdivided layers separated by rocky banks, each layer hosting ever more wicked sinners) is a little unusual, and so is the very precise measurement he offers of Satan himself. But the punishments, tortures, and torments he describes are rather run-of-the-mill by the standards of those who went before—derivative rather than original—and so is his use of a wise guide (Virgil in his case, as opposed to Virgil's own use of a sibyl).

How deep, and how big, was Dante's innermost pit? So deep that Dante describes sliding down Lucifer's enormous body to the southern hemisphere, where he sees stars. So great was his poetry, though, and so convincing his imagery, that he had his readers more than half-persuaded he had actually been there. Even Galileo, in what is surely not one of his signature achievements, calculated backwards from the presumed size of Satan, and Dante's notion that Satan's navel marked the exact centre of the earth, before reporting to an audience of clerics in Florence that hell must be somewhere around 650 kilometres beneath the surface of the earth—or, if you read his calculations another way, that the Dome of Hell must have a roof at least 640 kilometres thick to support it. Where the cone reaches the surface is Jerusalem. The River of Hell, or the Styx (the stories vary), runs around hell, separating it from the outside world. Satan himself is portrayed in the uttermost depths of hell, frozen in place.

Even these descriptions, while vivid, were not particularly original. What does distinguish the poem is Dante's willingness, even eagerness, to name names and assign blame. This was new—many early visions of hell recounted the sufferings there, but hardly ever named the sinners directly, particularly the author's contemporaries. Even Virgil, who was somewhat of a name-dropper in *The Aeneid*, only named those already in Elysium who had successfully passed judgment; the wretched in the pit remained anonymous.

This willingness to tattle no doubt had its origins in the turbulent politics of early fourteenth-century Italy, the period in which the *Commedia* was written. The fact that many of the people he encounters in hell are Florentines may be partly due to the poet's rancorous exile from his beloved city. There is no point in going into the details of this history itself, but as Florence became one of the pre-eminent mercantile cities on the Continent, it was wracked by a series of internecine wars between the so-called Ghibelines, who were allies of the Holy Roman Emperors, and the Guelfs, who were allies of the Holy See—a struggle that would consume the city for more than a century (the conflict was later codified and simplified as Black versus White). Dante was himself a casualty of these wars, his downfall caused by his opposition to the occupant of the Roman See at the time, Boniface VIII.

Dante's visit to the inferno began, as Virgil's did, "in a darksome wood." There he is threatened by a lion "rabid with hunger" and a she-wolf, but he soon encounters the great poet himself, to whom he professes his admiration as "the fount whence in a stream so full doth language flow." Indulging in a little harmless sucking up, Dante boasts:

> My master thou, and author thou,
>   alone!
> From thee alone I, borrowing,
>   could attain
> The style consummate which
>   has made me known.

In any case, Virgil, whose Aeneas has been there before, agrees to show Dante through hell. The passage—the entrance gate with its sigil "Ye who make entrance, every hope resign!"; the crossing by the reluctant Charon and the rest—are familiar from earlier tales. But who did Dante encounter there?

In canto 3, even before entering hell proper, Dante saw a shade he recognized: "I saw and knew of him, the search to close, whose dastard soul the great refusal made." By this he meant Pope Celestine V, whose refusal to perform the duties required of a pope led to his abdication a mere five months into his papacy, thereby allowing the ascension of the hated Boniface. He took his place in hell among the cowardly fence-sitters, or as Virgil tells it, those who neither honoured virtue nor disavowed it, who would never reach heaven nor be admitted to hell, along with "caitiff angels" (those angels who neither obeyed God nor joined Satan, an unpardonable sin), but would be left eternally to wail and complain "in uncouth accents and angry cries." Dante knew their fate: they were to be perpetually naked, fiercely stung by wasps and hornets, blood mingling with their tears sucked up by loathsome worms. And serve them right, in his view.

In the first circle (Limbo), Dante and Virgil encounter those worthy souls who lived before Christianity and baptism, and therefore could not be saved, a grim doctrine still debated by church fathers in the twenty-first century. Homer lived in that circle, for example, and so did Virgil, though he didn't encounter himself showing Dante around. These were people who were otherwise benign, but didn't rate saving because Jesus hadn't yet

been born—the virtuous heathens. Julius Caesar was to
be found there as well, and so was Marcia (Cato's wife)
and Julia, Caesar's daughter and later wife to Pompey.
More surprisingly, there were a few "Muhammadans"
as they were then called: Saladin (in the thirteenth and
fourteenth centuries the very epitome of a just Islamic
ruler), Avicenna, the Islamic physician whose canon was
the Bible (if we can use that word) for medical people for
centuries, and Averroes, the twelfth-century Cordovan
philosopher whose great commentary on Aristotle was
subsequently translated into Hebrew and then into Latin.
Aristotle himself was there, and Democritus, the founder
of atomic theory.

The second circle was the first of punishment, home
of the lustful, buffeted by storms (though seducers were
worse off, and lower down in hell). This circle contains
a judicious catalogue of carnal sinners, and was where
Dante began to settle old scores. Daringly Dido, Aeneas's
beloved, was there too, because for Aeneas she broke the
vow of chastity she made on her husband's death. Helen
of Troy was there. Alongside her is a more contemporary figure, Francesca, heroine of a famous scandal of
Dante's time: in 1275, she was married to Gianciotto (a.k.a.
"Deformed John") Malatesta, son of the lord of Rimini.
The marriage being one of political convenience, she fell
in love with Paolo, her husband's handsome brother, at
which point Gianciotto surprised the lovers and slew them
on the spot. In a brief diversion, Lancelot and Galahad
are there, because of their love for Guinevere. Cleopatra
and Tristan also rate a mention.

The third circle, the home of gluttons, is tormented by cold and filthy rain. Dante spends little time there, with only a perfunctory swipe at the worst offenders. Ciacco, a famous libertine and glutton (made famous by Boccaccio in *The Decameron*) can be found here, though Dante clearly doesn't think he was such a terrible fellow since he pauses to converse with him about how bad things really are. There is also another glancing mention of Boniface, and the "greedy and faithless" Charles of Valois, in hell for his capture of Florence.

The fourth circle was where the avaricious and the prodigal were to be found, condemned to roll weights in semi-circles, each trying desperately to access the other, to no avail. Dante found a few notorious sinners there, including cardinals and popes, but professed himself astonished that he could pick out no acquaintances of his own, saying to Virgil, "master, surely among all these I ought some few to recognize, who by such filthy sins were held in thrall." He did see a crowd "with shaven crowns." When he asks Virgil who they were, the elder poet responds:

> All of them squinted so
> In mental vision while in life they were,
> They nothing spent by rule.
>   And this they show,
> And with their yelping
>   voices make appear
> When half-way round the
>   circle they have sped,
> And sins opposing them asunder tear.

Each wanting thatch of
hair upon his head
Was once a clerk, or pope, or cardinal,
In whom abound the ripest
growths of greed.

The fifth circle was for the wrathful and the sullen. Nothing much to be said about them except to observe their torments, although the pagan Phlegyas gets a mention for burning the temple of Apollo at Delphi in revenge because the god had defiled his daughter—his appearance here remains mysterious. One of Dante's contemporaries does make a cameo: Filippo Argenti, a rich Florentine related to the great family of the Adimari, and an opponent of Dante's—his great sin was that he confiscated Dante's property after the poet's banishment from Florence. Elsewhere, Boccaccio describes him as a cavalier, very rich, and so ostentatious that he once shod his horse with silver, hence his surname.

The sixth circle is where the arch heretics are to be found, entombed in red-hot sepulchres. The tombs of the Epicureans, for example, are there—and no wonder: Epicurus was a Greek philosopher around 300 BC who was an "atomic materialist," which in practice meant he attacked everything he decided was superstitious and smacked of pseudo-divine management; the early Christians found his writings dangerous and fought to suppress them. This is also why Emperor Frederick II is here. Frederick, who reigned from 1220 to 1250, waged constant war with the popes for dominance of Italy. But it was not for this reason that Dante had him here, but rather for his radical free thinking. Otherwise the sixth circle is mainly populated by demons; there are picturesque descriptions of the circle's minarets, serving as bulwarks against the lower inferno, as well as the hellish Furies with snakes for their tresses, Medusa, Tisiphone (the moon), and the Gorgons. Still, there was one pope in the sixth: Pope Anastasius II, who reigned from 496 to 498 during the schism with Constantinople—his attempt at conciliation with the patriarchate of Constantinople was condemned by the Roman hierarchy as heretical. (Some think Dante meant the Byzantine emperor, Anastasius I, and simply got it wrong.)

The seventh circle has three rings of increasing awfulness: violence against neighbours (including tyrants and murderers); violence against the self (suicides) or against things (squanderers); and violence against god (blasphemers), including sodomites, and usurers. Dante lists some prominent sodomites, no doubt to their dissatisfaction. Suicides, bizarrely, are transformed into strange trees, while squanderers "are rent by bitches." One of the suicides is Pier delle Vigne, who rose from poverty to become chief counsellor to Frederick II; he committed suicide by bashing his brains out against a wall, reportedly because he tried to betray Frederick in favour of the hated pope. (Dante also acknowledged that he was a great poet.) Another contemporary of Dante's, and another suicide, was one Lano, a member of a "club of prodigals" who ran through their fortunes. Lano refused to escape from a battle, preferring to die than live in poverty. Another of the prodigals found here was Jacopo da Sant'Andrea, who was said to literally throw money away, and who once burned a house to the ground just to see the fire.

The Cretan Minotaur was the guardian of this circle. Alexander is here, but whether the Great or another tyrant is not known. The whole city of Sodom is here, obviously, but so is Cahors, a city in Languedoc that had a reputation as a hotbed of usurers, which seems a little unfair. Ezzelino Romano, the ruler of Veneto and an ally of Frederick II, is here because of his renowned cruelty, and so is Guy of Montfort, who murdered his cousin (among others) in a "river of blood"—also a reference to the Hadian river, Phlegethon.

Dante and Virgil also spy Azzolino of Romano, the Ghibeline leader, son-in-law of Frederick II, who was imperial vicar of the Trevisian Mark ("Cruelty, erected into a system, was his chief instrument of government, and in his dungeons men found something worse than death"). He died in 1259 of a wound received in battle. When urged to confess his sins by the monk who came to shrive him, he declared that the only sin on his conscience was negligence in revenge. Attila the Hun was here also, though James Romanes Sibbald, the eminent translator of Dante, thinks Dante confused him with Totila, the last of the Ostrogothic kings, who died in the sixth century. Here, too, is Pyrrhus of Epirus, who made the great error of warring on Rome. Lastly, to Dante's evident satisfaction, is Rinier of Corneto, who in Dante's time pillaged the Papal States with robbery and violence.

The third ring of the seventh circle contained nothing but burning sand and "great herds of naked souls, most piteously weeping every one."

And while that crowd was staring at me
    thus,
 One of them knew me, caught
    me by the gown,
And cried aloud: "Lo, this is marvellous!"
And straightway, while he
    thus to me held on,
I fixed mine eyes upon his
    fire-baked face,
And, spite of scorching, seemed
    his features known,
And whose they were my
    memory well could trace;
And I, with hand stretched
    toward his face below,
Asked: "Ser Brunetto! and
    is this your place?"
"O son," he answered, "no
    displeasure show,
 If now Brunetto Latini shall some way
Step back with thee, and
    leave his troop to go.

And so Dante dallies, holding converse with the scholar he revered in life, and as Sibbald writes, "he was the first to refine the Florentines, teaching them to speak correctly, and to administer State affairs on fixed principles of politics." While they speak, Dante is careful to stay on the narrow path, while the Fires of Sodom rain down on Brunetto's upturned face. Dante asks Brunetto who else was with him that he might recognize:

And he [said] to me: "To hear of some
   is well,
But of the rest 'tis fitting to be dumb,
And time is lacking all their
   names to spell.
That all of them were clerks,
   know thou in sum,
All men of letters, famous and of might;
Stained with one sin all from
   the world are come.
Priscian goes with that
   crowd of evil plight,
Francis d'Accorso too; and
   hadst thou mind
For suchlike trash thou
   mightest have had sight
Of him the Slave of Slaves
   to change assigned
From Arno's banks to
   Bacchiglione, where
His nerves fatigued with
   vice he left behind

Priscian, it seems, was a great grammarian of the
sixth century: he is listed here for no apparent reason.
D'Accorso, who died in 1294, was professor of civil law
at Bologna, and seems to have been an exemplary character in life; perhaps Dante had something on him no
one else knew. The "slave of slaves" reference is to Andrea
Mozzi, bishop of Florence in 1286. He was Dante's pastor

during his early manhood, and was said to be a man of dissolute manners.

The eighth circle has mostly to do with fraud of some kind: panders and seducers, scourged by demons; flatterers, immersed in excrement; simonists (where you can find a few more popes), head down in rock clefts, their feet tormented by flames; diviners, astrologists, magicians, art frauds, all with their heads on backwards; barrators plunged into boiling pitch, guarded by demons with prongs (curiously, many Sardinians are here); hypocrites, with caps of lead; thieves, bitten by a serpent, turned to ash and then restored, over and over; fraudulent counsellors, clothed in flames (Ulysses is here and so are a bunch of politicians from Romagna); sowers of scandal and schism, circling, perpetually wounded and then healed again (Muhammad is among them); falsifiers of metal (alchemists), plagued by scabs, lying on the earth scratching; counterfeiters of others' persons; counterfeiters of coins; counterfeiters of words (liars).

Dante then caught sight of a strange procession, a group of sinners whose heads were screwed on backwards, "and thus the face of every one round to his loins was turned . . . and their tears between their buttocks fell." One of these was Amphiaraüs, another of the seven kings who besieged Thebes, who foresaw his own death and sought by hiding to evade it (he was turned in by his furious wife).

The most prominent pope among the simonists in this circle was Nicholas III, famous in life for promoting his relatives to prominent churchly positions (Nicholas himself admitted he "favored the cubs" in his family—his family name was Orsini, or "little bears"). Because he is head down in a rocky cleft, he somehow mistakes Dante for Pope Boniface VIII, a galling mistake.

Dante name-drops quite a bit here: Guidoguerra, a Guelf leader; the cavalier James Rusticucci; the influential Florentine Tegghiaio, son of Aldobrand, of the Adimari family; William Borsiere, a famous wit; and Venedico Caccianimico, a Bolognese noble, brother of Ghisola, "whom he inveigled into yielding herself to the Marquis of Este, lord of Ferrara." Mostly, their sins are assumed, not spelled out. One whose sin is so spoken was that of Giovanni Buiamonte, known as the greatest usurer of them all. Others include Alessio Interminei, "so liberal in his flattery that he spent it even on menial servants."

There were more: Tiresias, who changed his sex in life, according to Ovid, "till for a man a woman met the sight, and not a limb its former semblance bore"; Manto, "whose flowing tresses hide her bosom, of which thou seest nought, and all whose hair falls on the further side" (Manto was a prophetess of Thebes and the city of Bacchus); and Michael Scot, "who knew the black art's inmost game"— Scot was an alchemist and the court astrologer to Frederick II, and much later a minor character in Walter Scott's *The Lay of the Last Minstrel* (in which his name was spelled with two *t*'s, though he was no relation to the poet); he famously foresaw his own death from a stone landing on his head.[1] Finally, another astrologer familiar to Dante: Guido Bonatti, renowned for being notorious without being noble, a damning judgment.

The ninth circle, the deepest and final, is where the residents need no introduction, as the saying goes. This is the central pit or well, where the last river of hell finally freezes. It is here that treacherous fraud is punished. Giants like Nimrod live here. Among them: Count Ugolino della Gherardesca (a.k.a. Gaddo), who was locked up in a tower ("the Tower of Hunger") with his four sons and left to die there. A nobleman of Pisa, he had been involved with Ghibeline/Guelf politics, and ran afoul of both factions. When the tower was finally opened, and the five corpses found still in chains, there were ghastly signs of the cannibalism that had transpired. Hard to see from all this why Gaddo was in hell, and not his jailers, but there it is.

This ninth circle itself has four rings, each one named after a prominent traitor. Caina (Cain) is the circle named for traitors against their kin—they are immersed in ice; Antenora (named after Antenor of Troy, who was Priam's counsellor during the Trojan War), where traitors to homeland or party can be found (the traitors gnaw at each other's heads); Ptolomaea (after Ptolemy), where traitors against their guests jut out from ice, their eyes sealed by frozen tears; and Judecca (Judas), reserved for traitors against their benefactor, who are completely covered in ice. Here you finally find Lucifer (or Dis), the emperor of the realm, his three mouths eternally rending Judas, Brutus, and Cassius. Judas is in the central jaws, head first, Brutus and Cassius feet first.

His poetic fancy at its height, Dante then slides down Lucifer's hairy flanks to his middle, the centre of the earth, before swinging around so he'll emerge head first in the southern hemisphere, where he catches a glimpse of strange constellations. As he climbs back up, he emerges into his own world to see the stars of dawn; the journey to the uttermost pit has taken twenty-four hours. It is now the morning of Easter Sunday, Resurrection Day, and Dante is free to travel to his next destination, Purgatorio, where we lose interest in him.[2]

Milton's hell contains no sinners, because there weren't any then. Lucifer fixed that

THERE WEREN'T ANY sinners in Milton's hell, at least not to start, because thus far there had been no one to actually sin. The first sinners, Adam and Eve, were only created well into the tale, and even they never went to hell. Indeed, little of the story is actually about hell, except for its opening scenes.

Paradise Lost is the story of the loss of innocence, of how Adam and Eve were created and how they came to lose their place in the Garden of Eden (located by Milton somewhere in present-day Lebanon, or possibly Libya). But the real hero of the tale, its main protagonist, more prominent even than God, was Lucifer—the not-yet-Satan, the Bringer of Light—and his downfall. I mentioned in an earlier chapter the opinion that Lucifer had drawn more bad press over the eons than he really deserved (and how God, in that view, could legitimately be perceived as a bit of a stick-in-the-mud). Well, in Milton's telling Lucifer is far from the grotesque black and hairy demon of Dante and the early Christian mystics. Instead, as Stephen Orgel and Jonathan Goldberg point out in the introduction to their 2008 edition of *Paradise Lost*, "he is a figure of genuinely heroic stature who cannot bear not being first—pride is the tragic flaw, the original sin. The classic model is Achilles, the flawed hero, but the greatest of heroes nonetheless. Lucifer's choice, not Eve's and Adam's, really constitutes the great moral exemplum in the poem. To say that the angels have free will but can only choose to obey is saying nothing at all: freedom implies, at a minimum, more than one choice. It is the rebel angels who make obedience meaningful—there is no notion of good without a notion of evil: we know things by their contraries."

This is not to say that hell was unpopulated. These "rebel angels" were legion: by Milton's estimate, "maybe the greatest half of all the angelick Body" rebelled and sided with Lucifer, "an host innumerable as the stars of night, or stars of morning, dew drops, which the Sun impearls on ev'ry leaf and ev'ry flower." That's quite a crowd and, again, doesn't say much for God's management skills. Still, for having raised "impious war in heaven and Battle Proud," the rebels were hurled "with hideous ruin and combustion, down to bottomless perdition."

And there the saga opens. Satan, as he is now known, meets Beelzebub (Hades) in hell, and attempts to enlist him in a second war against heaven. The two are lounging in a lake of fire at that point, a fire that gives off no light. Once they regain land, Satan suggests trying war again, to avenge his shameful defeat. Surely, he insists, all is not lost—we still have an unconquerable will, the thirst for revenge, an appetite for hate, and the courage never to submit:

That glory never shall [God's] wrath or
    might
Extort from me. To bow
    and sue for grace
With suppliant knee, and
    deify his power
Who, from the terror of
    this arm, so late
Doubted his empire—that
    were low indeed;
That were an ignominy and
    shame beneath
This downfall; since, by fate,
    the strength of Gods,
And this empyreal substance,
    cannot fail.

Our arms are not worse since our defeat, he declared,
and our foresight is much advanced, and so it is worth
trying again:

We may with more successful hope
    resolve
To wage by force or guile eternal war,
Irreconcilable to our grand Foe,
Who now triumphs, and
    in th' excess of joy
Sole reigning holds the
    tyranny of heaven.[3]

Satan clearly is keen on substituting the "mournful gloom" of hell for the celestial light, but Beelzebub is not so sure, and, in a speech full of guile and misdirection and flattery ("Oh leader of those armies bright which, but th' Omnipotent, none could have foiled!"), calls a gathering of the hellish elite: Moloch, "horrid king, besmeared with blood of human sacrifice and parents' tears"; then Chemos, "the obscene dread of Moab's sons"; Baal and Ashtoroth, who had both male and female parts (Astoreth, or Astarte, was the queen of heaven to the Phoenicians, with crescent horns); Thammaz (Ishtar's sometime consort), "whose annual wound in Lebanon allured the Syrian damsels to lament his fate"; Rimmon, who "against the House of God was bold"; and finally Belial, "than whom a Spirit more lewd Fell not from heaven, or more gross to love Vice for itself. To him no temple stood or altar smoked; yet who more oft than he in temples and at altars, when the priest turns atheist, as did Eli's sons, who filled With lust and violence the house of God?"

This motley crowd gathers on a hill, "whose grisly top belched fire and rolling smoke, and shone with a glossie scurff." There they build a royal camp, trenched a field and threw up a rampart; in this they were led by Mammon, "the least erected Spirit that fell from heaven; for even in heaven his looks and thoughts were always downward bent, admiring more the riches of heaven's pavement, trodden gold, than aught divine."

Quite a crew, as Beelzebub readily admits.

Then he calls all these and more to the newly created all-demon city of Pandemonium for a great consult. First Moloch has his say, calling for war and ever more war

against heaven until victory is assured, or oblivion: "No!
Let us rather choose, armed with hell-flames and fury, all
at once o'er heaven's high towers to force resistless way,
turning our tortures into horrid arms against the Tor-
turer; when, to meet the noise of his almighty engine, he
shall hear infernal thunder, and, for lightning, see black
fire and horror shot with equal rage among his angels."

But Beelzebub has a wilier way:

> What if we find
> Some easier enterprise? There is a place
> (If ancient and prophetic
>   fame in heaven
> Err not)—another World,
>   the happy seat
> Of some new race, called
>   Man, about this time
> To be created like to us, though less
> In power and excellence, but
>   favored more
> Of him who rules above. . . .
>
> Thither let us bend all our thoughts, to
>   learn
> What creatures there inhabit,
>   of what mold
> Or substance, how endued,
>   and what their power
> And where their weakness:
>   how attempted best,

By force or subtlety. Though
    heaven be shut,
And heaven's high Arbitrator sit secure
In his own strength, this
    place may lie exposed,
The utmost border of his kingdom, left
To their defense who hold
    it: here, perhaps,
Some advantageous act
    may be achieved
By sudden onset—either with hell-fire
To waste his whole creation, or possess
All as our own, and drive, as
    we were driven,
The puny habitants; or, if not drive,
Seduce them to our party,
    that their God
May prove their foe, and
    with repenting hand
Abolish his own works.

That is, Beelzebub suggests, God has favoured this new creature called Man, and if we can "seduce him to our party" (which should obviously be easy enough) we will have won a great victory through guile. Here is the key to the whole riddle: Lucifer could have merely said, "Well, we tried but lost, God was too much, let's give it up and go home." Or he could have joined with Moloch, and re-fought the lost fight. But he did neither. Instead, after much speechifying and with the approval of the mob, Satan assumes the task of subverting Adam and

Eve. He flies off, leaving through the nine gates, with the help of his incestuous offspring Sin and Death, and sets off to eavesdrop on Eden.

Thus endeth, to Milton, hell.

AFTER THAT, THE story is familiar enough from Genesis and other places. Satan finds the newly crafted Adam and Eve, becomes jealous, takes on the role of the serpent, mulls over the Trees of Life and Knowledge, and the temptation by Satan follows. God, who seems to have missed much of what is going on, commands the archangel Michael to escort the two new sinners from Eden—but not to hell, which for Milton is now out of the picture. If they lead virtuous lives henceforth, they can, in time, be reunited with God. After that comes Noah, the second creation of man, and the rest: reassured, Adam and Eve turn away, hand in hand with Michael, and wander out into the world.

Satan, and Lucifer, and Hell, and Beelzebub, and Moloch, and Mammon, and Belial—gone. Their role in the story is over.

CHAPTER 16

A BRIEF DETOUR
TO HEAVEN

Why is heaven so . . . bland?

THE HUMAN IMAGINATION HAS BEEN PROLIFIC IN its descriptions of hell, as we have seen. We have many eyewitness accounts and dreams of where it is, what it is, how its denizens behave, and what it is like to be there; tourists to hell have been two-a-penny over the ages, and we have followed some of their adventures. Not so much with heaven. You can comb the literature as much as you like, but heaven remains elusive. This may in part reflect the fact that most of the world's religions don't have a heaven at all, only a hell, so we are left with a reduced corpus, mostly from the major monotheisms (though even their writing is surprisingly thin when it comes to heaven). And much of what has been written is the worst kind of literary cliché. Clearly the idea of such beatific magnificence has intimidated all but the very brave, or, more frequently, enabled the very superficial—I give you streets paved with pure gold, clear as glass, a decorator's banal vision. Bright lights are common (sometimes described as "awful" bright lights); there is lots of dancing and singing and crying hosannas, and souls flitting about, though seldom described. Sometimes there is grass, and meadows, and more rarely a river or two; ever-bearing fruit trees can occasionally be found.

Unlike hell, tourists to heaven have been few. In the last decade or so in the United States there has been a mini-industry of morning-television explications of having been to heaven and back, but these have all, obviously enough, been easily debunked. Alex Malarkey has publicly disavowed his 2010 book, *The Boy Who Came Back from Heaven*; Colton Burpo's story of his own trip to heaven in 2011, recounted in his book *Heaven Is for Real*—in which he described a blue-eyed Jesus, bizarrely bobbing up and down, and in which he chats with John the Baptist—has yet to be retracted, but is only given credence in the outer fringes of the Christian right, and in the pages of the *Daily Mail*. There is also the contentious book *Proof of Heaven*, taken *sort of* seriously at first because it was written by a neurosurgeon, Eben Alexander, but soon dismissed as a new-agey fantasy (possibly because Alexander reported, among other fantastical events, that he was in a deep coma for seven days, during which time, often guided by a beautiful girl riding a giant butterfly, he flew around the invisible, spiritual side of existence, and there encountered God, whom Alexander frequently refers to as Om, the sound he recalls as "being associated with that omniscient, omnipotent and unconditionally loving God"). Scientific training, evidently, is no defence against radical foolishness.[1]

I liked Robin Williams's picture of heaven better: seats always near the front, Mozart and Elvis playing, and God as a stand-up cracking religious jokes. More earnestly, C.S. Lewis, in *The Problem of Pain*, called heaven "totally unspatial and non-temporal, giving the mind no basis for images and nothing to imagine," which is a bit unhelpful. Who wants to go *there*?

I couldn't find many harps in the stories, except in the visions of ten-penny preachers, but there are sometimes gates, pearly or not. Still, there are plenty of descriptions of the "residence of God, including Jesus Christ [which] is where the dead martyrs and saints are to be found; this is the location of the throne of God and where the holy angels surrounding his throne sing day and night, Holy, Holy, Holy is the Lord our God."[2]

Whether you find this exhilarating or tedium person-ified depends on your perspective and your idea of joy.

Conservative Protestants believe, if I interpret their credo correctly, that heaven is a wonderful place where there is no pain, disease, sex, or depression, and where people live in the presence of Jesus Christ in new-and-improved spiritual bodies that are immune to death. Once again, you can choose to be thrilled at this. Or at parts of it. Or not. Whatever your view, it is not particularly descriptive or helpful in building a picture of what the heavenly geography actually looks like.

So where can we turn?

Plutarch had a go at heaven. His version is nicely bucolic.

PLUTARCH, THE GREEK (and later Roman) writer most famous for his biographical studies, did have one go at heaven, or Elysium, in his case. In his *Life of Sertorius*, he was quite specific about it, if rather off-message on its whereabouts. He seemed, rather, to be writing from a farmer's point of view:

> [Elysium] is two in number, separated by a very narrow strait; they are ten thousand furlongs distant from Africa. . . . They enjoy moderate rains at long intervals, and winds which for the most part are soft and precipitate dews, so that the islands not only have a rich soil which is excellent for plowing and planting, but also produce a natural fruit that is plentiful and wholesome enough to feed, without toil or trouble, a leisured folk.
>
> Moreover, an air that is salubrious, owing to the climate and the moderate changes in the seasons, prevails on the islands. For the north and east winds which blow out from our part of the world plunge into fathomless space, and, owing to the distance, dissipate themselves and lose their power before they reach the islands; while the south and west winds that envelope the islands sometimes bring in their train soft and intermittent showers, but for the most part cool them

with moist breezes and gently nourish
the soil.[3]

If you weren't a farmer in life, that sounds like a lot of
work, what with all that plowing and so forth, though I
suppose it would be good to be a farmer with no pests
to deal with, and no harsh weather. Even so, not much
time for harps and hymns. Leave that for the Christians.

Dante, alas, wasn't interested in heavenly landscaping

NOR DOES HE really know where heaven is to be found,
except that it is "up there." Dante, who seldom disap-
points, has ten heavens, or spheres, one more than there
are levels in hell, one to each planet, including the moon,
and one to the sun and "fixed stars." Since his was still
a geocentric universe, with the earth at the centre of
everything and all the other stars and planets revolving
around it, these heavens were relatively easy to place. The
revolution of each sphere creates a different musical note,
so the sky is bursting with the marvellous "music of the
spheres," but as to what each sphere actually looks like
Dante is generally silent.

Much of his *Paradiso* is even gabbier than his *Inferno*,
and in it he name-drops even more shamelessly, but then
his interest is in personal redemption and not heaven as a
place—he is concerned with a close investigation of what
kind of people made it to heaven, not with geography or
topography. In only a few cantos is landscape mentioned.
For example, in the final canto, when Dante is finally

at the highest sphere of heaven, he sees a river flowing
between two flowered riverbanks, like rubies set into gold:

> As when the lightning, in a sudden
>   spleen
> Unfolded, dashes from the
>   blinding eyes
> The visive spirits dazzled
>   and bedimm'd;
> So, round about me,
>   fulminating streams
> Of living radiance play'd, and
>   left me swath'd
> And veil'd in dense impenetrable blaze.
> Such weal is in the love, that
>   stills this heav'n;
> For its own flame the torch
>   this fitting ever!
>
> No sooner to my list'ning ear had come
> The brief assurance, than I understood
> New virtue into me infus'd, and sight
> Kindled afresh, with vigour to sustain
> Excess of light, however pure. I look'd;
> And in the likeness of a river saw
> Light flowing, from whose
>   amber-seeming waves
> Flash'd up effulgence, as they glided on
> 'Twixt banks, on either side,
>   painted with spring,
> Incredible how fair; and, from the tide,

> There ever and anon, outstarting, flew
> Sparkles instinct with life;
>   and in the flow'rs
> Did set them, like to rubies
>   chas'd in gold;
> Then, as if drunk with
>   odors, plung'd again
> Into the wondrous flood;
>   from which, as one
> Re'enter'd, still another rose.[4]

Well, that sounds attractive.

But Beatrice, Dante's great unrequited love in life (though here she seems mostly a scold), tells the poet that he should slake his thirst from the river; she adds, though, that nothing he is seeing is real, because he has not yet learned how to see properly. Dante hurries to the river, and as he bathes in its brilliance the water itself seems to change before his eyes—it is no longer straight, but round, and all the flowers and gems come into focus; they are really the two hosts of heaven—the angels and the blessed saints sitting in heaven's court.

So that doesn't help much.

The gaudiest heaven is that of Revelation

THE BIBLE ISN'T much more informative. We know more or less what Adam and Eve's paradise looked like, but it is unclear whether that really serves as heaven (though it is true that Genesis has God wandering through the shrubbery on more than one occasion, so if it isn't heaven, it's a close neighbour).

As Genesis says, God planted a garden "eastward in Eden," and

> there he put the man whom he had formed. And out of the ground made the Lord God to grow every tree that is pleasant to the sight, and good for food; the tree of life also in the midst of the garden, and the tree of knowledge of good and evil. And a river went out of Eden to water the garden; and from thence it was parted, and became into four heads. The name of the first is Pison: that is it which compasseth the whole land of Havilah, where there is gold; And the gold of that land is good: there is bdellium and the onyx stone. And the name of the second river is Gihon: the same is it that compasseth the whole land of Ethiopia. And the name of the third river is Hiddekel: that is it which goeth toward the east of Assyria. And the fourth river is Euphrates.

Genesis obviously thinks highly of gold and onyx as well as bdellium, a kind of resinous gum, but places those worthy substances outside paradise proper, in the land of Havilah, thought to be somewhere in Arabia.

It has to be said that all this contains a lot of superfluous detail, and not much that is decently descriptive.

THE ONLY REAL depiction of heaven in the Bible is in Revelation, and a gaudy thing it is too (notice those Pearly Gates!), with an over-the-top decor worthy of America's forty-fifth president. Wrote John of Patmos:

> And he [the angel] carried me away in the spirit to a great and high mountain, and shewed me that great city, the holy Jerusalem, descending out of heaven from God,
>
> Having the glory of God: and her light was like unto a stone most precious, even like a jasper stone, clear as crystal;
>
> And had a wall great and high, and had twelve gates, and at the gates twelve angels, and names written thereon, which are the names of the twelve tribes of the children of Israel:
>
> On the east three gates; on the north three gates; on the south three gates; and on the west three gates.
>
> And the wall of the city had twelve foundations, and in them the names of the twelve apostles of the Lamb.
>
> And he that talked with me had a golden reed to measure the city, and the gates thereof, and the wall thereof.
>
> And the city lieth foursquare, and the length is as large as the breadth: and he measured the city with the reed, twelve thousand furlongs. The length and the breadth and the height of it are equal.

And he measured the wall thereof, an hundred and forty and four cubits, according to the measure of a man, that is, of the angel.

And the building of the wall of it was of jasper: and the city was pure gold, like unto clear glass.

And the foundations of the wall of the city were garnished with all manner of precious stones. The first foundation was jasper; the second, sapphire; the third, a chalcedony; the fourth, an emerald;

The fifth, sardonyx; the sixth, sardius; the seventh, chrysolyte; the eighth, beryl; the ninth, a topaz; the tenth, a chrysoprasus; the eleventh, a jacinth; the twelfth, an amethyst.

And the twelve gates were twelve pearls: every several gate was of one pearl: and the street of the city was pure gold, as it were transparent glass.

And I saw no temple therein: for the Lord God Almighty and the Lamb are the temple of it.

And the city had no need of the sun, neither of the moon, to shine in it: for the glory of God did lighten it, and the Lamb is the light thereof.

And the nations of them which are saved shall walk in the light of it: and the

kings of the earth do bring their glory and
honor into it.

And the gates of it shall not be shut at
all by day: for there shall be no night there.

To save you the tedium of conversion, all those furlongs would make a 2,400 kilometre cube—big, but a
bit crowded for the billions who must live there today.
And okay, *technically* it is hanging down from heaven,
which is where God is, rather than being heaven itself,
but close enough. A solemn commentary on the website
godandscience.org speculates that this must mean there
is no gravity in this New Jerusalem, because "structures
of this size would automatically become a sphere in
[our] universe because of gravity." As for the glitter and
the bling, it reminds me of the story commonly told by
preachers, about the rich man who was so pious that he
persuaded God to bend the rules and allow him to bring
some of his possessions to heaven. Saint Peter, checking
him in, told him to open the heavy suitcase that was his
carry-on, and found it stuffed with gold bullion. "What!"
he exclaimed, "you brought *pavement* to heaven?"

Can anyone else shed any light?

WHAT ABOUT JUDAISM and heaven? Just as with hell,
Jewish views of heaven are generally dull stuff—largely
because Jewish culture generally focuses on the community, and on living virtuous lives in the present and on
earth. As the delightful website called jewfaq.org puts
it, "traditional Judaism firmly believes that death is not

the end of human existence; however, because Judaism is primarily focused on life here and now rather than on the afterlife, Judaism does not have much dogma about the afterlife, and leaves a great deal of room for personal opinion. It is possible for an Orthodox Jew to believe that the souls of the righteous dead go to a place similar to the Christian heaven, or that they are reincarnated through many lifetimes, or that they simply wait until the coming of the messiah, when they will be resurrected." Likewise, Orthodox Jews can believe that the souls of the wicked are tormented by demons of their own creation, or that wicked souls are simply destroyed at death, and thereafter cease to exist. Constant study is the be-all and end-all of Jewish heaven. In the Mishnah (the compilation known as the Oral Torah) a rabbi put it this way: "This world is like a lobby before the Olam Ha-Ba [the world to come]. Prepare yourself in the lobby so that you may enter the banquet hall." And again: "This world is like the eve of Shabbat, and he who prepares on the eve of Shabbat will have food to eat on Shabbat. We prepare ourselves for the Olam Ha-Ba through Torah study and good deeds."

The writer Dennis Prager has said, wryly: "I remember one of my yeshiva rabbis telling us students that heaven is eternal study of the Torah. Now this may well have sounded terrific to my rabbi, but all I recall is wondering what the alternative is like—and I actually *liked* studying the Torah."[5]

So, not much help there.

HOW ABOUT ISLAM? Can Islam help us out? To some degree, yes. Islam is not bad on the topography, geography, climate, and vegetation to be found in heaven (or more precisely, "paradise").

Paradise is located "above the seventh sky and underneath the Throne," which is so far not helpful. Still, there is much to be said for it. "Paradise is the abode of peace, enjoyment, and happiness. Allah prepared it for the Muslims. It contains rivers of pure honey, milk, and non-intoxicating wine, different from the wine of this world, and other everlasting enjoyments."

Heaven, in the Qur'an, is an "oasis of oases, rinsed with sweet waters, with rivers running on it and under it, and with springs opening unbidden."[6] Enjoyment in Paradise is experienced by both body and soul. As multiple Islamic commentaries describe it, Paradise has different levels, some of which are higher than the others, the highest reserved for the prophets. Residents will not grieve, grow old, or die, but will have everlasting bliss. Some Muslim commentators provide further hints. Ibn Kathir, who died in 1373, in his Quranic commentary had this to say: "The Prophet Muhammad was heard saying: 'The smallest reward for the people of paradise is an abode where there are 80,000 servants and 72 wives, over which stands a dome decorated with pearls, aquamarine, and ruby, as wide as the distance from Al-Jabiyyah [a Damascus suburb] to Sana'a [the capital of present-day Yemen].'"[7]

It must be a good size, though its girth in furlongs is not known. "The Muslims there will be as tall as Prophet Adam, that is, 60 cubits [about 27 metres]. All Muslims there will be at the age of thirty three. The men will be without beards and they will have the beauty of Prophet Yusuf [Joseph in the Bible], peace be upon him."

What about women, always a touchy issue in Islamic thought? There are those "72 wives," for a start, so the women will all have to share. "People will be married and have interaction [sic] with one another, there will be no single [people] there; even the infant who had died on the day he was born will enter Paradise and marry there. The female would be married in Paradise to whomever Allah has willed for her to marry. Those in Paradise will have ranks according to their piety. Those who will be rewarded with Paradise will never be sent out of it. . . . Wives of the human will be everlastingly his. . . . There are also the *houris*, they are females whom Allah created, they are not humans or *djinn* and they will be married to those men whom Allah had willed for them to marry."

These *houris* would be pleasant to be around. "If one of them would appear in this world, she would fill what is between the east and the west with nice fragrance."

And all will be clean, no mess to pick up or to disturb the peace. "In Paradise there will not be what the self hates; there is no menstrual bleeding, no urine, no feces, or sweat that produces dirt; the sweat of the dwellers of Paradise will be like the musk." No need, then, for septic systems or garbage collection.

It is not clear whether there are animals in Paradise (except for flying horses; see below), and if there are, it is unclear where the holy slaughterhouse is. There are certainly trees. "The people of Paradise will live in uninterrupted enjoyments which will be always renewed, so for every fruit which the believer cuts in Paradise another fruit would grow in its place, the fruit there looks like the jar; the trees in Paradise have trunks of gold. When the trees of Paradise move they would make a beautiful sound which moves the selves, it is nicer than the sound of music."

Residents can get around in one of two ways: they will have flying beds crowned with aquamarine, pearls, and rubies; or, alternatively, on "horses made of rubies with wings made of gold at the service of the people of Paradise . . . [which] transport the person to wherever he wants within a blink of an eye; they would not find difficulty in riding them." A nice touch that: driverless horses.[8]

Not very heavenly, is it?

EVEN SO, IF this is the best the human imagination can cook up for the everlasting glory of heaven . . . it is pretty thin gruel. If nothing else, it shows a striking poverty of invention, especially when set against the inventiveness of the many visions of hell discussed above, and against the magnificent scale of the actual universe, the universe without myth, the universe-as-it-is, the universe in which we actually pass our actual days.

As our knowledge of the scale of the universe increases—and as cosmologists discover thousands more planets circling suns just like our own—the notion that we should rely on an ever-attentive god to punish those we fail to punish ourselves comes to seems embarrassingly self-centred. Can god really be that parochial, some sort of divine chum who will balance the scales on our behalf, while we look on in complacency? Can we really call him

Dad instead of Father? At the same time, the mirroring notion that an ever-present tempter has caused, say, Adolf Eichmann, or Ted Bundy, to do their work has come to seem increasingly naïve. Instead, we move to an understanding that hell is internal, or, as Milton put it, that it comprises the gnawing of the worm within (in *Paradise Lost* he has Satan lamenting, "Which way I flie is hell; my self am hell").

Perhaps it would be a more interesting and magical world if Ereshkigal and Baal and Ishtar and Yama and Hades were real (though Satan not so much, nor Baal's unruly sister)—but alas, they're not. Except in the human imagination, where they belong.

What's going on is our fault, not theirs.

EPILOGUE

BELIEF IN GODS AND DEVILS HAS BEEN A FORCE FOR stability and order over the millennia, no? For good, even?

It is often so argued, anyway.

Yet consider what happened after Christianity supplanted the chaotic but essentially pliant polytheisms of the Greeks and Romans. After Theodosius declared Christianity the sole authorized religion of imperial Rome (in 380), the formerly put-upon Christians went on a revenge rampage: not just widespread vandalism of "pagan" temples and artifacts, in the Taliban manner, but countless lynchings and atrocities too. For example, as Catherine Nixey recounts, "in Alexandria in 415 CE, the philosopher and teacher Hypatia was mobbed, stoned, flayed, ripped to pieces and burned by a gang of Christians, who accused her of witchcraft." Thereafter classical learning, literature, and philosophy were all suspect. "Being pious in the new faith meant not only participating in public religious practice but also a moulding of hearts, minds, art, architecture and reading matter to fit the new 'reality.'"[1]

Was this political or religious? Or both?

Whichever it was, for more than a thousand long years after *that* (except for a few luminous intermissions, like the fleeting Carolingian Renaissance in the ninth century) church-driven obscurantism and intolerance reigned, witches and heretics were burned, the peasantry sank into a glum torpor (to emerge in furious violence every few half-centuries), literacy—such as it was—retreated to the monasteries and cloisters that offered feeble shelter in the intellectual gloom (the monks themselves ever fearful of the demon-ridden world without), knights and their masters warred and killed and pillaged, kingdoms came and went. No, the church didn't cause the Dark Ages; that was due more to the disintegration of empire, the dissolution of civic authority—and plague. And in any case, the *other* church, that of Islam, kept the bright flame of intellectual activity alive. But . . . the Christian church surely didn't help. For all those dismal centuries church fathers took seriously Saint Augustine's notorious admonition to abjure intellectual effort as inherently sinful. "There is another form of temptation, even more fraught with danger," the good saint told his followers. "This is the disease of curiosity. It is this which drives us to try and discover the secrets of nature which are beyond our understanding, which can avail us nothing, and which man should not wish to learn."

"Remind yourselves," Yuval Harari admonishes, "that centuries ago millions of Christians locked themselves inside a self-reinforcing mythological bubble, never daring to question the factual veracity of the Bible, while millions of Muslims put their unquestioning faith in the Qur'an. For millennia, much of what passed for 'news' and 'facts' in human social networks were stories about miracles, angels, demons and witches, with bold reporters giving live coverage straight from the deepest pits of the underworld."[2]

It wasn't just that a life without God and the devil was too frightening to contemplate; through much of this period, it was almost impossible to imagine a system of divine justice that didn't involve punishment, because hellfire had become a central tenet of Christian doctrine. The communitarian (not to say communist) ethos of Christianity's founders, with its injunctions to charity and humility, gave way to official rage. Shape up (listen to your betters) or ship out (be consigned to hell) had become the whole point.

It's not hard to find stern warnings in church councils, ancient and less ancient:

+ "If we do the will of Christ, we shall obtain rest; but if not, if we neglect his commandments, nothing will rescue us from eternal punishment." (Second Clement 5:5, 150 CE)

+ "No more is it possible for the evildoer, the avaricious, and the treacherous to hide from God than it is for the virtuous. Every man will receive the eternal punishment or reward which his actions deserve. Indeed, if all men recognized this, no one would choose evil even for a short time, knowing that he would incur the eternal sentence of fire. On the contrary, he would take every means to control himself and to adorn himself in virtue, so that he might obtain the good gifts of God and escape the punishments." (Justin Martyr, First Apology 12, 151 CE)

+ "For the unbelievers and for the contemptuous and for those who do not submit to the truth but assent to iniquity, when they have been involved in adulteries, and fornications, and homosexualities, and avarice, and in lawless idolatries, there will be wrath and indignation, tribulation and anguish; and in the end, such men as these will be detained in everlasting fire" (Theophilus of Antioch, To Autolycus 1:14, ca. 160 CE)

+ "To the lovers of evil shall be given eternal punishment. The unquenchable and unending fire awaits these latter, and a certain fiery worm which does not die and which does not waste the body but continually bursts forth from the body with unceasing pain. No sleep will give them rest; no night will soothe them; no death will deliver them from punishment; no appeal of interceding friends will profit them." (Hippolytus, Against the Greeks 3, 212 CE)

+ "But if anyone dies unrepentant in the state of mortal sin, he will undoubtedly be tormented forever in the fires of an everlasting hell." (A letter to the

Bishop of Tusculum, 1254, from Pope Innocent IV [1243–54])[3]

But still . . . Even in the medieval
despond, resisters could be found

AS PHILIP ALMOND put it in his profile of the devil, by "1550 it was as impossible not to believe in the devil as it was impossible not to believe in God." Or, as Arthur Conan Doyle wrote in his novel *The White Company*, "Man walked in fear and solemnity, with Heaven very close above his head, and Hell below his very feet. God's visible hand was everywhere, in the rainbow and the comet, in the thunder and the wind. The Devil, too, raged openly upon the earth; he skulked behind the hedgerows in the gloaming; he laughed loudly in the night-time; he clawed the dying sinner, pounced on the unbaptized babe, and twisted the limbs of the epileptic."

But could you reject both?

There were flickers of independent thinking among the embers of intellectual life, and here and there a skeptic was to be found, reprising the ancient Greeks and forerunners of the Enlightenment itself. Some think, indeed, that skepticism was widespread. John Arnold, professor of medieval history at Cambridge, has argued that even in medieval Christendom the notion of a single, unified faith was a mirage, and that there was always a spectrum of belief and unbelief. He maintains, therefore, that the dark vision conventionally ascribed to the Dark Ages is just not accurate.[4]

Take defiant Thomas Tailour of Newbury, England (to whom this book is deferentially dedicated), who was punished in 1491 for calling pilgrims fools, denying the power of prayer, and doubting the survival of the soul after death. At his trial for heresy, Tailour reaffirmed his ridicule of those who went as pilgrims to Santiago de Compostela in Spain, the reputed site of the tomb of the apostle James, because "seynt Jamys had no fote to come ayenst them no hand to welcome theym neither tonge to speak to theym," but was just a piece of stone, no more. When a man or woman dies in the body they also die in their soul, he declared, for as the light of a candle is put out by casting it away or in other ways quenched by blowing or shaking it, "so is the soul quenched by death." For this heresy he was sentenced to public penance, and was lucky to escape the death sentence, though he remained under threat of execution by burning should he repeat his offence.

Also in 1491, Isabel Dorte of Berkshire admitted that she had spoken openly ayenst worshipping no ymages of seynts and pilgrams doying, shewing that no man shuld wourship no stykes nor stonys ne nothing made or graven with mannysd hand. She was arraigned for heresy, and sentenced to go on a pilgrimage herself. Around the same time, William Carpenter was prosecuted for casting aspersions on the clergy, asserting that it were better to geve a poreman a peny to them adding hereto that offeryges be made but only for the availe and lucre of the pristis and not for the soule helthe. And Alice Hignell, also of Newbury (clearly a hotbed of freethinkers, or Lollard heretics, as they were called), was satirical about statues of saints and others: why could the Virgin Mary not do a simple thing like blow a cobweb off her [statue's] face? Hignell's sentence was not to go farther than four miles from home without a bishop's licence.[5]

Similar small trials and confessions can be found in the national archives of France, Italy, and Spain.

The Enlightenment and Voltaire's nose

THEN CAME THE Renaissance, and the Enlightenment, and the gradual accession of the Copernican world view, and a renewed interest in the *mechanics* of it all (*how* it worked), and a growing skepticism. By the seventeenth century, satirists like Voltaire could mock the notion that man is created in God's image ("The nose was of course designed to fit spectacles," as he put it); and he suggested, as some of the gnostic gospels had more than a millennium earlier, that perhaps the world was created by the devil at a moment when God was distracted, his attention momentarily elsewhere. (It is worth noting, however, that Voltaire was no atheist despite his pithy "si Dieu n'existait pas, il faudrait l'inventer"—he was just against false gods, Jehovah in particular.)

Still, it was slowly becoming safe to assert the non-existence of the devil. As Philip Almond says in his profile of the devil, "it wasn't until Spinoza (1632–1677) that the devil's existence [but not yet God's] was denied altogether. There was only one substance—God—who was identified with Nature. Satan [had become] unnecessary: 'For we have no need, as others do, to posit devils in order to have causes of hate, envy, anger, and such passions. We have come to know them sufficiently with-out the air of such fictions'"—thus mimicking Epicurus. And so at last savants could say without fear things that had been commonplace fifteen hundred years earlier. It wasn't atheism yet, but it wasn't far off.

As David Brooks of *The New York Times* put it in early 2017, "the Enlightenment included thinkers like John Locke and Immanuel Kant who argued that people should stop deferring blindly to authority for how to live. Instead, they should think things through from the ground up, respect facts and skeptically re-examine their own assumptions and convictions. Enlightenment thinkers turned their skeptical ideas into skeptical insti-tutions, notably the U.S. Constitution."[6] The American Founders' Enlightenment thinking certainly understood that religion could be a "mind-forg'd manacle," as William Blake once put it.

As the Enlightenment progressed, Satan lost some of his sting, though he was not yet toothless. Even as witty a reporter as Daniel Defoe, while he could "correct" Satan's biography, and was more than willing to point out Milton's many theological blunders, didn't really dismiss the devil altogether, though he was willing to shift some of the blame:

> Bad as he is, the Devil may be abus'd,
> Be falsly charg'd, and causelesly accus'd,
> When Men, unwilling to
>   be blam'd alone,
> Shift off these Crimes on Him
>   which are their Own.

Defoe *seemed* to be dismissing Satan in his 1726 book *The History of the Devil, As Well Ancient as Modern: In Two Parts*, but he was really only shifting focus:

> No wonder then that he has chang'd hands too, and that he has left off pawawing in these Parts of the World; that we don't find our Houses disturb'd as they used to be, and the Stools and Chairs walking about out of one Room into another, as formerly; that Children don't vomit crooked Pins and rusty stub Nails, as of old, their Air is not full of Noises, nor the Church-yard full of Hobgoblins; Ghosts don't walk about in Winding-Sheets; and the good old scolding Wives visit and plague their Husbands after they are dead, as they did when they were alive. The Age is grown too wise to be agitated by these dull scare-crow Things which their Forefathers were tickled with; Satan has been obliged to lay-by his Puppet-shews and his Tumblers, those things are grown stale; his morrice-dancing Devils, his mountebanking and quacking won't do now.

Sure, Defoe suggested, the old-fashioned stuff—the magicians and necromancers and warlocks and witches—were no longer efficacious, and could safely be ridiculed as rank superstition. But it wasn't that the devil had disappeared. It was just that he would be *smoother* now, more urbane, able to capture men's minds via trickery and persuasion and not by frightening the hell out of them. He didn't need to "pawaw" anymore; he just needed to attend salons.

So is Satan now toothless? Scoffed out of existence?

ON THE FACE of it, it does seem that hell, like Satan himself, has lost its sting. The phrases are now trotted out without any sense of their residual meaning. *To hell and gone. The hell with it. Go to hell. It is hellishly hot* . . . Hell is just an epithet, not a place; as Michael Gerson put it in the *Washington Post*, "For a lot of people, hell is little more than a mental holding place for Hitler."[7]

Carol Zaleski, in her *Encyclopedia Britannica* article on national hells, suggested that "In the modern world, especially in the West, cultural shifts caused by the Enlightenment, 19th-century liberalism, and the psychotherapeutic culture of the late 20th century have contributed to a decline in the belief in an everlasting hell." In this view, evil was caused by misfiring synapses and failed education, nothing more. Indeed, the whole idea of god and the devil began to seem increasingly obsolete, concepts unworthy of free men. Thus, the notion that men and women should bow down and worship some unseen abstraction came to seem more and more undignified (the very word "worship" is cringe-making in itself); similarly, the idea that anyone should debase himself as a miserable sinner just because a long-ago, know-nothing ecclesiastic says he should seems . . . primitive.[8]

Indeed, some prominent conservative Christians believe the whole Western tradition has gone badly off the rails. Christian Smith, a sociologist at Notre Dame, asserts that "Moralistic Therapeutic Deism" has displaced authentic Christianity as the true religion of American Christians: "the perfect religion for a self-centered, consumerist culture," as Rod Dreher put it in *The New York Times*.[9] Dreher himself is a prominent conservative, but (and?) also a prominent gloomster. His solution, if it can be called that, calls for Christians to strategically withdraw from our "degraded" culture, leaving the rest of us to collapse into irrelevance.

It's true that the Roman Catholic Church's official Catechism still insists on the validity of hell as an actual place where actual sinners go to be actually punished. ("The teaching of the Church affirms the existence of hell and its eternity. Immediately after death the souls of those who die in a state of mortal sin descend into hell, where they suffer the punishments of hell, eternal fire.") The online *Catholic Encyclopedia* says much the same. The church hierarchy may be undecided about it, but the authors are steadfast: only "atheists and Epicureans" do not believe in it.

But wait a minute . . . The Vatican has also said that "the chief punishment of hell is eternal separation from God, in whom alone man can possess the life and happiness for which he was created and for which he longs." And even this clever hedge has been diluted—by the Vatican itself. Pope John Paul II suggested that the church was rapidly backing away from hell as a real place, saying instead that the Bible uses a "symbolic language which must be interpreted correctly." A correct interpretation, in his view, would define hell as "the state of those who freely and definitively separate themselves from God, the source of all life and joy." Confusingly, an evangelical document issued in 2000 declared that while biblical images of burning lakes "are not to be taken literally, they do symbolize the horrors that are in store for people who reject Christian teachings," which is known as having it both ways.

In the middle of 2017, the newly elected head of the Jesuits, the Venezuelan Arturo Sosa, pooh-poohed the whole idea of a malicious fiend—he, too, said the devil was just an idea, an expression of man's alienation from God. From this perspective, then, hell is not a punishment imposed externally by God but rather the inevitable development of premises already set by people in this life. As Sosa put it, "The very dimension of unhappiness which this obscure condition brings can in a certain way be sensed in the light of some of the terrible experiences we have suffered which, as is commonly said, make life hell." So much for the vengeful Saint Augustine's assertion that "knowledge of the torments of the damned is part of heavenly bliss" (though it's true Augustine did suggest that those who committed lesser offences, like overeating and laughing too much, might be let off after a bout of purgatorial fire). And Francis, the current pontiff, suggested that even atheists, if basically nice folk, could get to heaven too—and more easily than hypocritical Catholics at that. Cue conniptions in the Vatican hierarchy.

Another brief flurry of ecclesiastical shock-and-horror came just before Easter 2018, when an Italian journalist suggested that the pope had mused to him that hell wasn't a real thing but merely a convenient metaphor. This was hurriedly walked back by the ideologues of the Curia, but in fact it would have surprised no one if Francis had in fact said what he was quoted as saying.

But hell is hanging in, despite it all. And so is Satan

AND YET . . . THE idea of hell and its punishments persists, and in more than one not-so-obscure corner of the religious universe. As David Brooks put it in his column on the Enlightenment, "Enlightenment figures perpetually tell themselves that religion is dead (it isn't)." Removing hell from Christian doctrine leaves a hell-sized hole in the afterlife narrative: major religions are not used to not having answers. If there is nothing to fear, why be sinless? Thus, as Almond says, "The existence of the Devil, and his capacity to act in history, nature and human lives, remains for many Christians, both Protestant and Catholic, a satisfactory explanation of natural misfortune and human suffering, mitigated by the paradoxical conviction that, at the end of the day, Satan is carrying out God's will, and that, at the end of history, he will be defeated and eternally punished for doing so."[10]

Carol Zaleski again: "Defenders of the belief regard this [disbelief in hell] as a lamentable loss of nerve, of faith, and of moral seriousness. Hell may not be wished away, in their view, but must be conquered—by the merciful savior who liberates the spirits from bondage, by the overpowering force of divine forgiveness, or by a final battle, the ultimate outcome of which, some hope, will be hell emptied, hell despoiled."

Islam, for its part, still officially believes in hell, and this is true not just of the jihadis and other fundamentalists now peopling our universe with such ferocious fecundity: believers don't only accept the joys of martyrdom; they know that unbelievers are to spend eternity in hell, a place every bit as real as paradise. As the Qur'an has it, the existence of hell is a testimony to God's sovereignty and justice, and stands as a warning of the stark choices to be made—between righteousness and iniquity, eternal life and eternal death. At the end, God will bring his creation to a close, raise the dead, and judge them every one, committing each to the fate he deserves, the joys of paradise or the terrors of hell. "They will long to leave the fire, but never will they leave therefrom; and theirs will be a lasting torment."[11] Imam Kamil Mufti is adamant: "Hell exists at the present time and will continue to exist forever. It will never die down, and its inhabitants will remain in it forever. The . . . unbelievers will reside in it forever."[12]

Nor is it just "official" Islam that acknowledges the potency of Satan. Islam Issa, author of *Milton in the Arab-Muslim World*, suggested in a 2017 column in *The Guardian* that Muslims generally believe in the devil's existence more than any other religious group. "Belief in his day-to-day impact remains a part of popular culture, which links the devil to sinning, anger, nightmares and, in more remote regions, black magic and exorcism. Many Muslims still enter rooms with their right feet and eat with their right hands so the devil doesn't join them. While Satan isn't mentioned in Genesis, the Qur'an has well over a hundred references to him, and far from being silenced in Islamic tradition, he plays a key role in differentiating truth from falsity."[13]

Buddhism and Hinduism have scant need to abolish hell. They may tactfully avert their eyes, but hell remains. There has to be some mechanism whereby the soul can be chastised as one painfully learns the true path to fulfillment, and hell (if only as a way station) still fits the bill neatly.

In the West, it seems, the secular project is holding in many European countries, but elsewhere, including America and Russia, and to a lesser degree Britain and France, it is in trouble. How else, in England, to interpret the declaration by the Anglican bishop of Carlisle that the country's most recent floods were a definitive judgment that the country was on the wrong path—the path defined as the "moral degradation" of allowing more rights for homosexuals?

It's predictable that many *outré* branches of Christianity, including some of the more fundamentalist fire-and-brimstone sects, still cling to the older notions of hell. Even in 2016, you could still see billboards across parts of the American South declaring that "Hell is Real"; and some churches still operate "hell houses," in which terrified teenagers are herded by "demons" and shown graphic strobe-lit scenes of violent assaults, suicides, and drug takers here on earth. So much, so predictable. But you'd be hard pressed to find an adherent of even the more mainstream Christian doctrines who denies hell altogether.

As recently as 2004, Gallup polled Americans of all backgrounds for their views on hell, and found to its own

evident astonishment that despite the supposed seculariz-
ing of society the number of people who believed that god
would punish people in the afterlife had actually increased,
significantly, in a decade—from 50 to 70 percent (it was
80 percent for evangelicals). Even stranger, half of those
who said they never went to church said they nonetheless
definitely believed in hell, while 3 percent of those who
didn't believe in any god at all still believed in hell. In 2011,
an Associated Press poll found that 8 in 10 Americans
believed in angels—and for those who never went to
church the ratio was still 4 in 10. Similarly, 73 percent of
Americans believe that Jesus was born of a virgin (more
women, 78 percent, than men, 69 percent). The gap is a
little different in Canada: more than half of Canadians
believe in heaven, but only a third in hell.

To put all this in perspective on the credulity meter, it's
also true that in 2009 the Pew Research Center reported
that 1 in 5 Americans had experienced ghosts and that 1
in 7 had consulted a psychic.[14] And then, consider that
in April 2012, 1 in 10 Americans was convinced that
Barack Obama was the Antichrist, and they didn't mean
it politically—they meant for sure, for real, that Obama
was inhumanly evil.

Consider also that T.M. Luhrmann, a regular *New
York Times* contributor, revealed in 2013 how startled
she was "when a young woman I was interviewing told
me that God had spoken to her audibly." The column in
which she revealed this drew a response from Reverend
Michael P. Orsi of Naples, Florida, who reminded readers
that the "audible voice of God reported by Joan of Arc
and Francis of Assisi was not psychologically induced by

prior intense prayer . . . [but was real] . . . Also, both have been judged by history to be quite sane."[15]

Sane? Not sane? A thirteen-country study conducted in 2017 and reported in *Nature Human Behaviour* found that it is widely believed that serial killers are much more likely to be atheists than religious folk—which, obviously enough, suggested to the authors that ostensibly secular societies remain intolerant of non-believers.[16]

And there's more. Rob Bell, a prominent evangelical pastor at the Mars Hill megachurch in Grand Rapids, Michigan, set off a firestorm among his fellows in 2016 when he published a book called *Love Wins*, in which he argued that an all-loving God could not possibly consign billions of non-Christians to eternal suffering in hell (he called the notion "misguided and toxic"). For such views he was roundly condemned by, among others, the prominent Calvinist John Piper, who gave Bell the honour of being "farewelled," the equivalent of pronouncing someone anathema and drumming them out of church. (It didn't help that Bell also allowed women into leadership positions in his church.) Bell was widely denounced as a "rogue" and accused by traditionalists of heresy. Justin Taylor, another evangelical, wrote, "It is unspeakably sad when those called to be ministers of the Word distort the gospel and deceive the people of God with false doctrine," and he accused Bell of "moving farther and farther away from anything resembling Biblical Christianity."

Love as false doctrine . . . Yikes! Bell soon "left" Mars Hill.

It is worth remembering, too, that the late American Supreme Court justice Antonin Scalia, referred to in many obituaries as one of the foremost legal minds of his time, said in an interview with *New York* magazine that he believes in Satan. "Of course!" he said. "Yeah, he's a real person. Hey, come on, that's standard Catholic doctrine! Every Catholic believes that."[17]

Somewhat further down on the intellectual scale, consider the Florida college student accused of randomly killing an elderly couple and chewing on the dead man's face; his defence, if it can be called that, was that he was fleeing a demon called Daniel. In his flight, he stripped off his clothes and dashed into a random garage, where he promptly killed the people he found there and started gnawing away. Not his fault—Daniel's.

WHAT, TOO, TO make of a very strange piece published in *Vanity Fair* in December 2016, written by William Friedkin, director of the horror movie *The Exorcist?* The story takes as its starting point an exorcism performed in the Vatican by the church's "chief exorcist," Father Gabriele Amorth, which Friedkin was allowed to watch (actually it was the ninth exorcism ritual performed on the young woman, who is identified only as Rosa; apparently exorcisms can take ages—Amorth has been exorcising one man for sixteen years). In any case, it was the father's belief that Rosa's affliction stemmed from a curse that her brother's girlfriend, who was said to be a witch, had brought against her. The brother and girlfriend were part of a powerful demonic cult, apparently. Had Rosa sought medical help? Gone to a psychiatrist? Not at all. "It was useless to go to doctors. My problem is caused by evil spirits."

Amorth told Friedkin that "Satan is pure spirit. . . . He often appears as something else, to mislead . . . an exorcist requires specific training and must be thought to have a personal sanctity. . . . He can be exposed to dangerous behavior and personal threat. His prayers often cause a violent response as he attempts to shine a beam of light into the darkness." Asked whether he really had said that the devil is in the Vatican, Amorth agreed: "Yes, today Satan rules the world. The masses no longer believe in God. And yes, Satan is in the Vatican."

And then Francis—yes, Pope Frank himself—suggested in 2017 that priests who hear troubled confessions from parishioners should not hesitate to call in an exorcist. As *The Guardian* reported in March 2018, the eighty-year-old pontiff told priests at a Vatican seminar on the art of hearing believers recount their sins that "a good confessor has to be very discerning, particularly when he has to deal with real spiritual disorders. Disorders could have their roots in all manner of circumstances, including supernatural ones," he suggested.

The *Vanity Fair* piece has nothing of the skeptic about it; it is presented in an uncritical reportorial style, and includes the interesting datum that there are currently four exorcists in Rome and perhaps three hundred around the world. At one point Friedkin professes himself an agnostic, but in the same sentence casts doubt on his own agnosticism: "I believe that the power of God and the human soul are unknowable." I had to pinch myself when I wrote these paragraphs, and went back to the article in question. No, there was no sign of satire, and if it was thought to be fake news, there were no hints.

I mean, demonic possession in Sumeria in 3500 BCE, sure . . . but *now*?

It seems so. In 2013, the Jesuit theologian James Martin put it this way: "There are some Gospel stories that still, 2,000 years later, do not lend themselves so easily to scientific explanations, stories in which the demon is able to identify Jesus as the Messiah, at a time when others around him (including his closest followers) still had no clue about Jesus's identity; stories in which the demons speak of themselves, oddly, in the plural, as when they identify themselves as 'Legion'; stories in which the demons enable people to do frightening physical feats, such as bursting through chains. . . . In our own day, too, there are credible stories of possessions that defy any rational explanations. Since entering the Jesuits . . . I have read about, and heard, stories from very reliable (and highly rational) witnesses who have assisted at exorcisms, or who have seen terrifying things. . . . To my mind, the possibility of possessions is not hard to believe."[18]

Carl Sagan once pointed out (in *The Demon-Haunted World*) that demonic possession was still very much a current idea. "In a 1992 'spiritual warfare manual' called *Prepare for War*, Rebecca Brown informs us that abortion and sex outside of marriage 'will almost always result in demonic infestation'; that meditation, yoga and martial arts are designed so unsuspecting Christians will be seduced into worshiping demons; and that 'rock music didn't just happen,' it was a carefully masterminded plan by none other than Satan himself." And then, in 2017, came reports of a growing number of non-church or "private" exorcists operating in ostensibly secular France, along with "a host of . . . healers, mediums, kabbalists, shamans and energiticians," whatever energiticians are. A piece in *The Economist* quoted one of the exorcists, Philippe Moscato, who it found after he "de-spooked" (the magazine's word) a Paris apartment, as suggesting that three parts of France are particularly vulnerable to "black magic": Paris, Lyon, and the French Riviera, where local mafia are said to be active; Moscato was confident that this could be countered by sufficiently strong exorcists. The demand for these, he said, spiked after prominent terrorist attacks in France in 2015. Apparently, many victims of possession are reassured at the ease of booking an exorcist online.[19]

Cogent arguments for hell can still be found, here and there

THE ARGUMENT THAT there *must* be a hell was partly derived, as I suggested in an earlier chapter, from the knowledge that, in our part of the cosmos at least, the moral universe seems out of whack, and wicked people prosper far more often than they should. So there must be a hell in order to balance life here on earth, and to consign malefactors to their just desserts. This is an argument still put forward even by sophisticated believers. Related is the notion that god was taking a chance when he created us and gave us free will. He rolled the dice on our probity, this argument goes; failed to come up sixes; and so folded.

Still, he couldn't have done otherwise. If he created man in his image, after all, his creatures must be as free as he.

In 1943, for example, C.S. Lewis wrote in *The Problem of Pain*: "Why, then, did God give [humans] free will? Because free will, though it makes evil possible, is also the only thing that makes possible any love or goodness or joy worth having. A world of automata—of creatures that worked like machines—would hardly be worth creating. . . . The happiness which God designs for His higher creatures is the happiness of being freely, voluntarily united to Him and to each other. . . . And for that they must be free. Of course, God knew what would happen if they used their freedom the wrong way: apparently he thought it worth the risk." Lewis also wrote the following: "God whispers to us in our pleasures, speaks in our conscience, but shouts in our pain: it is his megaphone to rouse a deaf world." Lewis was responding to what other philosophers of religion call the "ontological argument," a curious proof-of-god that in essence states this: God is perfect. Existence is an essential attribute of perfection, therefore, god exists. And therefore, damnation is also part of perfection. This circuitous locution has been attributed to Saint Anselm, who died in 1109.

Lewis once said that he would prefer not to believe in hell, "but it has the full support of Scripture and, specially, of Our Lord's own words; it has always been held by Christendom; and it has the support of reason." Even so, Lewis's hell was rather more Jewish than mainstream Christian, dreary rather than tormented: hell was a place where it always rained, no one was satisfied, and your neighbours hated you. Oh, and the doors were locked from the inside . . .

The philosopher Jerry Walls, in a complicated 1972 book called *Hell: The Logic of Damnation*, made somewhat the same point: the doctrine of hell, he says, is intelligible from the standpoint of human freedom, since the idea of a decisive choice of evil is a coherent one, and therefore that some versions of hell are "compatible not only with God's omnipotence and omniscience, but also with a strong account of his perfect goodness."

Contemporary defences of hell can still be found here and there. For example, Adrian Reimers, in his curious *Hell and the Mercy of God*, published in 2017 by the Catholic University of America Press, is convinced of Satan's corporality, and he suggests that "hell is the place where Satan reigns. It is the realm of power, manipulation, and anti-love. . . . It is a state of satanic abuse and enmity."

A more sophisticated apologia for hell is offered by Ross Douthat, *The New York Times*'s house conservative:

> Doing away with hell, then, is a natural way for pastors and theologians to make their God seem more humane. The problem is that this move also threatens to make human life less fully human.
>
> Atheists have license to scoff at damnation, but to believe in God and not in hell is ultimately to disbelieve in the reality of human choices. If there's no possibility of saying no to paradise then none of our no's have any real meaning either. They're like home runs or strikeouts in a children's game where nobody's keeping score.

In this sense, a doctrine of universal
salvation turns out to be as deterministic as
the more strident forms of scientific mate-
rialism. Instead of making us prisoners of
our glands and genes, it makes us prisoners of God himself. We can check out any
time we want, but we can never really leave.

The doctrine of hell, by contrast,
assumes that our choices are real, and,
indeed, that we *are* the choices that we
make. The miser can become his greed,
the murderer can lose himself inside his
violence, and their freedom to turn and be
forgiven is inseparable from their freedom
not to do so.[20]

The physicist Sean Carroll, whose *Discover* essay I
quoted in the chapter on hell's physics, was scathing in
response: Douthat, he wrote, "does us all the favor of
reminding us how certain ideas that would otherwise
be too ugly and despicable to be shared among polite
society become perfectly respectable under the rubric of
religion. In this case, the idea is: certain people are just
bad, and the appropriate response is to subject them to
torment for all time, without hope of reprieve. Now that's
the kind of morality I want my society to be based on."[21]

It seems to me that when Douthat asserts that to
"believe in God and not in hell is ultimately to disbelieve
in the reality of human choices," this can be read not as
a persuasive argument for hell, but as a not-so-oblique
argument against the existence of heaven, and thus of god.

As Christopher Hitchens put it in the introduction to *The Portable Atheist,* if you don't believe in god "it will not be long until you are politely asked how you can possibly know right from wrong. Without holy awe, what is to prevent you from resorting to theft, murder, rape, and perjury? It will sometimes be conceded that non-believers have led ethical lives, and it will also be conceded (as it had better be) that many believers have been responsible for terrible crimes. Nonetheless, the working assumption is that we should have no moral compass if we were not somehow in thrall to an unalterable and unchallengeable celestial dictatorship. What a repulsive idea!"

The free-will justification for evil

IN OUR TIME Alvin Plantinga is the pre-eminent explainer-in-chief of this ugly notion. An evangelical Protestant, he stoutly maintains that God is a (real) person who not only created and maintains the universe and its laws, but also intervenes specially in the world via the miracles related in the Bible and in other ways. As part of this argument, Plantinga asserts that faith is a source of belief "'that goes beyond the faculties included in reason.' God endows human beings with a *sensus divinitatis* that ordinarily leads them to believe in him. In addition, God acts in the world more selectively by 'enabling Christians to see the truth of the central teachings of the Gospel.'"[22]

Plantinga has mounted what he calls the free will defence of hellish punishment, a gloss on C.S. Lewis that essentially amounts to this: God's creation of persons with morally significant free will is something of tremendous value; God could not eliminate much of the evil and suffering in this world without thereby eliminating the greater good of having created persons with free will with whom he could have relationships and who are able to love one another and do good deeds; God therefore allows some evils to occur (humans indulging in what Plantinga calls "transworld depravity") that are smaller in value than a greater good to which they are intimately connected. Therefore, people are free in the most robust sense of that term—and because of this, when they do what is right, they can properly be praised. Moreover, when they do wrong, they can be rightly blamed or punished for their actions, thereby neatly evading a tricky sticking point in Christian theology: should not a god with divine foreknowledge have been able to avoid evil in the first place?

It is all Adam's fault

HOW THEN TO differentiate, if at all, between moral evil (which you could argue people bring on themselves) and natural evil, which happens without human agency? (An asteroid falling on your head would be an example of the latter; so would cancer in a small child.)

Plantinga's solution is that one caused the other, that all natural evil followed as the result of the world's first moral evil, the sin of Adam and Eve—that all the world's evils have their source in that one evil act.[23] In this theory, if Adam hadn't eaten that damned apple, there would be no earthquakes, or plagues, or tornadoes, or errant asteroids.

Other believers are not so sure, though they concede that this "problem of evil"—or theodicy, as it's technically known—has for years been an atheist's best friend. At its simplest formulation it is this: if god is so great, if god is all-powerful, if god is omniscient, omnipotent, and omnibenevolent—if god is just and merciful and the rest—why does evil exist in the first place? (Atheists have their own answer; indeed, the philosopher Hans Küng has called the problem of evil "the rock of atheism.") But, Plantinga aside, it is a question that still vexes the religious, and for them shows no signs of solution. Indeed, ordinary people still find it important. Pollster George Barna was once commissioned (by the journalist Lee Strobel) to ask people to respond to this question: "If you could ask God only one question and you knew he would give you an answer, what would you ask?" By far the most common response was this: "Why is there pain and suffering in the world? If God is all-powerful, all-knowing and perfectly good, why does he let so many bad things happen?"

Some religious traditions attempt a solution by suggesting that the world was the dual creation of benevolent and evil forces in constant combat. Bad things therefore happen to good people because god is not omnipotent: an independent evil power does the work. But the idea of a weak god never caught on in the monotheisms, for reasons that are rather obvious—the whole *point* of monotheism is the creation and governance of the universe.

It is interesting to watch theologians and preachers tying themselves in knots over this apparently simple issue. What follows is a small collection of those knots.

I'm not going to source them—their exact origins are not important; there are hundreds just like them.

- "God has given us freedom of choice. Having this freedom means that we can rebel against God and make choices that are contrary to his desires. Since we can say that evil is anything contrary to God's perfect and holy will, then anyone who chooses anything contrary to God's perfection is committing evil. But this is the risk of being able to have freedom of choice. Evil and suffering are the result of making bad free choices."

- "As for natural disasters and sickness, Biblically, Adam represented not only all of his descendants, but he was also the head of the created order since he was given dominion over the earth. Therefore, when he fell, sin entered into the world, and with it the effects of being fallen spread to the earth as well as to humanity."

- "God killed every human except Noah [and his family] in the flood. Were any of these people killed unjustly? No! The Bible says specifically *all* people (again, excepting Noah and his family) had become corrupted . . . and were *continually* plotting evil. So . . . no innocent people were killed in the flood."

- "God is loving, but God's love requires God's justice. As I discipline my three children when they disobey, God disciplines us if we don't meet his requirements. God would have been completely just and loving in destroying all of us for our disobedience to him. It is only through his extraordinary love and grace that we are allowed into his presence."

◆ "Natural evil—the pain of disease, the intermittent and unpredictable destruction of natural disasters, the decay of old age, the imminence of death—takes away a person's satisfaction with himself. It tends to humble him, show him his frailty, make him reflect on the transience of temporal goods, and turn his affections towards other-worldly things, away from the things of this world. No amount of moral or natural evil, of course, can guarantee that a man will [place his faith in God]. . . . But evil of this sort is the best hope, I think, and maybe the only effective means, for bringing men to such a state."

If there is a common thread to all these, it is that the problem is not suffering, but *undeserved* suffering. It *cannot* be undeserved, because, well, god is god . . .

What to believe, then, if you can't believe all this?

TO PUT IT plainly: the multiple (and conflicting) depictions of the *Inferno* and the *Paradiso* in all the foregoing chapters are folk tales, no more; as such, they are on a par with spiritualism, Ouija boards, hauntings, hobgoblins, and the rest. More inventive than hauntings, true, and deeper than mediums talking to the dead, with more room for mystery and the sublime. More comforting for believers too (both the heaven and the hell parts); there is much solace to be had in belief.

Which leaves the rest of us where? There is no hell, and no devil. There is no heaven, and no god.

Inventions, all.

Even so, how can we be *sure* there is no devil? With the same level of confidence as saying that there are no fairies, that there is no Santa Claus, that there are no ghosts, or that there is no magic—or levitation, teleportation, telepathy, out-of-body experiences, miracles, an afterlife, or anything else outside the bounds of what Sean Carroll calls "poetic naturalism." There is no evidence that stands up to scrutiny for any of it. To be sure, the lack of evidence does not necessarily justify atheism; it is barely possible that the universe we occupy had a creator, who then wandered away, perhaps with other things on his mind, or maybe even a committee of creators. In that single sense, agnosticism could be justified—and modern cosmology offers a razor-thin opening to this notion.

Even so, the burden, it seems to me, is on the believer. How is the believer credibly to assert—now, in the light of what we do know—that heaven and hell are in any way real? How is the believer to show that the universe, in all its immensity, was (Hitchens again) "set in motion for the express purpose of creating and influencing life on a minute speck of a planet, billions of years later, at the margin of the whirling nebulae and amid the extinction of innumerable other worlds? . . . What kind of designer or creator is so wasteful and capricious and approximate? What kind of designer or creator is so cruel and indifferent?"[24]

Most believers don't even try to grapple with these matters, but rely instead on inner certitude. Here's an immaculate example: "Intellectually, the problem is that religion is essentially reasonable and atheism is unreasonable and the consequences of the militancy of contemporary atheism are not only unreasonable but offensive to reason. Few things in our murky lives could be more obvious and indisputable than that there must be some force in the cosmos that causes spiritual insight, authenticated miracles, and is able to grasp the notion of the timeless, the limitless, and the fact that at some point in our past there was some kind of creation."

That's practising Catholic Conrad Black, a former newspaper proprietor, in a column for the Canadian *National Post*, lamenting the colonization of intellectual thought by what he calls "militant atheism," or sometimes "aggressive atheism." (Over the years, Black has made occasionally persuasive political and social pronouncements, albeit camouflaged in an often baroque vocabulary, but his dismissal of atheists as "aggressive" and "militant" while describing their views as "elitist sniggering" is a bit rich.) As is normal in these circumstances, no evidence is offered for these pronouncements, except to note that recruitment to the clergy is increasing and attendance at services is steady or rising, and then the bald assertion that "few things . . . could be more obvious and indisputable" than the existence of a creator, somewhere, somehow, of some kind, and that miracles have been "authenticated."

Well, no. And no. It isn't. And they haven't. No evidence is offered because there is none.

No miracles. Not one. Not ever.

THE REAL PROBLEM is with this idea of the supernatural. So far—and science has looked, with a level of scrutiny that is mind-bogglingly intense—no evidence whatsoever has turned up that anything can exist outside the natural world, and scientists have never found a miracle, not one, not ever. Which is not to say that we understand everything, only to say that there is no barrier to understanding except our own as-yet-incomplete knowledge. How, for example, can there be a creation without a creator? What came before the Big Bang? Conventional post-Einstein science asserts that the question is meaningless. Since time itself began at the singularity—the Big Bang—there could not have been a "before" to be, well, before. There wasn't even nothing, there just wasn't anything. (Physicists seem to have no trouble with this counterintuitive notion. Lawrence Krauss, for example, wrote a book, *A Universe from Nothing: Why There Is Something Rather than Nothing*, demonstrating that not only can something emerge from nothing—that is, not have a cause—but that something will *always* emerge from nothing.)

The intelligent design argument (that the universe is too complicated to have emerged spontaneously *ex nihilo*) is just one of the theistic theories that have succumbed to our increasingly intricate knowledge of how the world really does work—the ineffable is effable after all. Nor is this a new argument, exactly. The Greek philosopher Democritus had an answer for the question of why the cosmos seemed so well set up for the existence of life: perhaps, he said, there were an infinite number of worlds, not just one, and so we have just been lucky—in this, he anticipated the many-universes theory by a couple of thousand years.

A more sophisticated version of the argument from design points out that the parameters of the Big Bang were perfectly designed to produce a universe that sustained life: if the Big Bang had differed in strength as little as 1 part in 1,060, the universe would have either quickly collapsed back in on itself, or expanded too quickly for stars to have formed. Democritus's theory serves to answer this too: perhaps there are other universes even more amenable to sustaining life than ours; and (it can be added) if ours is the only universe, why did the creator allow such vast quantities of waste, massive galaxies with just one tiny corner hospitable to life? Couldn't he have done better? Any competent designer could have.[25]

As Louise Antony argued in an interview with the philosopher Gary Gutting, "I deny that there are beings or phenomena outside the scope of natural law. That's not to say that I think everything is within the scope of human knowledge. Surely there are things not dreamt of in our philosophy, not to mention in our science—but *that* fact is not a reason to believe in supernatural beings. I think many arguments for the existence of a god depend on the insufficiencies of human cognition. I readily grant that we have cognitive limitations. But when we bump up against them, when we find we cannot explain something—like why the fundamental physical parameters happen to have the values that they have—the right conclusion to draw is that we just can't [yet] explain the thing. That's the proper place for agnosticism and humility."[26]

Sean Carroll, in his 2016 book *The Big Picture*, has a simple way of explaining why there can be no life after death: life is a process rather than a substance. In this, he essentially reprises and updates Thomas Tailour's 1491 candle metaphor for the soul: "When a candle is burning, there is a flame that clearly carries energy. When we put the candle out, the energy doesn't 'go' anywhere. The candle still contains energy in its atoms and molecules. What happens, instead, is that the process of combustion has ceased. Life is like that: it's not 'stuff'; it's a set of things happening. When that process stops, life ends. Life is a way of talking about a particular sequence of events taking place among atoms and molecules arranged in the right way." Put another way, if you want to believe in an afterlife (while being perfectly well aware that the body decays), you are obliged to think that there is a thing independent of the body, called the soul. Otherwise the afterlife can't work.[27] But there is no such "thing."

Adam Gopnik, in a *New Yorker* essay on atheism and belief, makes the same point: "What [atheists], whatever their numbers, really have now . . . is a monopoly on legitimate forms of knowledge about the natural world. They have this monopoly for the same reason that computer manufacturers have an edge over crystal-ball makers: the advantages of having an actual explanation of things and processes are self-evident. What works wins. We know that men were not invented but slowly evolved from smaller animals; that the earth is not the center of the universe but one among a billion planets in a distant corner; and that, in the billions of years of the universe's existence, there is no evidence of a single miraculous intercession with the laws of nature. We need not imagine that there's no heaven; we know that there is none, and we will search for angels forever in vain."[28]

Ross Douthat is dismissive of this view. "How little they know of religion who mostly secularism know," he wrote in a *New York Times* column. He says that Gopnik and others fail to grasp "a fairly elementary point—that the possible conceptions of God are not exhausted by the lightning-hurling sky-god and the mostly-irrelevant chairman of the board." Indeed, sophisticated believers "do believe that religion can be intellectually rigorous without making prayer empty and miracles impossible."[29]

Even so, dismissal is not refutation. For refutation, we wait in vain.

We still have to deal with cruelty, though, and evil

DESPITE ALL THIS, civil society has in many ways already self-corrected from hell and eternal punishment. In a roundabout fashion, our views of the afterlife have edged closer to those of traditional African societies, which generally lacked a hell or a devil; the elders knew that malefactions had to be dealt with by the living, and they did so, not always wisely, but at least decisively. In the "West," if there is still such an entity, burning women as witches was regarded as a perfectly civilized activity until relatively recently. Now, a village pyre would bring not just prosecution but horrified condemnation, at least in most contemporary societies. Yet as we grow less tolerant of cruelty, the exploits of cruel and evil men fill popular literature and the imagination of ordinary people. And we know, *pace* the Holocaust, ISIS, and Pol Pot, that ordinary people can inflict cruelties no less abhorrent than the demons of hells past.

Self-evidently, then, a lowered public tolerance for cruelty hasn't lowered the amount of cruelty we still inflict; evil men still do evil things, only without any help from the devil and without any hindrance from god. One thing religion did contribute was its sense of fundamentality—the sense that there are things in the universe that, as it were, "throw the last stone."[30] That was comforting to many, lifting a burden they felt unable to bear. That doesn't happen anymore. There is no longer a final arbiter, which may be why so many people have turned to the newly minted gods of authoritarian communism, fascism, and "populism"—and back to religious fundamentalism.

At least in our society, jurisprudence hasn't invoked the supernatural since the last witches went to the stake (the last recorded execution in England was after a woman and her young daughter caused a thunderstorm by taking off their stockings), and the argument for eternal hellfire has devolved into a squabble between punishment for life and punishment by death, between revenge and the possibility of personal redemption and rehabilitation. As far as the law is concerned, death is the end of everything, as it should be. *Tout finis.*

The systems we create are therefore *our* systems, not *his*; they are infinitely malleable, and require constant vigilance, frequent updating, and unending skepticism from an engaged citizenry. This adds uncertainty to an already uncertain world, but it's what we've got.

NOTES

Chapter 1

1   This from the philosopher Adam Kotsko in *The Prince of This World*.

2   This episode was recounted in the epilogue to a book called *Into Africa: A Journey through the Ancient Empires*, which I co-wrote with Sheila Hirtle. It was published by Key Porter Books in 1999.

3   Act 5, scene 1.

4   From *God Is Watching You: How the Fear of God Makes Us Human*, by Dominic Johnson.

5   This from "Born to be Conned," a *New York Times* piece by Maria Konnikova (December 5, 2015). Konnikova was writing about the wider human predilection for being conned, but it serves for religion too.

6   *The Histories of Polybius*, vol. 1.

7   Quoted by Karl Popper in *The Open Society and Its Enemies. Volume 1: Plato*.

8   See an excellent summary of the early church's development of the hell myth by R. Craig Hogan, on the website 30ce.com.

9   Quoted by David Ganz in his essay "Charlemagne in Hell," *Florilegium* 17 (2000).

10 This from Swinden's 1727 opus, *An Enquiry into the Nature and Place of Hell*.

Chapter 2

1   These were excavated by a team of British and American archeologists headed by Leonard Woolley. (For trivia buffs,

Agatha Christie's *Murder in Mesopotamia* was inspired by these royal tombs; indeed, Christie herself later married Woolley's assistant.)

2   This from chapter 22, "The State of the Dead," www.sacred-texts.com/neu/celt/rac/rac25.htm.

3   See John W. Buckley, *Prophecy Unveiled: Exploring the Incredible Truths That Lie Hidden in the Bible.*

Chapter 3

1   Rossella Lorenzi quotes Strabo in "Pluto's 'Gate to Hell' Uncovered in Turkey," April 3, 2013, http://amra26.blogspot.com/2013/03/plutos-gate-uncovered-in-turkey.html.

2   https://motherboard.vice.com/en_us/article/xyy3nk/archaeologists-in-turkey-discover-an-ancient-gate-to-hell.

3   According to the International Volcanic Health Hazard Network, if CO_2 is 25 percent or more of the ambient air, "convulsions occur and rapid loss of consciousness ensues after a few breaths. Death will occur if level is maintained."

4   Rob Preece, "The Door to Hell: Take a Look inside a Giant Hole in the Desert which Has Been on Fire for More than 40 Years" *Daily Mail*, July 27, 2012.

5   This from Bill Arnold and Bryan Beyer, *Readings from the Ancient Near East: Primary Sources for Old Testament Study.*

6   From Morris Jastrow's 1915 book *Descent of the Goddess Ishtar into the Lower World*, in his *The Civilization of Babylonia and Assyria.*

7   Qur'an 15:43–44

8   As usual, hell-on-line.org offers a decent bibliography for the Lough Derg, with many scholarly citations.

9   See "Hell: A Rough Guide," *Economist*, December 22, 2012.

10   Quotes from Swinden's *An Enquiry into the Nature and Place of Hell* are from a digitized copy of a book in the library of the University of California, Los Angeles.

11   Some of these "locations" are from hell-on-line.org.

12   "The Geography of Xibalba," from the *Ancient History Encyclopedia.*

13   The full inscription is this:

        Through me to the city dolorous lies the way,

> Who pass through me shall pains eternal prove,
> Through me are reached the people lost for aye.
> 'Twas Justice did my Glorious Maker move;
> I was created by the Power Divine,
> The Highest Wisdom, and the Primal Love.
> No thing's creation earlier was than mine,
> If not eternal; I for aye endure

14 See Leonard Lesko, *The Ancient Egyptian Book of Two Ways*.

15 Virgil, *The Aeneid*.

16 *Encyclopedia of Hell*, 173–4.

17 See also the Zoroastrian *Book of the Judgments of the Spirit of Wisdom*, from the ninth century CE.

18 Various editions of this tract are extant, including a Project Gutenberg release, and one issued in the Grimm Library in England in 1908.

19 Also via http://www.avesta.org/mp/dd.htm#p4.

Chapter 4

1   This from Ovid's *Metamorphoses* (A.D. Melville translation), iv 451ff.

2   Wikipedia has useful entries on each named.

3   This translation from H.G. Evelyn-White of the Essex University Centre for Myth Studies.

4   *Metamorphoses*, Book 5 (Melville translation again).

5   *Encyclopedia of Hell*, 277–8.

6   Elaine Pagels, *The Origin of Satan*, 39.

7   See Mark Twain, *Letters from the Earth*.

8   See for example *The Testimony of Truth*.

9   Quoted by Philip Almond in *The Devil: A New Biography*, 42.

10 This disparaging review from Edward E. Foster, editor of *Three Purgatory Poems*.

11 The text is from *The Visions of Tundale Together with Metrical Moralizations and Other Fragments of Early Poetry, Hitherto Unedited*, edited by W.B.D.D Turnbull and published in Edinburgh by Thomas G. Stevenson in 1843.

12 Matthew Hopkins, *The Discovery of Witches*, 17–18 (Kindle edition).

13   Kramer and Sprenger's work has been published online in the 1486 edition, translated by the Rev. Montague Summers.

14   For this I am indebted to Malcolm Gaskill from the November 30, 2017 issue of the *London Review of Books*.

15   From Francis Grose's *Dictionary of the Vulgar Tongue*.

16   An unsourced account on unexplainedstuff.com, but backed up by a scholarly translation of his major work, reviewed by Elspeth Whitney in *Renaissance Quarterly* 60, no. 4 (2007).

17   Whitney again.

18   This from the *Encyclopedia of Hell*, 209.

Chapter 5

1   *The Gospel of Nicodemus* was formerly called *Acts of Pontius Pilate*. The text can be found at sacred-texts.com.

2   From the 1924 Clarendon Press edition of *The Apocryphal New Testament*, translated and introduced by M.R. James. The text is also available at http://gnosis.org/library/gosbart.htm.

Chapter 6

1   The story of Ereshkigal and Nergal is from several sources, including Stephanie Dalley's masterful *Myths from Mesopotamia* and from a piece called "Nergal and Ereshkigal Re-enchanting the Mesopotamian Underworld," at http://www.gatewaystobabylon.com/religion/nergalereshkigal2000.htm. Direct quotes come from the latter.

Chapter 7

1   This from the Wikipedia entry on the Pyramid Texts.

2   www.britannica.com/topic/hell.

3   This from the piece on Gehenna by Kaufmann Kohler and Ludwig Blau in the *Jewish Encyclopedia*.

4   These passages from Enoch are from sacred-texts.com, in a 1917 translation by R.H. Charles. More on Enoch and the Watchers in a later chapter.

5   Daniel 12:2.

6   http://www.jewishvirtuallibrary.org/pharisees-sadducees-and-essenes.

7   See Robert Garland, *The Greek Way of Death*.

8   Eileen Gardiner's hell-on-line.org has a good survey of these matters.

9   Thomas Sheehan, in *The First Coming: How the Kingdom of God Became Christianity*, a 1986 exploration of religious origins. Sheehan is a philosopher at Stanford University.

10   From http://www.avesta.org/mp/dd.htm#p4. Avesta is the online Zoroastrian archive. The translation is by E.W. West.

11   The quote is from the *Encyclopaedia Britannica*.

12   Some of this from http://www.hinduwebsite.com/hinduism/h_death.asp.

13   *The Systematic Philosophy* [*Abhidharma kosabhasyam*] by Vasubandhu (Buddhist [Sanskrit], 4th–5th century CE). From hell-on-line.org.

14   From the *Ancient History Encyclopedia*.

15   This list from www.buddhistdoor.com/OldWeb/bdoor/archive/.

16   This from Eileen Gardiner, hell-on-line.org.

17   Quoting Carol Zaleski in the *Encyclopaedia Britannica*.

18   *Encyclopedia of Hell*, 22.

19   Wikipedia has a clever entry on this document.

20   This from a 1921 translation by G.R.S. Mead, the full text of which can be found at http://gnosis.org/library/psoph.htm. According to a Nag Hammadi document, Jesus explained her to his disciples as follows: "Son of Man consented with Sophia, his consort, and revealed a great androgynous light. Its male name is designated 'Saviour, begetter of all things.' Its female name is designated 'All-begettress Sophia.' Some call her 'Pistis.'"

21   *Encyclopedia of Hell*, 264

22   See https://en.wikipedia.org/wiki/Apocalypse_of_Paul.

Chapter 8

1   This from "Hell: A Rough Guide," *Economist*.

2   Quoted by Philip Almond, *The Devil*, 192.

3   I was also led to Shower by Philip Almond.

4   This interesting list from Eileen Gardiner, hell-on-line.org, describing the torments of various Chinese hells.

5   The quote is from Charles Horne's 1917 translation; I have also drawn on a translation from the Pahlavi by Martin Haug, published in Bombay and London in 1872.

6   Matthew 13:41.

7   Isaiah 66:24

8   *The Apocalypse of Peter* was first published (in French) by Abbé Sylvain Grebaut in *Revue de l'Orient Chrétien*, in 1910. Greek and Ethiopic texts differ slightly.

9   Excerpts from *The Apocalypse of Paul* from *The Apocryphal New Testament* edited by M.R. James.

10   From http://skepticsannotatedbible.com/quran/.

11   See islamreligion.com.

12   Adamnán material and quotes from the 1908 (London) edition, reissued by Project Gutenberg in 2015.

13   This from hell-on-line.org.

14   Innocent III was a prolific commenter on hell, as well as a masterful politician. His rather gloomy views of humanity's nature are best seen in his most enduring work, *On the Misery of the Human Condition*, available at https://www.montville. net/cms/lib/NJ01001247/Centricity/Domain/825/On%20 the%20Misery%20of%20the%20Human%20Condition.pdf.

15   https://diyubianxiangtu.wordpress.com/2009/04/28/the-hell-of-sword-tree/.

16   *The Middle-Length Discourses of the Buddha*, published by the Buddhist Publication Society in Kandy, Sri Lanka. This version translated from Pali and edited by Bhikkhu Bodhi, and found on lirs.ru, an online Buddhist library.

17   These descriptions are taken from a doctoral thesis by Andrea de Antoni titled *Hell Is Round the Corner: Religious Landscapes, People and Identity in Contemporary Japan* (University of Venice, 2010), http://dspace.unive.it/handle/10579/921.

18   From a comment thread at https://www.quora.com/What-is-hell-like-in-Hinduism#.

Chapter 9

1   Eileen Gardiner describes similar durations in her hell-on-line.org reference to *The Sutra on the Eighteen Hells*, which I have not been able to find anywhere else.

2   Some of this is also from a Wikipedia entry on the Problem of Hell, which asserts that "the problem of hell can be viewed as the worst and most intractable instance of the problem of evil."

Chapter 10

1   *Book of Enoch,* chapter 6.
2   Mark Twain, *Letters from the Earth,* 26–7 (Kindle edition).
3   Quoted by Michael Howard in "Enoch and the Watchers," available at http://www.newdawnmagazine.com.

Chapter 11

1   Multiple versions of this epic remain in print in English. Some include the so-called twelfth tablet, some omit it. I have consulted several texts, one edited by Morris Jastrow at Yale (1920), now in a Project Gutenberg edition (Jastrow is rather sniffy about some of the other translations); another distributed by the Assyrian News Agency at www.aina.org, edited by Nancy Sandars; a third from a Stanford University book edited and translated by Maureen Gallery Kovacs, available at www.ancienttexts.org/library/mesopotamian/gilgamesh/. For a translation of the Twelfth Tablet, see Stephanie Dalley's splendid *Myths from Mesopotamia.*
2   From David Ferry's 1992 verse translation.
3   This last section from Dalley, *Myths from Mesopotamia.*
4   This from Morris Jastrow's *The Religion of Babylonia and Assyria,* in a Project Gutenberg edition.
5   There are multiple versions of this story, including many that have been expressly rewritten for websites that include the words "crystal" or "moonbeam" in their titles, for Ishtar has been adopted by the more misty reaches of feminism. Most of my excerpts, on the other hand, are adapted from a 1915 translation of the myth from Akkadian by Morris Jastrow under the title *Descent of the Goddess Ishtar into the Lower World.*
6   This quote is from https://inanna.virtualave.net/tammuz. html.

7   My sources for this story of the Assyrian prince are an essay by
UCLA professor Seth Sanders ("The First Tour of Hell: From
Neo-Assyrian Propaganda to Early Jewish Revelation") and
an essay on the website of the Universität Duisburg-Essen,
Institut für Evangelische Theologie, which in turn quotes
Benjamin Read Foster, *Before the Muses: An Anthology of
Akkadian Literature*, vol. 2.

8   This passage and the others of the Baal saga translated by
J.C.L. Gibson in *Canaanite Myths and Legends*.

9   Also from Gibson, *Canaanite Myths and Legends*.

Chapter 12

1   Much of this is from a tendentious and condescending book
on "Chinese superstitions" by a Jesuit priest, one Henry Doré,
which was translated from the French by another Jesuit, Father
Michael Kennelly, and published by the T'Usewei Printing
Press, Shanghai, in 1920. (The copy I consulted is from the
Gettysburg College Library's rare book collection, digitized
by Microsoft.) Again, I am grateful to Eileen Gardiner for
pointing me in this direction. The other observations are
from visits to Fengdu.

2   *The Great Maudgalyayana Rescues His Mother From hell, from
the Tun-huang Pien-wen Manuscript*, translated by Eugene
Eoyang, available at isites.harvard.edu/fs/docs/icb.../Maudg-
alyayana%20Saves%20His%20Mother.pdf.

3   Details of this story can be found in many places, but I have
drawn from the same tendentious book as before, *Researches
into Chinese Superstitions*, by the Jesuit missionary Henry
Doré. Doré's mission seems to have been mostly to show
how superstition-prone the Chinese were—this in contrast,
of course, to the rigours of Jesuit theology, but at least he
did tell the actual tales at length. This is available at https://
archive.org/stream/researchesintocho6dor/researchesinto-
cho6dor_djvu.txt.

Chapter 13

1   This and other quotes from the Orpheus story from Edith
Hamilton's 1942 book *Mythology*. She herself drew on

Apollonius, Ovid, and Virgil. The book was republished in 2015 by the New Canadian Library edition in 2015.

2   From greeka.com.

3   Some of the others, for the diligently curious, were "Phaedra and Procris and woeful Eriphyle, shewing on her the wounds of her merciless son, and Evadne and Pasiphaë; Laodamia goes in their company, and she who was once Caeneus and a man, now woman, and again returned by fate into her shape of old."

4   Excerpts from *The Aeneid* come from the Project Gutenberg translation by J.W. Mackail; verse excerpt from a translation by John Dryden for the Internet Classics Archive.

5   These excerpts are from *The Book of Arda Viraf* translated by Martin Haug.

Chapter 14

1   Peter Ackroyd, in a work called *The Roaring Girls of Queer London* (New York: Abrams Press, 2018).

2   This from a translation by M.R. James of a manuscript in the Bodleian Library, which he (James) provisionally dated to the ninth century. He was not much impressed, calling it a late and clumsy compilation based on the Assumption legends and *The Apocalypse of Paul*.

3   Gregory the Great, pope from 590 to 604, reigned at a time of multiple invasions and outbreaks of plague, and his *Dialogues* took comfort in a number of back-from-the-dead tales, including a legionary who had personally witnessed the horrors of hell and had been sent back to warn mortals of what was in store if they didn't shape up—the forerunner of many such allegories that turned up over the course of the next millennium.

4   The words in quotes in the above two paragraphs are from David Ganz's essay "Charlemagne in Hell."

5   Also quoted by Ganz.

6   Again, quotes are from Ganz's essay.

7   This from *The Birth of Purgatory*, by Jacques Le Goff, medieval historian and former editor of the journal *Annales*.

8   Edward E. Foster (ed.), *Three Purgatory Poems*.

9   This is a familiar quote, appearing in many books and texts, including the commentary by Saint Teresa herself, called *Of Certain Outward Temptations and Appearances of Satan. Of the Sufferings Thereby Occasioned. Counsels for those who Go On.* See for example the website carmelitemonks.org.

Chapter 15

1   Philip Almond, *The Devil*, 82.

2   Quotations from Dante are from the Project Gutenberg edition, translated by James Romanes Sibbald; the commentary is largely drawn from Sibbald's notes.

3   The quotes from Milton's text are from the Project Gutenberg edition of *Paradise Lost*.

Chapter 16

1   See Brian Bethune, "Why So Many People—Including Scientists—Suddenly Believe in an Afterlife," *Maclean's*, May 7, 2013.

2   See for example www.biblestudytools.com.

3   This from Plutarch, *Life of Sertorius*, vol 8, 2.

4   Quotations from *Paradiso* from the Project Gutenberg edition, translated by Rev. H.F. Cary.

5   Dennis Prager, "Is There a Heaven and a Hell?" *Jewish Journal*, June 15, 2012.

6   Garry Wills, *What the Qur'an Meant and Why It Matters*.

7   See "Houris, Heavenly Maidens In Islam," available at www.muslimhope.com/HourisheavenlyMaidensInIslam.htm.

8   http://www.alsunna.org/Description-of-Paradise-in-Islam.html#gsc.tab=0.

Epilogue

1   Catherine Nixey, *The Darkening Age*.

2   This comes from an interview with the *Observer* on August 5, 2016, titled "Humans are a post-truth species."

3   These examples of the church's early views come from the book *The Church Teaches on Hell* by John Clarkson, available at http://catholic-church.org/grace/growing/hell/tct.htm.

4   As Arnold's CV puts it, "he is especially interested in questioning medieval belief, and has argued against long-standing ideas of the Middle Ages as an age of faith." Most notably, this idea is explored in *Belief and Unbelief in Medieval Europe* (2005).

5   Quotations and examples are from Diana Webb, *Pilgrimage in Medieval England*. Good explication can also be found in John Arnold's *Belief and Unbelief in Medieval Europe* (2005), where some of the same instances are cited.

6   See "The Enlightenment Project," *New York Times*, February 28, 2017.

7   "Bernie Sanders's Crusade Against . . . Believing in Hell?" *Washington Post*, June 12, 2017.

8   Bertrand Russell made similar points in his tract *Why I Am Not a Christian.*

9   "Trump Can't Save American Christianity," August 2, 2017.

10   Almond, *The Devil*, 220 ff (epilogue).

11   5:32.

12   See "A Description of Hellfire (Part 5 of 5): The Horrors of Hell," available at www.islamreligion.com/articles/383/.

13   See "Why Arab Muslims Love Paradise Lost—and Their Leaders Hate It," *Guardian*, September 1, 2017.

14   This from T.M. Luhrmann, "Conjuring Up Our Own Gods," *New York Times*, October 14, 2013. Luhrmann is a reliable purveyor of the more credulous side of Christian apologetics.

15   See Molly Worthen, "A Great Awakening," *New York Times*, April 29, 2012.

16   Quoted in Benedict Carey, "Research Points to Bias Against Atheists, Including in Mainly Secular Societies," *New York Times*, August 7, 2017.

17   "In Conversation: Antonin Scalia," *New York*, October 6, 2013.

18   This from his book *Jesus: A Pilgrimage*. Martin writes regularly for *America*, a Jesuit magazine.

19   "Why Exorcisms Are on the Rise in France," *Economist*, July 31, 2017.

20   "A Case for Hell," *New York Times*, April 24, 2011.

21   From "Hell," *Discover*, April 25, 2011.

22   Quoted by Thomas Nagel in his review of Plantinga's *Where the Conflict Really Lies: Science, Religion and Naturalism*, in the *New York Review of Books*, September 27, 2012.

23   An interesting survey of all this, including a discussion of Plantinga, by James R. Beebe ("The Logical Problem of Evil") can be found in the *Internet Encyclopedia of Philosophy*, at http://www.iep.utm.edu/.

24   Christopher Hitchens, in his introduction to *The Portable Atheist*.

25   The Democritus material from Tim Whitmarsh, *Battling the Gods: Atheism in the Ancient World*.

26   The interview was published in *The New York Times* under the title "Arguments Against God," February 25, 2014.

27   This last from the neuroscientist Dick Passingham, in an interview on fivebooks.com.

28   Gopnik, "Bigger Than Phil: When Did Faith Start to Fade?" *New Yorker*, February 14 and 24, 2014.

29   See "Among the Believers," *New York Times*, February 13, 2014.

30   This phrase is from William James, American philosopher and psychologist, who died in 1910.

BIBLIOGRAPHY

Books

Alighieri, Dante. *The Divine Comedy of Dante Alighieri: The Inferno*. Translated by James Romanes Sibbald. Project Gutenberg, 2012. http://www.gutenberg.org/ebooks/41537.

——. *The Divine Comedy, Volume 3, Paradise*. Translated by Charles Eliot Norton. Project Gutenberg, 1999. http://www.gutenberg.org/ebooks/1997.

Almond, Philip. *The Devil: A New Biography*. Ithaca, NY: Cornell University Press, 2014.

——. *Heaven and Hell in Enlightenment England*. Cambridge: Cambridge University Press, 1994.

Arnold, Bill, and Bryan Beyer. *Readings from the Ancient Near East: Primary Sources for Old Testament Study*. Grand Rapids, MI: Baker Academic, 2002.

Arnold, John. *Belief and Unbelief in Medieval Europe*. New York: Bloomsbury Academic, 2005.

Barrow, John D. *New Theories of Everything*. Oxford: Oxford University Press, 2008.

Bernstein, Alan. *The Formation of Hell: Death and Retribution in the Ancient and Early Christian Worlds*. Ithaca, NY: Cornell University Press, 1993.

Boswell, Charles Stuart, trans. *An Irish Precursor of Dante: A Study on the Vision of Heaven and Hell Ascribed to the Eighth-Century Irish Saint Adamnán, with Translation of the Irish Text*. London: David Nutt, 1908; Project Gutenberg, 2015. http://www.gutenberg.org/ebooks/50021.

Buckley, John W. *Prophecy Unveiled: Exploring the Incredible Truths That Lie Hidden in the Bible*. College Station, TX: Virtual Bookworm, 2007.

Buddha. *The Middle-Length Discourses of the* Buddha. Kandy, LK: Buddhist Publication Society, 2003.

Carroll, Sean. *The Big Picture: On the Origins of Life, Meaning, and the Universe Itself*. New York: Dutton, 2016.

Clarkson, John. *The Church Teaches on Hell*. Rockford, IL: Tan Books and Publishers, n.d. Also available at: http://catholic-church.org/grace/growing/hell/tct.htm.

Dalley, Stephanie, trans. *Myths from Mesopotamia: Creation, the Flood, Gilgamesh, and Others*. Oxford: Oxford University Press, 2009.

Defoe, Daniel. *The History of the Devil, As Well Ancient as Modern: In Two Parts*. Project Gutenberg, 2010. http://www.gutenberg.org/ebooks/31053.

Doré, Henry. *Researches into Chinese Superstitions*, Vol. 6. Translated by Fr. Michael Kennelly. Shanghai: T'Usewei Printing Press, 1920.

Doyle, Arthur Conan. *The White Company*. London: Smith, Elder & Co., 1891.

Dworkin, Ronald. *Religion without God*. Cambridge, MA: Harvard University Press, 2013.

Ferry, David. *Gilgamesh*. New York: Farrar, Straus and Giroux, 1992.

Foster, Benjamin Read. *Before the Muses: An Anthology of Akkadian Literature*. Vol. 2. Bethesda, MD: CDL Press, 1993.

Foster, Edward E. *Three Purgatory Poems*. Kalamazoo, MI: Medieval Institute Publications, 2004.

Gardiner, Eileen. *Medieval Visions of Heaven and Hell: A Sourcebook*. London: Taylor and Francis, 1993.

——. *Visions of Heaven and Hell Before Dante*. New York: Italica Press, 1989.

Garland, Robert. *The Greek Way of Death*. London: Duckworth, 1986.

George, Andrew. *The Epic of Gilgamesh*. London: Penguin Classics, 2003.

Gibson, J.C.L., ed. *Canaanite Myths and Legends*. Edinburgh: T&T Clark International, 1956.

Grayling, A.C. *The God Argument: The Case against Religion and for Humanism*. New York: Bloomsbury, 2013.

Grose, Francis. 1811. *Dictionary of the Vulgar Tongue*. Project Gutenberg, 2004. http://www.gutenberg.org/ebooks/5402.

Hamilton, Edith. *Mythology: Timeless Tales of Gods and Heroes*. 1942. Reprint, New York: New Canadian Library, 2015.

Harari, Yuval Noah. *Sapiens: A Brief History of Humankind*. Oxford: Signal, 2014. Kindle edition.

Haug, Martin, trans. *The Book of Arda Viraf*. Bombay and London, 1872.

Hitchens, Christopher, ed. *The Portable Atheist: Essential Readings for the Non-believer*. New York: Da Capo Press, 2007.

Hoffmann, R. Joseph, ed. *Sources of the Jesus Tradition: Separating History from Myth*. Amherst, NY: Prometheus Books, 2010.

Homer. *The Odyssey*. Translated by Emily Wilson. New York: W.W. Norton, 2017.

Hopkins, Matthew. *The Discovery of Witches*. Project Gutenberg, 2004. http://www.gutenberg.org/ebooks/14015.

James, M.R., trans. *The Apocryphal New Testament*. Oxford: Clarendon Press, 1924.

Jastrow, Morris, ed. *Descent of the Goddess Ishtar into the Lower World*. Philadelphia, PA: J.B. Lippincott, 1915.

——. *An Old Babylonian Version of the Gilgamesh Epic*. Project Gutenberg, 2006. http://www.gutenberg.org/ebooks/11000.

Johnson, Dominic. *God Is Watching You: How the Fear of God Makes Us Human*. New York: Oxford University Press, 2016.

Kotsko. Adam, *The Prince of This World*. Stanford: Stanford University Press, 2017.

Kovacs, Maureen G., trans. *The Epic of Gilgamesh*. Stanford: Stanford University Press, 1989.

Krauss, Lawrence. *A Universe from Nothing: Why There Is Something Rather than Nothing*. New York: Atria Books, 2013.

Kvanvig, Jonathan L. *The Problem of Hell*. New York: Oxford University Press, 1993.

Le Goff, Jacques. *The Birth of Purgatory*. Hoboken, NJ: Wiley-Blackwell, 1991.

Lesko, Leonard, ed. *The Ancient Egyptian Book of Two Ways*. Los Angeles: University of California Press, 1972.

Manuschihr, Dastur. *Religious Judgments*. Translated by E.W. West. Edited by Joseph Peterson. 1996. http://avesta. org/mp/dd.htm.

McCabe, Joseph. *The Existence of God*. London: Watts and Co., 1933.

Meyer, Marvin W., ed. *The Nag Hammadi Scriptures*. San Francisco: HarperOne, 2009. Kindle edition.

Milton, John. *Paradise Lost*. Edited by Stephen Orgel and Jonathan Goldberg. Oxford: Oxford University Press, 2008; Project Gutenberg, 1991. https://www.gutenberg. org/files/20/20-h/20-h.htm.

Naff, Clay Farris. *Free God Now: How to Liberate Yourself from Old Time Religion and Just Maybe Save the World*. Self-published, 2012.

Nixey, Catherine. *The Darkening Age: The Christian Destruction of the Classical World*. London: Macmillan, 2017.

Ovid. *Metamorphoses*. Translated by A.D. Melville. Oxford: Oxford University Press, 2008.

Paine, Lauran. *The Hierarchy of Hell*. New York: Hippocrene Books, 1972.

Pagels, Elaine. *The Gnostic Gospels*. New York: Vintage, 1979.

——. *The Origin of Satan*. New York: Random House, 1995.

——. *Revelations: Visions, Prophecy and Politics in the Book of Revelation*. New York: Viking, 2012.

Peers, E. Allison, ed. and trans. *The Life of Teresa of Jesus: The Autobiography of Teresa of Ávila*. n.d. http://www.carmelitemonks.org/Vocation/teresa_life.pdf.

Plantinga, Alvin. *Where the Conflict Really Lies: Science, Religion and Naturalism*. Oxford: Oxford University Press, 2011.

Plutarch. *Lives of the Noble Grecians and Romans*. Edited by Arthur Hugh Clough. Project Gutenberg, 1996. http://www.gutenberg.org/ebooks/674.

Polybius. *The Histories of Polybius*. Vol. 1. Translated by Evelyn Shuckburgh. Project Gutenberg, 2013. http://www.gutenberg.org/ebooks/44125.

Poole, Kevin R., ed. and trans. *Chronicle of Pseudo-Turpin*. New York: Italica Press, 2014.

Popper, Karl. *The Open Society and Its Enemies. Volume 1: Plato*. London: Routledge, 1945.

Russell, Bertrand. *Why I am not a Christian: And Other Essays on Religion and Related Subjects*. New York: Touchstone/Simon and Schuster, 1957.

Sandars, Nancy, ed. *The Epic of Gilgamesh*. London: Penguin Classics, 1960.

Sheehan, Thomas. *The First Coming: How the Kingdom of God Became Christianity*. New York: Random House, 1986.

Shower, John. *Heaven and Hell, or, The unchangeable state of happiness or misery for all mankind in another world occasion'd by the repentance and death of Mr. Shetterden Thomas, who departed this life April 7, 1700, aetat. 26: preach'd and publish'd at the desire and direction of the deceased . . .* London, 1700.

Swinden, Tobias. *An Enquiry into the Nature and Place of Hell*. London: T. Astley, 1727.

Tugendhaft, Aaron. *Baal and the Politics of Poetry*. London: Routledge, 2017.

Turnbull, W.B.D.D, ed. *The Visions of Tundale Together with Metrical Moralizations and Other Fragments of Early Poetry, Hitherto Unedited*. Edinburgh, 1843.

Turner, Alice K. *The History of Hell*. New York: Harcourt, 1993.

Van Scott, Miriam. *Encyclopedia of Hell*. New York: Thomas Dunne, 1998.

Virgil. *The Aeneid of Virgil*. Translated by J.W. Mackail. Project Gutenberg, 2007. http://www.gutenberg.org/ebooks/22456.

Walls, Jerry L. *Hell: The Logic of Damnation*. Notre Dame: University of Notre Dame Press, 1992.

Webb, Diana. *Pilgrimage in Medieval England*. London: A&C Black, 2007.

Whitmarsh, Tim. *Battling the Gods: Atheism in the Ancient World*. New York: Vintage, 2015. Kindle edition.

Wills, Garry. *What the Qur'an Meant and Why It Matters*. New York: Viking, 2017.

Wright, Robert. *The Evolution of God*. New York: Little, Brown and Co., 2009. Kindle edition.

Gnostic and Non-canonical Gospels

The Apocalypse of Peter
The Apocalypse of Paul (a.k.a. *The Vision of Paul*)
The Apocalypse of Mary (a.k.a. *The Apocalypse of the Virgin*, a.k.a. *The Apocalypse of the All-Holy Theotokos Concerning the Punishments*)
The Book of Enoch
The Gospel of Nicodemus (a.k.a. *The Acts of Pontius Pilate*)
The Nature of the Rulers
The Origin of the World
The Questions of Bartholomew

Me

BIBLIOGRAPHY

The Testament of the Twelve Patriarchs
The Testimony of Truth

Sacred Texts

The Bible (King James version)
The Qur'an

Christian Tracts

Memoirs of St. Teresa of Ávila, Of Certain Outward Temptations and Appearances of Satan. Of the Sufferings Thereby Occasioned. Counsels for those who Go On
The Vision of Drythelm (reported by the Venerable Bede)
Malleus Maleficarum
Tableau de l'Inconstance des mauvais Anges

Egyptian Texts

The Book of Am-Tuat
The Book of Caverns
The Coffin Texts
The Book of the Dead
The Book of the Earth
The Book of Gates
The Book of Two Ways

Mesopotamian Texts

The Book of Arda Viraf
The Epic of Gilgamesh
Descent of an Assyrian Crown Prince to the Underworld
Descent of the Goddess Ishtar to the Underworld

Asian Texts

The Tibetan Book of the Dead

Academic Journals

Florilegium (Journal of the Canadian Society of Medievalists)

General Reference

Ancient History Encyclopedia
Encyclopaedia Britannica
Jewish Encyclopedia

Useful Websites

aina.org
ancienttexts.org
avesta.org
hell-on-line.org
jewfaq.org

INDEX

Islam: *vs.* Christianity,
    282–3; existence of hell,
    294; notion of devil in,
    294–5; notion of God's
    authority, 131; paradise
    in, 276–8; soul in, 131
Islamic hell: bridge motif,
    54–5; entrances to, 54;
    food served in, 145–6;
    hellfire, 145; keepers of, 62;
    location of, 45, 130; torment
    of infidels in, 131, 294
Issa, Islam: *Milton in the
    Arab-Muslim World*, 294

J

Jacopo, da Sant'Andrea, 250
Jahannam (Islamic hell), 130
Jambudvīpa, 123, 125
James, M.R., 325n2
James VI, King of Scotland, 82
Jastrow, Morris, 323n1, 323n5
Jehovah (God of Israel),
    63, 74, 167, 172
Jehovah's Witnesses, 35
Jesus: conversation with
    St. Bartholomew, 91–3;
    descent into hell, 65–6, 89,
    92–4; as the Messiah, 300;
    on Sophia, 321n20; on
    torments of hell, 141, 142–3
Jewish tradition: afterlife in,
    22–3, 32, 44–5, 108–11;
    demons in, 64; hell in, 31,
    128–9; notion of heaven
    in, 274–5; soul in, 276;
    vision of death, 275
Job (biblical figure), 72–3

Job, the Book of, 72
John, of Patmos, 272
John, the Baptist, 78
John Paul II, Pope, 291
Joyce, James, 157–8
Jubilees, the Book of, 174

K

Kamil, Mufti, 294
Kant, Immanuel, 160, 288
Kennelly, Michael, 324n1
King of Glory, 89, 90
Kotsko, Adam: *The Prince
    of This World*, 14
Kramer, Heinrich, 83, 116
Krauss, Lawrence: *A Universe
    from Nothing*, 312
Ksitigarbha, monk, 126
Kumaya (prince of Ninevah),
    190, 191–2, 323n7
Küng, Hans, 307
Kur (Mesopotamian
    afterworld), 30, 31, 41
Kwoh, Governor of Szechuan
    province, 50–1, 199–200

L

Laetoli footprints, 6–7
l'Ancre, Pierre de: reputation,
    84–5; *Tableau de l'Inconstance
    des mauvais Anges*, 84
Lateran Council (1215), 136
Lethe, river, 113, 115
Leto (Greek goddess), 65
Lewis, Crystal St. Marie, 160
Lewis, C.S.: *The Problem
    of Pain*, 266, 302

A Note About the Type

THE BODY OF THIS BOOK is set in *Adobe Jenson*. It is an old-style serif typeface drawn for Adobe Systems by its chief type designer Robert Slimbach. Its Roman styles are based on a text face cut by Nicolas Jenson in Venice around 1470, and its italics are based on those created by Ludovico Vicentino degli Arrighi fifty years later.

THE ACCENTS ARE SET in *Celestial* and was designed by Ramandhani Nugraha at Fortunes Designs. Celestial is based on Victorian handlettering.

PHOTO: PAUL ORENSTEIN

MARQ DE VILLIERS is the Governor General's Award–winning author of *Water*, and sixteen other books. Marq lives in Port Medway, Nova Scotia.